COLLECTING THE GLOBE

A VOLUME IN THE SERIES

Public History in Historical Perspective

Edited by

Marla R. Miller

COLLECTING THE GLOBE

The Salem East India Marine Society Museum

George H. Schwartz

University of Massachusetts Press
Amherst and Boston

Printed in the United States of America

ISBN 978-1-62534-472-4 (paper); 471-7 (hardcover)

Designed by Jen Jackowitz
Set in Granjon and Agobe Garamond Pro
Printed and bound by Maple Press, Inc.

Cover design by Sally Nichols
Cover art: Michele Felice Cornè, East India Marine Society Museum sign, 1803.
Oil on canvas, 15 x 41¾ in. Peabody Essex Museum Collection, M235.

Library of Congress Cataloging-in-Publication Data
Names: Schwartz, George H., author.
Title: Collecting the globe : the Salem East India Marine Society Museum / George H. Schwartz.
Description: Amherst : University of Massachusetts Press, [2020] | Series: Public History in Historical Perspective | Includes bibliographical references and index.
Identifiers: LCCN 2019019893 | ISBN 9781625344717 (hardcover) | ISBN 9781625344724 (pbk.)
Subjects: LCSH: Salem East India Marine Society Museum. | East-India Marine Society of Salem. | Maritime museums—Massachusetts—Salem. | Shipping—Massachusetts—Salem—History. | Salem (Mass.)—History, Naval.
Classification: LCC F74.S1 S43 2020 | DDC 355.0099744/5—dc23
LC record available at https://lccn.loc.gov/2019019893

British Library Cataloguing-in-Publication Data
A catalog record for this book is available from the British Library

FOR JANNA, HANNAH, AND VIVIAN

CONTENTS

ACKNOWLEDGMENTS

This book is the culmination of a journey started in 1984, when I first visited the Peabody Essex Museum (then the Peabody Museum of Salem) as a young boy on a spring vacation to New England. Creating it would not have been possible without the help of many people along the way. I am grateful for the support and assistance of current and former colleagues at the Peabody Essex Museum. From the beginning, Dan Finamore, the Russell W. Knight Curator of Maritime History, encouraged my research on the East India Marine Society. As a friend and mentor, he provided endless feedback on my work and shared my enthusiasm for large and small discoveries. I am grateful to curators Sarah Chasse, Karina Corrigan, Karen Kramer, Dean Lahikainen, Paula Richter, William Sargent, Trevor Smith, Daisy Wang, and Janey Winchell, who helped with object-related questions. Adam Brooks, John Childs, Matthew Delgrosso, Natasha Gallagher, Alyssa Langlais, Dave O'Ryan, Claudine Scoville, Katherine White, and Eric Wolin of the registration and collections departments allowed me to consult the museum's object archives. Claire Blechman, Carla Galfano, Shayna Nestor, Bob Packert, and Allison White generously provided all the images of, and permissions for, museum objects. Kathryn Carey and Mimi Leveque conserved several objects so they could be photographed by Kathy Tarantola, and Bob Monk happily took me to see the East India Marine Hall attic to research the names written on and carved into many support beams. Sid Berger, Anne Deschance, Kathy Flynn, Tamara Gaydos, Jennifer Hornsby, Catherine Robertson, and Ruth Stewart at the Phillips Library were unflagging in their enthusiasm for my project, willingly pulled any material I requested, and awarded me a Francis E.

Malamy Fellowship for the fall of 2014, which was instrumental in allowing me to finish my research in a timely manner.

This book originated as a Ph.D. dissertation, and my doctoral committee at Boston University supported my work in many ways. My advisor, Professor Emeritus Keith Morgan, directed my study in museology and offered critical feedback on my writing. Professor William Moore provided essential material-culture context for this study and was always available for advice. Professor Emerita Patricia Hills promoted my work at an early stage and contributed essential feedback as I worked to weave aspects of antebellum American culture into the dissertation. I am also grateful to Marilyn Halter, Kim Sichel, Nina Silber, John Thornton, James A. Winn, Thomas Glick, and the many other professors associated with the American and New England Studies Program for their support; the Boston University Center for the Humanities and the Graduate School of Arts and Sciences for fellowships and awards in the summer of 2014 that allowed me to finish my research and writing; and my graduate colleague C. Ian Stevenson for invaluable publishing guidance.

At the University of Massachusetts Press, I would like to thank Matt Becker, Courtney Andree, Sarah Culver, Rachael DeShano, Sally Nichols, and Dawn Potter for helping shape my manuscript. I am also grateful to the independent reviewers of my work for their suggestions to strengthen it.

Other individuals made important contributions to this project. I am indebted to Professor Dane Morrison of Salem State University for his guidance and willingness to share material from his book *True Yankees* before it was published. I am grateful to Michelle Tolini Finamore, the Penny Vinik Curator of Fashion Arts at the Museum of Fine Arts, Boston; Amanda Hollis Brusky, an associate professor of Politics at Pomona College; and Tom Jefferies for their guidance on book proposals. Joan Vaughan Ingraham and Allan Vaughan, the master and clerk of the Salem Marine Society, allowed me access to their institution's rich archive and showed a keen interest in my work. At Tufts University, Professor Cynthia Robinson, the director of the Museum Studies Program, Professor Elizabeth B. Lemons, Professor David Proctor, and Professor Alisha Rankin all gave me guidance on grant support; and Dean Nancy Bauer, with the help of Laura DiBacoo, Angela Foss, and Michelle Pare, approved funds toward a subvention. Thanks also to John Barker at the Hawaiian Mission Houses Historic Site and Archives, Janet Bloom of the Clements Library at the University of Michigan, Naomi Boneham at the Scott Polar Research Institute, Elizabeth Burgess at the Harriet Beecher Stowe Center, Vicki Catozza at the Western Reserve Historical Society Library Research Center, Bruce Kirby at the Library of Congress, Thomas Knoles at the American Antiquarian Society, Molly Kodner at the Missouri History Museum Library and Research Center, Valerie-Ann Lutz at the American Philosophical Library, Caroline Moseley at the Bowdoin College Library, Rebecca Petersen at the Z. Smith Reynolds Library at Wake Forest University, Elizabeth Rogers at the J. Willard Marriott Library at the University of Utah, Dean Smith of the Bancroft Library at the University of California at Berkeley, Steven Smith of the Historical Society of Pennsylvania, Kathy Steiner at the Henry Ford Museum, Olga Tsapina at the Huntington Library, and Sarah Wilcox at the New York Historical Association Research Library for answering my research questions. In addition, I thank Professor Stephen Houston of Brown University, Professor Emeritus Stephen Whitfield of Brandeis University, Professor Stephen Mrozowski of the University of Massachusetts Boston, and Harvard University's president Larry Bacow for encouraging my graduate work and guiding me toward American Studies; Dennis Carr at the Museum of Fine Arts, Boston, for sharing his research on zograscopes; Catherine Mazur-Jefferies of Boston University and Daniel Tober of Columbia University for their help with Greek and Latin translations; and Professor Lisa Delissio of Salem State University for her feedback on the East India Marine Society's guide for preserving specimens.

The greatest level of support came from my family. My parents, Joel and Rhoda Schwartz, who nurtured my academic pursuits and passion for objects from an early age, were an invaluable source of help and guidance, and my brother, Mark Schwartz, and sister-in-law, Cathy Kaneti, constantly encouraged my work. I also thank my in-laws, Arnold and Claire Berkman, for their support; my brother-in-law, Eric Berkman, for his feedback and advice on my graduate school applications; and the rest of my extended family and close friends. Above all, though, I am thankful for the love and strength of my amazing wife, Janna, and my wonderful daughters, Hannah and Vivian. They provided endless cheer and reassurance. I would not have completed this book without them, and for that reason and others I am eternally grateful.

COLLECTING THE GLOBE

Introduction

"A CABINET, THAT EVERY MARINER MAY POSSESS THE HISTORY OF THE WORLD"

> As you surmounted the flight of steps that ushered you abruptly into the [East India Marine Society's] hall . . . you felt as if touched by an enchanter's wand . . . shooting from the present moment into past ages—into the caverns of the earth and the bosom of the ocean.
>
> —Hannah Flagg Gould (1788–1865),
> "The Greek Antique," *Godey's Lady's Book*, January 1, 1847

To escape the "prosaic streets" of Salem, Massachusetts, in the first half of the nineteenth century, local residents and travelers from across the United States and the globe came to the East India Marine Society Museum (1799–1867). Located on the town's main thoroughfare, Essex Street, the museum transported individuals to another world, into an "atmosphere redolent with the perfumes from the east."[1] Before entering, visitors were greeted by a small horizontal sign painted in 1803 by Michele Felice Cornè (1752–1845), a Neapolitan artist who had immigrated to Salem four years earlier in order to avoid fighting in the Napoleonic Wars (see figure 1).[2] In the center of this painting, a ship with the American flag flying from her stern sails out of Salem Harbor toward an expanse of open blue-green sea. A small tender holding a dozen people, doffing their hats and gesturing toward the departing vessel, trails off the ship's stern. Another American flag, aglow against pinkish clouds, flies above Fort Pickering (built in 1643). On the left side of the foreground, a woman in Empire dress—perhaps an allusion to Columbia, the personification of America at the time—sits on a rocky cliff, extending her open arms and gesturing the viewer toward the vast stretch of water. Two putti hold a banner with the words "East India

Marine Hall," labeled in 1825, when the Society's first permanent museum building was constructed.[3]

Cornè received several commissions from the East India Marine Society in the early nineteenth century for portraits of famous mariners and paintings depicting historical scenes and overseas trading grounds. His sign captured a nautical scene visitors would have readily understood and was intended to heighten their anticipation for the voyage they were about to embark on. The beckoning woman he depicted was inviting people to come see the four corners of the globe inside the gallery, to imagine what might lie behind the museum's walls.

The sign also visually encapsulated the East India Marine Society's fusing of American identity with the sea. Inside the museum's door, this concept was presented to the public through the display of objects collected from all over the world. Visitors to East India Marine Hall entered the building and then walked down a narrow corridor to reach the foot of a staircase on the left. At the base of the first set of stairs, nothing was visible apart from a landing, but when they reached the top and made a 180-degree turn up a second staircase, the enormity of the hall was palpable (see figure 2). As one visitor recalled, "The entrance into such an apartment has a fine effect upon the mind"; once the "spectator *ascends* the staircase, rising, say 12 or 15 steps, the farther side of the apartment . . . meets the admiring eye." Light filled the 100-by-45-foot room; and though there were floor cases with many objects and "High walls, completely covered

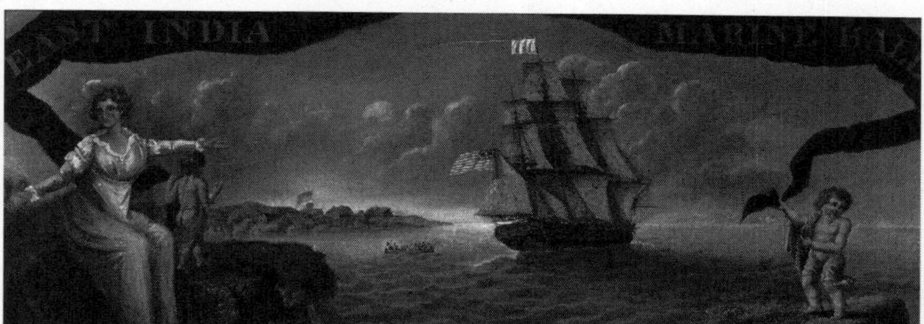

FIGURE 1. Michele Felice Cornè, East India Marine Society Museum sign, 1803. Oil on canvas, 15½ x 41¾ in. Peabody Essex Museum Collection, M235. © 2006 Peabody Essex Museum, Salem, MA. Photography by Mark Sexton.

with the curiosities of the far distant Indies," the twenty-three-foot high ceiling made the gallery appear spacious and filled "the eye, roving with wonder over every part."[4]

Almost immediately the visitors would have felt surrounded by the sea. Looking left toward the south end of East India Marine Hall, they would have seen a birchbark canoe and a sealskin kayak perched above floor cases. In between was a six-foot, seven-inch sculpture of the Hawaiian god Kūkaʻilimoku that had once stood in front of a coastal *heiau,* or temple, of King Kamehameha I (1758–1819) (see figure 3). Beyond the five tall arched windows they could see Salem's wharves, ships, and harbor. To the north, two models of Malay ships hovered above identical floor cases (see figure 4). Just behind—flanked by two specimens of the large Southeast Asian sea sponge *Cliona patera,* or "Neptune's cup"—was an early nineteenth-century plaster-cast copy of the classical sculpture known as the Laocoön Group (circa 27 BCE to CE 68) depicting the Trojan priest and his sons wrestling with great sea serpents. This cast stood in front of seven more arched windows that looked out onto Essex Street, revealing the commercial businesses that supported Salem's maritime ventures.

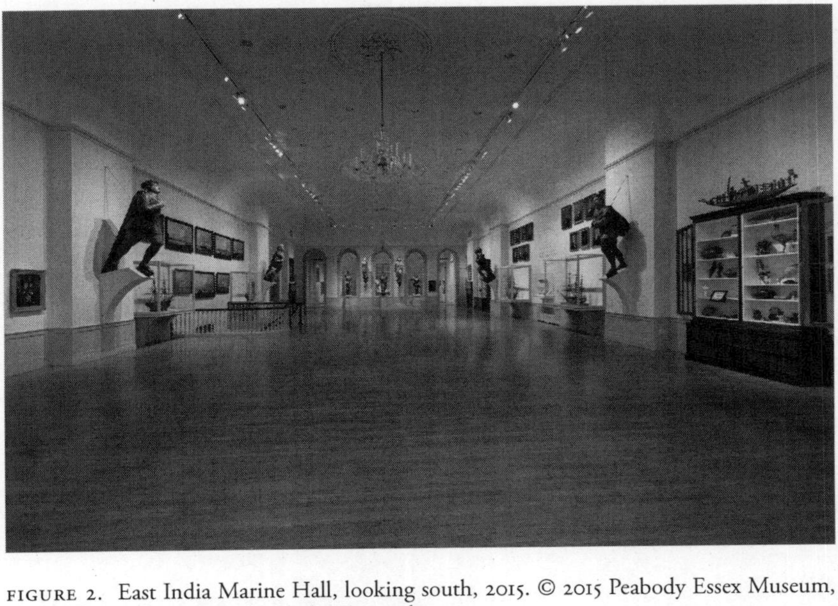

FIGURE 2. East India Marine Hall, looking south, 2015. © 2015 Peabody Essex Museum, Salem, MA. Photography by Kathy Tarantola.

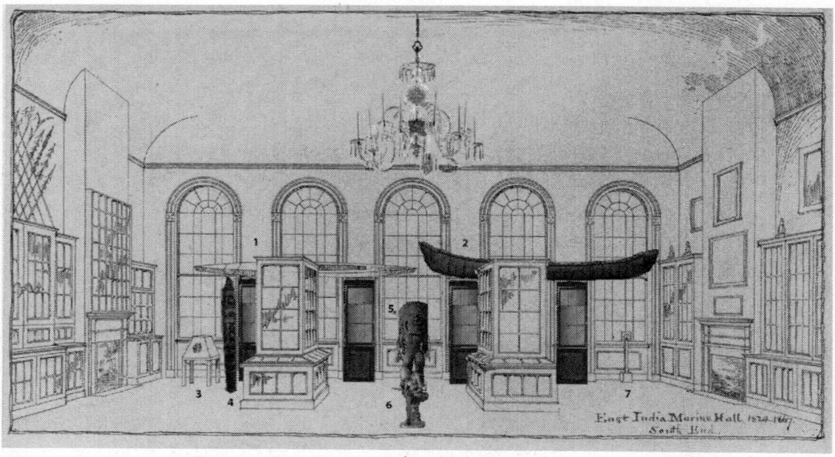

FIGURE 3. James Henry Emerton, *East India Marine Hall, 1824–1867, South End*, 1879. Ink on paper, 6½ x 11¾ in. Peabody Essex Museum Collection, M303.2. © 2016 Peabody Essex Museum, Salem, MA. Photography by Kathy Tarantola. Images of objects overlaid by the author.

Key to objects: 1. Sealskin kayak; 2. Birchbark canoe; 3. Perspective table; 4. *Virshakashta* (memorial post) from India; 5. Figure of Kūkaʻilimoku; 6. *Boy with Thorn*; 7. Sundial owned by Governor John Endicott.

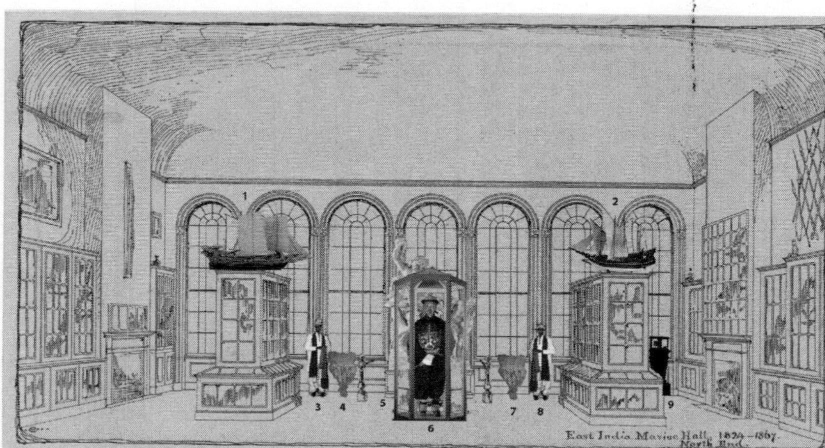

FIGURE 4. James Henry Emerton, *East India Marine Hall, 1824–1867, North End*, 1879. Ink on paper, 6½ x 11⅞ in. Peabody Essex Museum Collection, M303.4. © 2016 Peabody Essex Museum, Salem, MA. Photography by Kathy Tarantola. Images of objects overlaid by the author.

Key to objects: 1. Malay pirate ship; 2. Malay trading ship; 3. Figure of an Indian man; 4. Neptune's cup; 5. Laocoön Group; 6. Figure of a Canton merchant; 7. Neptune's cup; 8. Figure of an Indian man; 9. Heaven and the Day of Judgment terminal rosary bead.

The East Indies also greeted visitors right away. Seated life-size portrait figures of merchants Raj Kissen Mitter (1811–72) and Rajinder Dutt (1818–89), the most prominent Indian agents trading with Americans in the 1830s and 1840s, flanked either side of the staircase. A larger group of East Indian figures were displayed in the center of the floor, enclosed by a low iron railing; and standing figures of Chinese and Indian merchants were positioned in front of the north windows (see figures 5 and 6). Over the stairwell was a palanquin from Calcutta (today Kolkata) donated by five East India Marine Society members in 1803. This object was used by members in their annual parade through Salem during the first two decades of the nineteenth century, which took place near the anniversary of the Society's founding: a public display of their worldly mercantile success through global objects. Just in front of the palanquin was a box containing an eagle, noted in the newspaper the *Christian Watchman* as "the bold *eagle*, as if ready to soar to the sun," an allusion to American ascendancy in the world.[5]

The majority of the collection was displayed on the east and west walls. There were eight chimney flues in the hall, but only four had active fireplaces. All were used to display objects; the active ones held fireboard paintings of international and local ports by Cornè and another local artist, Samuel Bartoll (1786–1837). Between the chimneys were mahogany and glass bookcases that held the Society's books, shells, and minerals.

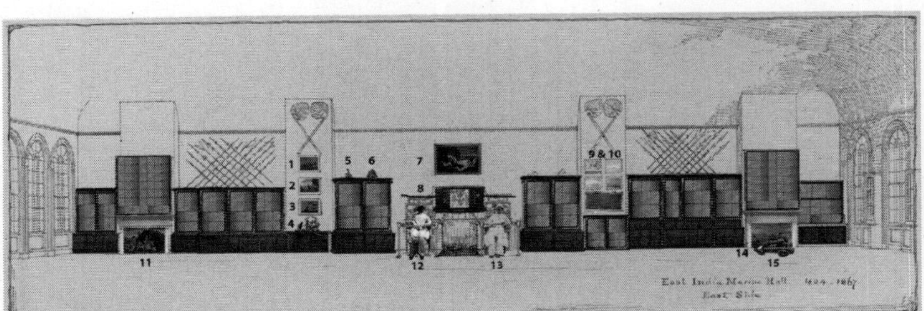

FIGURE 5. James Henry Emerton, *East India Marine Hall, 1824–1867, East Side*, 1879. Ink on paper, 6⅝ x 18¼ in. Peabody Essex Museum Collection, M303.3. © 2016 Peabody Essex Museum, Salem, MA. Photography by Kathy Tarantola. Images of objects overlaid by the author.

Key to objects: 1, 2, and 3. Naval prints donated by Benjamin Tanner; 4. *The Sick Chamber* by Lucy Cleveland; 5. Indian religious sculpture; 6. Chinese religious sculpture; 7. *The Death of Abel*; 8. Palanquin; 9 and 10. Print scenes of Calcutta and a view of Gibraltar; 11. *Native Encampment* by Michele Felice Cornè; 12. Figure of Rajinder Dutt; 13. Figure of Raj Kissen Mitter; 14. *Landing of the Pilgrims* by Samuel Bartoll; 15. Chinese cannon from the fort at Ningpoo.

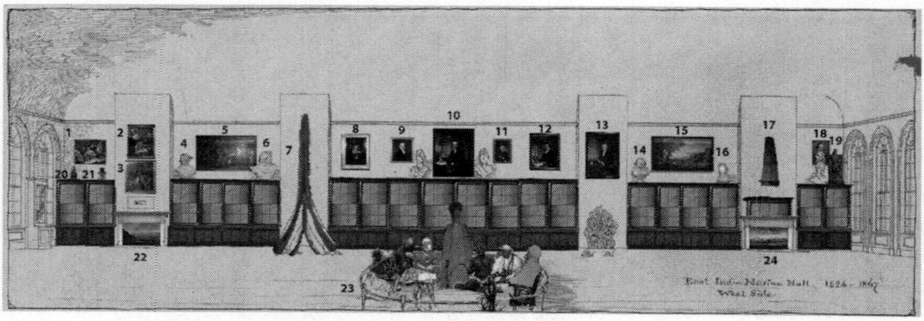

FIGURE 6. James Henry Emerton, *East India Marine Hall, 1824–1867, West Side*, 1879. Ink on paper. 6⅜ x 17¾ in. Peabody Essex Museum Collection, M303.1. © 2016 Peabody Essex Museum, Salem, MA. Photography by Kathy Tarantola. Images of objects overlaid by the author.

Key to objects: 1. *Columbus and the Egg* by Michele Felice Cornè; 2. *Susanna and the Elders* by Delano [full name unknown]; 3. *Game Piece* by Vervoort [full name unknown]; 4. Bust of Diana; 5. *The Adoration of the Magi* by Van Wyck [full name unknown]; 6. Bust of Apollo; 7. Sperm whale jaws; 8. Portrait of Governor John Endicott by James Frothingham; 9. Portrait of John Quincy Adams by Charles Osgood; 10. Portrait of Nathaniel Bowditch by Charles Osgood; 11. Portrait of Eshing by Guan Zuolin (Spoilum); 12. Portrait of Elias Hasket Derby by James Frothingham; 13. Portrait of Joseph Peabody by Charles Osgood; 14. Bust of John Adams; 15. *View of the Temple of Apollo and Athens* by Theodore Fisher; 16. Bust of Napoleon; 17. Harp from Japan; 18. Portrait of Captain Cook by Michele Felice Cornè; 19. Figure of Durga; 20 and 21. Religious statuary from India; 22. *View of Cape Town* by Michele Felice Cornè; 23. Figures of Indian merchants and inhabitants; 24. *View of the Foreign Factories in Canton* by Michele Felice Cornè.

Mantel cases above the two fireplaces on the east wall contained insects, and the standing floor cases held a mix of natural history specimens and other artifacts.

Perched on top of many wall cases were busts of American patriots such as John Adams, European philosophers, and classical deities such as Apollo and Diana. Portraits of the Bombay (today Mumbai) merchant Nusserwanjee Maneckjee Wadia (1753–1814) and the Cantonese merchant Eshing—both trading partners of Society members—were exhibited alongside maritime heroes such as Captain James Cook (1728–79). Busts of American military heroes sat next to Southeast Asian religious sculptures. These were labeled simply as "idol" in the printed catalogue available for personal consultation in the museum; the true meaning of these complex figures was likely unknown to visitors. Still, many were exhibited on the same plane that western objects were. Perched above a viewer's head, they imparted a notion of reverence and human frailty in the presence of supernatural forces.

Portraits of revered mariners, shipowners, and Society members as well as eighteenth- and nineteenth-century versions of Renaissance paintings hung directly above and behind the busts and small statues on the west side of East India Marine Hall. On the east wall's chimney flues were a few patriotic prints of American naval victories during the War of 1812 and British prints of India, both topped by overlapping fans. An intricate pattern of crisscrossed spears and clubs from the Pacific Islands hung above the bookcases on the east wall. This arrangement resembled Ishmael's depiction of the entrance to the Spouter-Inn in Herman Melville's *Moby-Dick*: "The opposite wall of this entry was hung all over with a heathenish array of monstrous clubs and spears . . . You shuddered as you gazed, and wondered what monstrous cannibal and savage could ever have gone a death-harvesting with such a hacking, horrifying implement."[6]

Together, the vast ensemble was an organized display of the natural, cultural, and spiritual world bound by the sea and open to visual inspection through the efforts of the American maritime trade. While this message was generally optimistic in tone, nineteenth-century American maritime life was often filled with danger: violent storms, seas frequently patrolled by hostile vessels, and encounters with people from cultures that were fighting against western incursion. A few objects exhibited in the museum directly engaged these negative associations, such as a journal "written with blood upon a Seal Skin" by shipwrecked sailors in the South Seas and the calendar stick of James Drown of Providence, who was stranded for more than 160 days on the remote South Atlantic island Tristan da Cunha in 1804 until he was rescued. These pieces of material culture were clearly identified in the museum catalogue, but the darker secrets within most of the objects were not readily available to visitors or Society members.

In the days before the Smithsonian Institution and Gilded Age museums such as the Metropolitan Museum of Art came into being, the United States was dotted with mostly for-profit oddity museums—notably, the showman P. T. Barnum's American Museum in New York City (1841–65)—and the scientific and artistic collections of learned societies such as the American Philosophical Society in Philadelphia.[7] The East India Marine Society Museum, unlike the houses of spectacle or the cabinets of learned societies open only to members, appealed to multiple audiences: educated individuals, those who sought wondrous forms of entertainment, and others. Acknowledged as a model for other institutions in the country and open to the public free of charge, the museum allowed visitors to circumnavigate the globe, gaining an understanding of the world and their place within it through objects collected via international exchange.

A stroll around this created space was both transformative and memorial, a reflection of America's and Salem's growing maritime presence in the world during the first half of the nineteenth century. One visitor remarked, "The various objects arranged around the hall could scarcely be enumerated within the compass of a volume," of interest to "the man of science, and amusement to the mere traveller."[8] For some people, a visit to the museum transported them to exotic lands not seen in their workaday world; for others, it brought back wistful memories of past adventures. Museum patrons read the objects on display much as modern museumgoers do: they were influenced by their personal tastes and cultural background.

As an institution, the East India Marine Society Museum mirrored America's founding democratic principles and their unequal application in the new country. While Society members attempted to offer authentic versions of the nation's global interactions, the collection and displays also reflected American expansionism at a time when the country was struggling with notions of race and citizenship. These dualities were evident in Society members' understanding of other cultures and their vision of who should be allowed into the museum.

Today, the East India Marine Society Museum lives on as the Peabody Essex Museum (PEM), America's longest continually operating museum. While the PEM has been soaring to great heights both nationally and internationally in the twenty-first century, its progenitor has been relatively forgotten outside of Salem or diminished as an "accidental cabinet of curiosities" that was rarely visited.[9] Few scholars have made more than a cursory examination of the East India Marine Society's substantial institutional archive and collection, which still exists at the PEM.[10] Unlike other early American museums, this vast collection was well documented for its time: internal and published catalogues almost always included donor names, dates of acquisition, and provenance information. In addition, East India Marine Hall still exists and contains installations connected to its nineteenth-century appearance. Nonetheless, beyond the scholarship of current and former museum staff members, very few people since the late 1800s have recognized the significance of the institution—acknowledged in its day as "the best in the Union"—to antebellum American culture.[11]

When twenty-two master mariners formed the East India Marine Society in 1799, Salem was at the epicenter of American consciousness. In a region devoid of good arable land, the ocean was the town's greatest resource, and serving before the mast was the accepted career path of most young men. Salem was founded as a year-round fishing post in 1626. By 1638, as small shallops and ketches came into use for longer voyages, the port was trading dried codfish with European countries such as Spain and Portugal.[12] African slaves were not a major part of Salem's trade, but local mariners and merchants profited from the "triangle trade" that brought West Indian sugar and molasses to New England, New England rum to the west coast of Africa, and African slaves to the English colonies in the West Indies for work on sugar plantations. Salem's major part in this trade pattern was sending waste fish to the West Indies to feed Caribbean slaves, providing horses to use in sugar mills, shipping wooden staves for making casks to transport molasses, and becoming a market for the commodities produced by slave labor (sugar, molasses, and indigo).[13]

Salem merchants soon expanded their sights beyond the North Atlantic and Caribbean in order to trade their staple products for finer goods. As commercial shipping grew, the town quickly developed into a thriving maritime community in the Atlantic world. Beginning in the eighteenth century, Salem's overseas trade increased. Local vessels traded with Spain, Portugal, and the Azores, and while the town continued to thrive as a small fishing community, a few successful shipowners assembled several waterfront lots in the 1760s and began construction of larger commercial wharves.

After the Revolutionary War, some Salem merchants who had prospered during the conflict began investing their fortunes in the reestablishment of their fishing fleets and the reaffirmation of old trade relationships.[14] A few pioneering shipowners such as Elias Hasket Derby (1739–99), considered to be the first millionaire in the United States at the time of his death, took advantage of unfettered trade in the new republic and looked for expanded opportunities in areas around the Baltic Sea and in the Far East. Derby's ship *Atlantic*, commanded by his son and future East India Marine Society member Elias Hasket, Jr. (1766–1826), was the first American vessel to reach Surat, Bombay, and Calcutta in 1788.[15] Other Salem mariners, many of whom founded the Society or later joined the organization, followed suit and moved away from the familiar prewar routes and helped steer their ships into uncharted waters. Salem's golden age of maritime commerce had begun, and the town grew to be an entrepôt. Because skilled mariners were the port's best feature and most marketable commodity, Salem vessels peddled a litany of goods around the world in the face of hostile British, French, Malay, and Barbary ships and took great economic risks.[16] In return, they carried home prized cargo and objects from distant lands.

The historian Daniel Vickers notes, "Today it is difficult to reimagine an early American past when the frontier extended in all directions and when the Atlantic, rather than the continental West, stood at the center of our country's geographic consciousness. In that world, Salem was not peripheral but fully enmeshed in the central historical developments of the age."[17] In this environment, Salem's pioneering captains formed a new marine society—the Salem East India Marine Society. Unlike other marine societies, whose primary focus centered on providing relief to the widows and children of deceased members, this organization had loftier ambitions beyond benevolence. Membership was limited to Salem masters (captains) and supercargoes (the business agents onboard ships) who navigated the seas near or beyond the Cape of Good Hope or Cape Horn, and among the founding objectives of the organization was the call "to form a Museum of natural and artificial curiosities."[18]

Between 1799 and 1867, more than 330 members fulfilled the Society's collecting mission, donating manmade and natural objects obtained from many ports of call around the globe. They also accepted gifts from individuals outside of the organization—from other mariners, trading partners, and the public. In addition, the Society commissioned works from local artists such as Cornè to fill perceived gaps in its institutional narrative. Through these multiple networks, the Society amassed more than 6,400 objects during its history—from Pacific island sculptures, to flora and fauna, to western art.[19]

This collection of material culture was at the nexus of global interaction, connected to the maritime trade that dominated international relations during the early days of the new republic. When displayed in the East India Marine Society Museum, these expressions of cultural identity had a profound impact on visitors. While Salem's maritime clout would weaken throughout the century, the reputation of the museum did not. In 1841, the *Salem Gazette* remarked, "We do not think it is too much to say that our city owes to this society, next to its 'witches' one of its greatest attractions to strangers, in its rare and beautiful collection of curiosities," which was "maintained by . . . the remarkable liberality, public spirit, and enlightened zeal, which have always characterized the proceedings of the members."[20]

In 1905, Edward Sylvester Morse (1838–1925)—director of the East India Marine Society Museum's second incarnation, the Peabody Academy of Science (1867–1915)—remarked that "a student of history must be the one to properly bring together the records of the East India Marine Society."[21] This book takes up his call, weaving the museum into the fabric of antebellum American life for the first time. By providing significant new insights on its influence in collecting, exhibiting, and interpreting international objects in the early United States, it will demonstrate how the Society used its collection to support a vision of America's identity tied to the sea.[22]

Chapter One

ORIGINS

A Noble company, that early band,
Who left their homes to sail across the sea,
And distant voyages to the Orient planned.
The land of wealth and dark Idolatry.
Behold their Monument!—the rich and rare,
Gathered with cost and pains from every clime,
And in this spacious hall preserved with care,
To interest and instruct the future time.

—Reverend Jones Very, excerpt from
"The East India Marine Museum," 1865

When the East India Marine Society was formed on the last day of August 1799, Salem captain Jonathan Carnes (1757–1827) was homeward bound from the East Indies. Carnes, who became a member of the Society shortly after his return, was emblematic of the post–Revolutionary War Salem mariners who took great risks opening American markets in the Pacific Islands, the Far East, the northwestern coast of North America, Africa, Russia, and the Near East. During a voyage to modern-day Indonesia in 1795, Carnes learned of a location on the west coast of Sumatra where he could obtain the valuable spice, pepper, directly from local inhabitants without interference from hostile Dutch and English ships. Back in Salem, he caught the ear of his uncle, Jonathan Peele, Jr. (1731–1809), a wealthy merchant. Peele outfitted a schooner named *Rajah*, and with Carnes as master the vessel set sail on one of the most important voyages in Salem's history. The *Rajah* returned to its home port in 1797 carrying the first cargo of wild black pepper to America, yielding a 700 percent profit and starting a fifty-year-long lucrative trade for Salem merchants.[1]

At this time, Salem was in the midst of a golden age of maritime commerce. These were the days, as nineteenth-century author Arlo Bates (1850–1918) romanticized, when "Derby Street was alive with bustle and excitement; when swarthy sailors were grouped at the corners, or sat smoking before the doors of their boarding-houses, their ears adorned with gold rings, and their hands and wrists profusely illustrated with uncouth designs in India ink; when every shop window was a museum of odd trifles from the Orient, and the very air was thick with a sense of excitement and of mystery."[2] At the height of Salem's commercial activity as the sixth-largest port in the United States (accounting for 5 percent of the nation's per-capita income), forty wharves lined the South River harbor (see figure 7).[3]

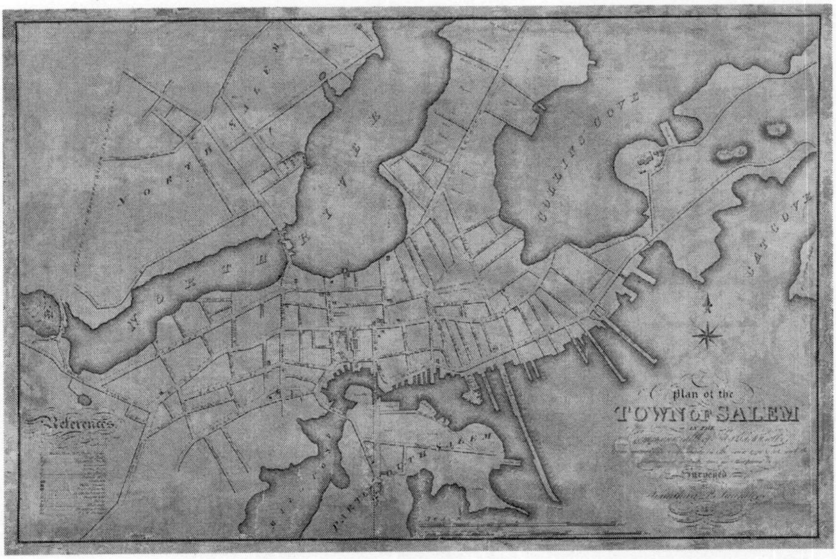

FIGURE 7. *Plan of the town of Salem in the commonwealth of Massachusetts: From actual surveys, made in the years 1796 & 1804; with the improvements and alterations since that period as surveyed by Jonathan Peele Saunders,* 1820. Printed paper, 21 x 31⅝16 in. Peabody Essex Museum Collection, LIBG3764.S2-S286-C.2. © 2016 Peabody Essex Museum, Salem, MA. Photography by Kathy Tarantola. Saunders was an East India Marine Society member. The museum is one of thirteen buildings plotted on the map and noted in the key as "E.I.M. Museum."

By 1807 Salem's mercantile fleet consisted of approximately two hundred vessels. This was the pinnacle of the local shipbuilding enterprise, when shipwrights such as Enos Briggs (1746–1819) were creating the port's famous East Indiamen. These ships were 75 to 100 feet long, 200 and 300 tons (the measure of a ship's cargo-carrying capacity), with a multiethnic crew of twelve to twenty-four sailors: one-quarter the size of their European equivalents.[4] Rounded barrel bottoms made these vessels sluggish, but they drew less water and were easier to handle. Salem's East Indiamen were therefore well equipped to navigate in and out of their local shallow harbor and small foreign ports while still having enough cargo space to make a voyage profitable, and they were safer and financially less risky than the larger ships of the period.

Salem's fleet included the first American vessels to enter many eastern ports—from Mocha (in modern-day Yemen), to Batavia (today Jakarta, capital of Indonesia), to Nagasaki, Japan. The port town valued the region so much that the motto "To the Farthest Port of the Rich East" was inscribed on Salem's official seal, created when it became a city in 1836. Likewise, merchants in the east held Salem in high esteem. Charles Timothy Brooks (1813–83), a Salem-born Unitarian pastor and poet, wrote:

> Some native merchant of the East, they say,
> (Whether Canton, Calcutta or Bombay),
> Had in his counting-room a map, whereon
> Across the fields in capitals was drawn
> The name of SALEM, meant to represent
> That Salem was the Western Continent,
> While in an upper corner was put down
> A dot named Boston, SALEM'S leading town.[5]

While Salem may have been synonymous with the United States among those who would never set foot on American soil, the port's rise in the antebellum period mirrored, in many ways, the rise of the burgeoning nation.

Salem's overseas trade was a complex affair; only those Yankee sailors who possessed keen nautical and business acumen were successful in acquiring goods and creating profits. In these heady days, a ship did not leave home with cargo intended for the final destination; instead, it carried New England resources such as dried fish and timber to trade along the way at several different ports. A vessel bound for the East Indies would typically exchange goods in Europe, then sail down the coast of Africa and around the Cape of Good Hope to the Isle de France to trade, and continue up the African coastline, along the rim of the Indian Ocean, to India, Batavia, or Canton (today Guangzhou). In all of these eastern ports, the ship's master and supercargo drove profitable bargains, often turning over cargoes (and, in some cases, the ship itself!) a dozen times for a great profit.[6] Due to these intricate trading patterns, Salem mariners obtained knowledge of distant cultures and also of the material objects associated with these new lands.

Once Salem ships returned home, and after duties were paid, most foreign merchandise such as pepper from Sumatra or tea and silk from China would go into shops or be sold at auction. Some cargo would be re-exported to Europe or other American ports. Mary Boardman Crowninshield (died 1840), the wife of then secretary of the navy Benjamin William Crowninshield (1772–1851), wrote to her husband in 1815 of "a most agreeable jaunt down to the wharf to see the prise [*sic*] goods." She discovered "the most elegant ladies clothing . . . books most elegantly bound . . . elegant pictures landscapes in colours . . . chintzes very beautiful table linens." This experience led her to exclaim, "I wish you could have been with me to HAVE SEEN THESE PRETTY THINGS."[7] Numerous advertisements for similar commodities were published daily in Salem newspapers, echoing Crowninshield's description of Salem's wharves and evidence that a wide array of goods were available to residents. In turn, Salemites used this vast assortment of commodities to create a cosmopolitan lifestyle normally associated with large European cities—using spices for meals, drinking tea in Chinese porcelain and English ceramic services, and imbibing spirits crafted in distant lands.

In postwar Salem, a burgeoning economy allowed local shipping merchants to emerge from their Puritan roots and become the port's most influential class, eclipsing the religious elite that had governed the town in the previous century.[8] Shipowners and captains developed new areas of the city to display their wealth, funding the construction of elegant Federal-style houses and public buildings. Their ships brought back more than fine goods and profit, though. A constant stream of material culture, both artwork and extraordinary objects referred to as "curiosities," flowed into the town. When Jonathan Carnes returned to Salem in October 1799 after the *Rajah*'s second voyage to Sumatra, his valuable cargo of pepper was matched in importance by a select few items from this distant land.

One might view these thirteen objects, which included a cup made from rhinoceros horn, an elephant's tooth, and various flora and fauna, as mere bric-à-brac. To Salem mariners, however, they were cultural reflections of their new trading partners and perhaps emblems of American free trade in the new republic.

The objects Carnes gave to the East India Marine Society were the first donation to the newly founded institution. Among them was a most unusual-looking pipe he acquired near Banda Aceh, Sumatra (see figure 8). Not one but two metal stems emanate from the central bowl like cattle's horns. The carved and decorated bowl is caked with a thick black tar, evidence that it was smoked at some point in time, but this dark patina does not reveal any further clues as to the object's origins and meaning. Was this an object for leisure, or was it intended for ritual purposes? Today, little is known about this curious pipe except that it is not native to Sumatra.[9] Its double-ended form, however, makes it one of the most symbolic objects in the Society's collection, unintentionally encapsulating the multiple meanings imbued within this organization.

In the early days of the United States, Salem was representative of a new kind of American town, one at the forefront of the American Enlightenment.[10] At this time, the town had two newspapers, ten churches, several

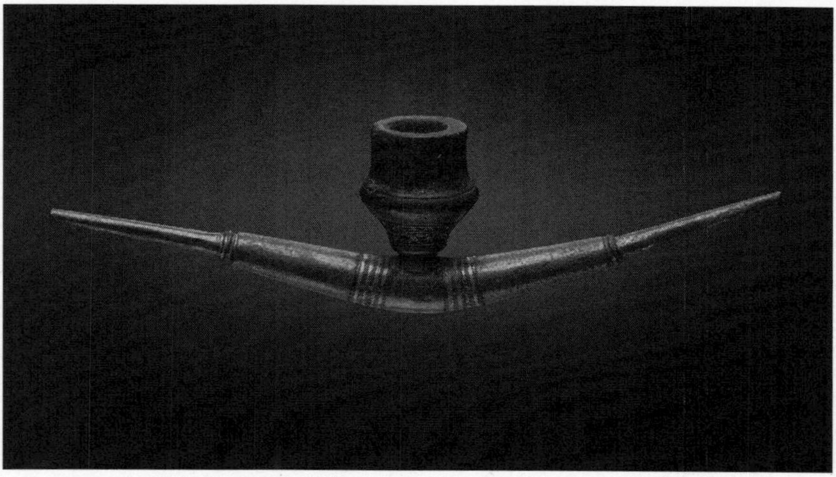

FIGURE 8. Two-stem smoking pipe, circa 1790, acquired by Captain Jonathan Carnes in Sumatra. Metal and wood, 2⅝ x 9½ x 1⅝ in. Peabody Essex Museum Collection, M18. © 2014 Peabody Essex Museum, Salem, MA. Photography by Walter Silver.

schools, banks, publishers, insurance companies, charitable organizations, libraries, bookstores, a municipal water system, and concert halls in addition to the East India Marine Society Museum. Salem could also boast of its national political importance in these years immediately following the formation of the country. Native-son Timothy Pickering (1745–1829) was George Washington's third secretary of state, and in the following decades, Salem mariners—many of who were Society members as well—became senators, congressmen, and cabinet members. The town was home to intellectuals who rivaled those in the nation's early capital, Philadelphia. For instance, Edward Holyoke (1728–1829), a well-respected scientist and physician who had lived through the transformative eighteenth century in Salem, was a founding member and later president of the American Academy of Arts and Science (founded in 1780 in Massachusetts).

As Salem developed into a global port, the first American collecting institutions took form in the country. During the first half of the eighteenth century, they were versions of the *Kunstkammer* (art chamber) of the late Renaissance and the *Wunderkammer* (wonder chamber) of northern Europe. Better known as *cabinets of curiosity*, these precursors to the modern museum were created by noble and elite circles and scholars or virtuosos and emphasized an object-based epistemology to obtain knowledge. While many cabinets highlighted the rare and unusual, the collections reflected a scientific and human impulse to classify the world. They also contained ethnographic material amassed and disseminated from exploration during the Age of Discovery. Thus, cabinets of curiosity were partly devices for learning, partly fantastical, and tinged with a hint of religious reliquaries. While there were regional differences, princely cabinets in sixteenth- and seventeenth-century Europe emphasized the rare and exotic; they were showpieces that enhanced the status of their owner. Among humanist scholars, cabinets served a more scientific purpose.[11]

At the end of the eighteenth century, European cabinets of curiosity were being replaced by large municipal or national institutions devoted to art: the universal survey museum.[12] The Louvre, established in Paris in 1793, was the first such institution open to the public. Through its classical architecture and arrangement of Old World and Renaissance art, the Louvre promoted French culture as the next step on the historical trajectory of western civilization.[13] The British Museum in London was similarly formed with an elitist ideology emphasizing the democratization of art for the masses.[14] Universal survey museums did not appear on American shores until the end of the nineteenth century, when industrialists such as Andrew Carnegie (1887–1919) and J. P. Morgan (1837–1913) helped establish the museums still familiar to us, such as the Metropolitan Museum of Art in New York City.

As private cabinets of curiosity fell out of fashion in Europe in the mid- to late eighteenth century, they emerged in America as the cabinets of learned societies in several colonial cities. For members of these institutions, the collections were local centers of scientific knowledge—essentially a form of a democratic enlightenment.[15] In the mid-Atlantic region, Philadelphia's American Philosophical Society, founded in 1743, pursued "all philosophical Experiments that let Light into the Nature of Things," according to its founding member, Benjamin Franklin (1706–90).[16] The collection featured scientific apparatuses, natural history specimens, Native American objects, and historical mementos such as the chair in which Thomas Jefferson (1743–1826) was believed to have written the Declaration of Independence. Further south, the Library Society of Charleston, South Carolina, started in 1773, collected material relating to local natural history and mechanical contraptions such as a telescope and a camera obscura, which served as visible indicators of the institution's purported scientific goals.[17] In New England, learned societies such as the Massachusetts Historical Society, founded in 1791, and the Anthology Society, founded in 1804 (which became the Boston Athenaeum in 1807), were primarily focused on creating exclusive subscription libraries but did promote collecting and displayed artwork.[18] Eventually, the majority of these institutions donated their cabinets to the large art and natural history museums that emerged during the Gilded Age (such as the Museum of Fine Arts in Boston).[19]

Along with the cabinets of American learned societies, there were a few larger museums in the early republic. Principle among them was the museum founded in 1786 by the artist Charles Willson Peale (1741–1827) and run by him and his family.[20] Peale's Philadelphia Museum (also known as Peale's American Museum), unlike those of learned societies, was open to all willing to pay the price of admission. Peale and his family attempted to construct a national museum for the new country, exhibiting the "natural and the uncivilized races of America," attracting the attention of Thomas Jefferson and other founding fathers.[21] The museum contained cases of natural history specimens such as a mastodon discovered by Peale himself. Portraits of Native Americans and Revolutionary heroes painted by the artist hovered above the cases; and the collection included European art, some biological oddities and technical devices, and other objects. With a mixture of science and patriotism, the Peale family envisioned their collection as the first wholly American museum. Yet like many museums in the late eighteenth and early nineteenth centuries, Peale's institution did not last. Political opposition and ideological differences eventually destroyed his vision, and the remnants of the museum run by his son, Rembrandt Peale (1778–1860), were dispersed to the commercial ventures of individuals such as P. T. Barnum (1810–91).[22]

For-profit sideshow-style museums also abounded throughout most of the nineteenth century. The British humorist Edward Peron Hingston (circa 1823–1876) satirized them:

> A "Museum" in the American sense of the word means a place of amusement, wherein there shall be a theatre, some wax figures, a giant and a dwarf or two, a jumble of pictures, and a few live snakes. In order that there may be some excuse for the use of the word, there is in most instances a collection of stuffed birds, a few preserved animals, and a stock of oddly assorted and very dubitable curiosities; but the mainstay of the "Museum" is the "live art," that is, the theatrical performance, the precocious manikins, or the intellectual dogs and monkeys.[23]

Accessible for a fee, these museums offered a mix of oddities such as double-headed creatures as well as visual art and live performances. Antebellum American culture lacked a distinction between high and low culture, between highbrow and lowbrow art. Entertainment such as Shakespearean plays, operas, and a variety of museums were not associated solely with elite circles but were enjoyed by all segments of society.[24] The Boston-based Columbian Museum (1795–1825), opened by Daniel Bowen (circa 1760–1856), a close friend of Peale's, advertised "the most entertaining place of amusement in the United States" filled with "Paintings . . . Waxwork . . . Musical clocks . . . Natural curiosities . . . Music, on the grand piano forte . . . [a] Menage of living animals," all accessible for half a dollar.[25] In New York City, Scudder's American Museum (1810–41), run by John Scudder (1775–1821), a former coastal sailor who used the money he earned at sea to acquire objects, offered the paying public "the most beautiful productions of nature," "WAX FIGURES of different characters," and "every kind of Curiosity, which may be pleasing to the eye," for twenty-five cents. Scudder's collection was ultimately purchased by Barnum to form his nationally famous house of spectacle: Barnum's American Museum.[26]

Within this mix of exclusive learned societies closed to the general public, institutions such as Peale's that were accessible to all for a fee, and the for-profit museums of Bowen and others stood the East India Marine Society Museum, created and run by mariners. This transnational group had a clear advantage in collecting objects as they spent the majority of their lives hopping from port to port, obtaining souvenirs to record and memorialize their experiences. The sailors who formed the East India Marine Society were able to construct an organization that could independently collect and interpret objects from around the globe on a greater scale than any other learned society of the day. In addition, by displaying their collections in a museum open to the public, Society members exhibited an enlightened desire to contextualize the tangible records of their overseas adventures within the international world now explored by American mariners.

The East India Marine Society, unlike many learned societies of the day, privileged maritime prowess over social connections and financial clout. According to the *New York Courier*, in Salem "few old gentlemen of any eminence in wealth, are to be found here who bear not the title of captain. This is not a barren militia title, indicated by epaulettes, &c. It is a marine honor, and most heroically has it sometimes been earned—not by the heroism of conquering nations, destroying the human race, and sating the wild ambition of little minds—but that heroism which battles the elements in the pursuit of independence, which braves the mountain waves for the glory of the nation's commerce, which penetrates every ocean in the honorable calling of a merchant and navigator."[27] The *Courier*'s bombastic characterization of American maritime enterprise as a patriotic endeavor that has emboldened the country, as opposed to the evils of imperial European powers, ignored the negative impacts of the nation's growth both at home and across the globe.

When the East India Marine Society was founded, Salem boasted few learned societies. The city's Social Library, which would later become the Salem Athenaeum, was the only public institution in the town when it was founded in 1760. Like the majority of American learned societies, the Social Library primarily collected published volumes, with two- and three-dimensional objects a secondary focus of its mission.

At this time, the collection and display of global knowledge in Salem was mostly a private affair. John Prince (1751–1836), the pastor of the Unitarian First Church in Salem and later a donor to the East India Marine Society Museum, formed a collection that he used to instruct students in the methods of experimental science. In addition, he entertained guests with performances employing his various optical instruments.[28] Nineteenth-century Salem politician Charles W. Upham (1802–75) recalled Prince's cabinet as a place where people "were introduced, through his admirable apparatus and specimens, to all the wonders of Astronomy, Optics, Pneumatics, Botany, Mineralogy, Chemistry, and Entomology." Prince's visitors were able "to explore the ruins of the old world, to traverse the streets of London, Paris, St. Petersburg, . . . to watch the successive aspects of an eruption of Ætna or Vesuvius, and literally to survey the whole earth and the glories thereof."[29]

William Bentley (1759–1819), the minister of the Salem East Church, also created a vast personal cabinet. Bentley was a renaissance man: a collector, a writer, an editor, a cleric, and more. Schooled at Harvard College, he developed a penchant for acquiring objects at an early age and created an extensive collection of books, flora, fauna, and curiosities. He also kept detailed diaries, starting in 1784, when he arrived in Salem at the age of twenty-five, until his death. His daily entries reveal active relationships with several of the founding members of the East India Marine Society before its formation, a network of exchange he used to procure books and objects for his personal collection. For example, Bentley wrote in his diary on February 26, 1787, that he "Delivered at Capt Gibaut's a written request to be forwarded to E. H. Derby . . . that he would purchase for me one, any, or all volumes of Bossuet's theological works, &c."[30] Bentley inventoried his collection indiscriminately in twenty-two pages of his diary, including the date he obtained an object and the donor.[31] He wrote, "Formed a Cabinet in June 1802 & here shall notice all articles obtained for it," and created a systematic display of his collection within his personal quarters that included a wide variety of objects, from "a tooth found in Salem Channel" to an "Egyptian Pipe and Tobacco from Alexandria."[32]

Many Salem mariners were parishioners at the East Church, such as John Gibaut (1767–1805), Bentley's mentee and one of the East India Marine Society's founders, and the Society's first president, Benjamin Hodges (1754–1806). These men (and likely others) considered Bentley an authority on collecting and asked for his assistance in crafting the Society's founding articles. In August 1799, Bentley "[c]omposed Articles xxiii for intended Society of Marines who have navigated the seas of Asia" and "delivered them to Capt. Gibaut." Three months later, "The first friends of the Institution met & chose a committee to compare & digest articles from the scetches given to them." However, "the members had met & signed the articles proposed by the Committee" rather than Bentley's.[33] Soon after, Gibaut and Hodges brought Bentley the Society's articles and "begged a revision of them," and he "promised whenever they are again exhibited to give my remarks in writing, as this liberal & important design has not yet the perfection its members intend to give it."[34]

In late 1799, according to Nathaniel Silsbee (1773–1850), "a few shipmasters who were standing together, on a cold day, 'under the lee' of the store on the end of Union Wharf (which I think belonged to Mr. Derby) where they were in the habit of congregating," first discussed forming a new marine society in Salem. During Silsbee's course of residence on shore, "in that interval between my voyages," he and twenty-one other Salem captains met at Benjamin Webb's (1754–1815) Sun Tavern on Essex Street to lay down the structure of this new society.[35] Taverns were among the most important public spaces for mariners and many others from across colonial American society: centers for commerce and news and meeting places for clubs and organizations. Silsbee signed the "List of subscribers agreeing to formation of organization" on August 31, 1799, and was assigned to the committee tasked with writing the Society's bylaws.

In the early days of the republic, marine societies covered the eastern seaboard from Maine to South Carolina, with organizations founded in Portland (1796), Portsmouth (1808), Newburyport (1772), Marblehead (1798), Salem (1766 and 1799), Boston (1742), Newport (1752), Providence (1798), New York City (1770), Philadelphia (1788), Baltimore (1798), and Charleston (1806). All adhered to one major principle: the goal of providing relief to the widows and families of sailors who "go down to the sea in ships, and nevermore return" and to sailors who had fallen on hard times.[36] In addition to benevolence, many marine societies supported improved navigation in and around their home ports.

These marine societies were comprised of local captains and supercargoes who paid an initial membership fee as well as dues at each meeting, which were invested to support charitable purposes and maritime endeavors. Some, such as the Newport Marine Society, allowed a few "persons of any other profession" to become members.[37] Each society's executive council consisted of a president, a committee of observation, a treasurer, a secretary, and other officers chosen annually by members. Several used analogous terms, such as "the box" (the container used to collect and hold charitable funds), or had similar articles in their bylaws, such as those prohibiting drunkenness and partisan politics at meetings.

In comparison to many of their European counterparts, benevolent marine societies were truly American endeavors. At their founding, the Marine Society in London (1756), the Hibernian Marine Society in Dublin (1775), and others were focused on increasing conscriptions into the Royal Navy. Later, they shifted their efforts to educating, maintaining, and apprenticing the orphans of naval and merchant seamen.[38] American marine societies, however, emerged due to a lack of governmental support for sailors. As the Baltimore Charitable Marine Society declared in 1798, "individuals, inadequate of themselves apart, . . . combine together in societies—strength is gained, and the hand of charity can stretch to a great distance—Aid a falling brother—save a sinking family—and prove fathers to helpless orphans. . . . Charity desires the happiness of mankind, and rejoices at their prosperity."[39]

The East India Marine Society created measures to ensure it had the financial stability for benevolent services. Prospective members were admitted by a vote of three-fourths of the members present at each of the six meetings held annually. Upon admission, they were required to pay $25 (approximately $471 today).[40] Afterward, they were assessed fifty cents at each meeting. In addition, members who did not have a legitimate excuse for missing a meeting, such as sickness or being away on a voyage, were fined twenty-five cents.[41] Failure to pay fines after two years, if not away from the state of Massachusetts or the victim of "shipwreck or unavoidable misfortune," could result in expulsion from the organization. By 1808, East India Marine Society funds were approximately $4,408.[42] Fifteen years later, Society funds—invested in bank and insurance stocks—had increased to $7,984.66, $78 of which was being distributed to beneficiaries.

The East India Marine Society provided relief not only to the families of members but also to members themselves when they fell on hard times. On September 5, 1810, the president and the committee of observation ordered "all demands upon Joseph Phippen . . . stating that by misfortune he has been unable to pay the assessments due to the society . . . be suspended . . . for the time being." Similarly, during the next meeting, the assembled members voted to grant Captain George Girdler Smith "such assistance from the funds of the Society, from time to time, as they shall judge best."[43] In 1819, the officers also waived the dues for Jonathan Carnes, William Mugford (1762–1841), and John Burchmore (born 1776) for similar reasons. Of the handful of members who sought assistance from the Society, none is more surprising than Carnes, who had prospered during the early years of the pepper trade. In addition to being absolved from paying dues, he received distribution funds until his death in 1827.[44] In Carnes's case, the dangers of the maritime experience extended beyond shipwrecks and storms to include unstable markets and personal financial misfortune.

At the dawn of the nineteenth century, Salem was the only American port that boasted two marine societies: the East India Marine Society and the Marine Society at Salem in New England (commonly known as the Salem Marine Society). The latter, founded in 1766, was formed "to relieve such of their Members as thro' Misfortune at Sea, or otherwise, or by Reason of old Age or Sickness, stand in Need of Relief"; to aid "the necessitous Families of deceased Members"; and "to communicate in Writing, to be lodged with the Society, the Observations they make at Sea of any Matters which may render Navigation, particularly on this Coast, easier & safer."[45] Its seal featured the motto "Where Virtue Reigns, the Unfortunate Find Relief," and until 1790 it was open only to Salem ship captains; after that point shipowners became eligible for membership.[46] With more than two hundred members on the rolls before the creation of the East India Marine Society, the Salem Marine Society supported the local maritime community financially, not least by improving the port's buoys and lighthouses to help ships navigate in and around local waters.

Maintaining two marine societies in one port might appear to be redundant. In fact, as Salem expanded its international presence, it was justified. The "Association of Masters or Commanders of Vessels who have been or are engaged in the East India trade from the town of Salem" who met in August 1799 recognized that the Salem Marine Society's focus on local and Atlantic waters did not reflect Salem's new global standing at the dawn of the nineteenth century. Thus, they agreed to form "a Society by the name of the East India Marine Society . . . making such rules & by-laws at future meetings as may be judged useful & necessary in obtaining any nautical or mercantile knowledge & information, especially relative to East India Voyages." Eighteen of the thirty men who signed the Society's founding articles at Webb's Sun Tavern in October 1799 were already Salem Marine Society members. Their signatures, therefore, symbolized the need for a new institution with goals that were "objects of Public & private utility and advantage."[47]

To distinguish themselves from all other American marine societies, the East India Marine Society limited membership to Salem supercargoes and masters with worldly nautical cachet: those who sailed near or beyond the Cape of Good Hope or Cape Horn. This founding provision created an exclusive maritime club, one that attracted the pioneering mariners in the town. Among its early members were those who had opened American trade across the globe, such as Benjamin Hodges, who arrived in Salem with tea from Canton in 1790 while commanding the brig *William and Henry*; Jacob Crowninshield (1770–1808), who brought the first elephant to the United States on the ship *America* in 1797; and Jonathan Lambert (1772–1814), who had taken the brig *Hope* to Mozambique in 1789 and later became the self-appointed ruler of Tristan da Cunha in 1811.[48]

The East India Marine Society's strict membership qualifications excluded many mariners who belonged to the Salem Marine Society, most notably Joseph Peabody (1757–1844). Peabody had gone to sea before the Revolutionary War and was one of Salem's most prosperous merchants into the 1840s. When President James Monroe came to Salem in 1817 and visited the Society's museum, he "waited upon" the merchant, according to local legend.[49] Peabody owned many ships that had rounded the Cape of Good Hope, but he never did so himself and was thus ineligible to join the Society. Over the course of the next sixty-eight years, members debated about revising or eliminating these rigorous nautical restrictions, but to no avail, even during periods with declining membership and financial hardships. In an ironic twist, the exclusivity and prestige inherent in this stipulation led to the Society's eventual demise in the twentieth century.

The East India Marine Society magnified its standing in Salem by expending financial resources on festivities.[50] One of its bylaws stipulated that the president and the committee of observation "order a Publick Dinner . . . for the members annually."[51] This provision, more typical of a fraternal organization than of a benevolent society, put social intercourse on the same platform as charity. During the first two decades of the nineteenth century, around each anniversary of the Society's founding, members would parade throughout Salem before retiring to their museum quarters for a lavish dinner accompanied by excessive drinking and smoking and numerous toasts. Local newspapers reported on the annual celebration, and these accounts were often reprinted in out-of-town publications, increasing the Society's national exposure. Such rich semiotic events, another material form of exhibition and spectacle, reveal a great deal about the East India Marine Society, the United States, and the global connections that existed in the early republic.

On the first Wednesday in January (after 1804 moved to the first Wednesday in November to avoid icy winter conditions), East India Marine Society members moved in procession through the streets of Salem after their business meeting. They dressed in outfits that were collected abroad or donated by East Indian merchants and carried portions of the museum collection. One fixture of these parades was the palanquin from Calcutta donated by five members in 1803, who felt "it may gratify the curious, will show the method of travelling in this country, and may answer a very good purpose on our festival day, in case any accident should happen [to] a member."[52] That year, the *Salem Register* recorded that the parade "moved in procession . . . accompanied with a band of Musick, to their Hall, in which an elegant dinner was provided by Capt. Benj. Webb."[53]

To foster a spirit of American patriotism, the East India Marine Society hired musicians and local military outfits such as the Salem Artillery or the Salem Mechanic Light Infantry to accompany the parade and afterward to dine with the members. Large crowds gathered annually, even in January 1804, when the weather was cold and the streets were icy. Two years later, the *New-York Herald* (via the *Salem Register*) reported that as the Society's procession passed Derby Wharf, "a salute was fired, and the colours on all the vessels in the harbour and the wharves were displayed."[54]

With the benefit of historical context, modern scholars have interpreted these parades as open displays of exoticism. Some have stressed the performance and entertainment aspects of these processions, in which Society members dressed in clothing obtained overseas to celebrate their economic success as a result of trade.[55] Others categorized them as an example of public exhibition in the antebellum period that reinforced racial stereotypes and created a spectacle for western audiences.[56]

In the early nineteenth century, these parades were also viewed through multiple lenses. Local coverage was often favorable, noting their "harmony and conviviality" and the spreading of global knowledge. The *Salem Gazette* in 1805 described how Society members "passed in procession . . . exhibiting in characteristic dresses, instruments, etc. of distant nations, equal proofs of bold enterprise and steady industry in our nautical and mercantile citizens."[57] In 1807, the *Salem Register* announced that the procession "in some measure inform[s] us of the customs, manners and arts of their inhabitants," declaring "that the object of this society is not a mere ostentatious parade, but the promotion of nautical and commercial knowledge, which the journals and observations deposited in the library by the member[s] on their return from distant voyages fully testify."[58]

Other contemporary interpretations were not as approving. In 1802, William Bentley sneered, "The dressing of one of their company in a Mandarin's dress was no compliment paid to themselves on the occasion. Might they not rather have given the dress to one of their Servants or have exhibited a figure to the wondering multitude."[59] Bentley's criticism might reflect his personal issues with the founding articles of the organization or his racial and class bias.[60] An article in the *New-England Galaxy* offered a similar critique of the parades in 1823. While noting that the Society was "one of the most useful and honorable associations in the country," the author believed that their "dignity is by no means impaired, by the omission, at their annual festival, of the grotesque and masquerade procession, which formerly paraded through the streets of Salem, to the infinite wonder and delight of all the boys in the place."[61] Like Bentley, the writer viewed the members' "masquerade" in the dress of other cultures with racial prejudice, as a disservice to their status.

An anonymous mariner who visited Salem in the 1830s provided an alternative account of these parades, alluding to the antipathy directed toward the East India Marine Society during its anniversary celebrations:

> For several years there was a procession and dinner, but the ridicule of the press has ended the processions, while the dinner is wisely retained. The procession was as good as Abolition itself, which it resembled, as much as Asia is like unto Africa. The officers had mandarin cloaks, and other oriental garbs, and the man that attends in the museum was robed like a Chinese, and carried a tail like a streamer, sweeping the ground. The palankeen was borne by

> four blacks, in trowsers and turbans. A boy sat within, dressed like a nabob, and another, like a slave, carried the hooka by his side . . . These good old times are over, the exhibition discontinued, and a Salem mariner is apt to look grave when the procession is mentioned, and to watch an opportunity to change the conversation.[62]

To the mariner, this complicated cultural and racial role play—white sailors wearing East Indian dress, the hiring of African American men as Indian palanquin bearers—was akin to "Abolition."[63] In his eyes, the parade was a public form of appreciation for other cultures or trading partners and also a means of displaying the town's and the country's prominence on the world stage. As for the unidentified Salem mariner mentioned at the end, we are left to wonder whether he shared the author's sentiments or held an opposing view.[64]

As these period and contemporary perspectives make clear, the Society's parades were not ordinary festive pageants. Rather, they were complex cultural statements that blurred the lines of race and American identity as seen by transnational mariners. On the one hand, these processions boldly proclaimed that "Jack Tar" was the preeminent agent in defining what it meant to be American; on the other, the viewer was left with a distorted view of who was included and excluded from this characterization of a "true Yankee."

When the public spectacle ended, the internal one began. East India Marine Society members entered their hall with invited guests, including the military outfit that accompanied the parade and a local religious official. The assembled group sat in fanback chairs around a great crescent-shaped table in the center of the hall and consumed a sumptuous array of food.[65] Benjamin Webb provided the first few anniversary dinners. In later years, they were prepared by John Remond (1786–1874), a native of Curaçao and the patriarch of one of the most influential free families of color in nineteenth-century America. Remond catered many important events in Salem, including a dinner organized for the Marquis de Lafayette (1757–1834) during his second visit to Salem on August 31, 1824.[66] While people of color were not allowed access to many public spaces in the antebellum United States—including the Society's museum from 1833–65 (discussed further in chapter 5)—they could prepare the food that white people ate. Caterers such as Remond exploited this duality and created a monopoly over an industry that few white individuals would enter. The

African American activist and writer W. E. B. Du Bois (1868–1963) characterized these businessmen "as remarkable a trade guild as ever ruled in a medieval city. [The caterers] took complete leadership of the bewildered group of Negroes, and led them steadily on to a degree of affluence, culture and respect such as has probably never been surpassed in the history of the Negro in America."[67]

Throughout each anniversary dinner, numerous toasts were delivered, accompanied by various types of liquor, from rum to brandy, as well as lemonade.[68] In addition, the Society served "Peabody punch", a highly alcoholic festive beverage attributed to Joseph Peabody, who purportedly created the recipe on his last voyage, in 1791, to the West Indies.[69] This drink was a global concoction: many of its ingredients—Jamaican rum, cognac, Madeira, limes, guava jelly, and green tea—were acquired from international ports of trade.

The Peabody punch was served from two nearly identical ceramic punchbowls, which had been commissioned in the port of Liverpool, England, by Benjamin Hodges's brother George (1765–1827), and donated to the Society in 1800 (see figure 9).[70] On the inside bottom of each bowl, the words "Salem East India Marine Society Instituted 1800" is inscribed, surrounded by a vinelike cartouche. The outsides of the bowls, like the cardinal points on a compass rose (north, south, east, west), are decorated with four scenes that fuse the institution with maritime commerce and American patriotism. One side depicts the Great Seal of the United States, while another features a circular print showing several stages in the construction of a ship and a verse from one of the most popular political songs of the time, "Ode. Adams and Liberty"—an allusion to the vast natural resources of American shipbuilding that would never be used again by foreign entities. These transfers and two others combined to form a patriotic tableau that was visible when the bowls were on display in the museum and when they were in use for Peabody punch, an elixir produced by American maritime trade and enterprise.[71] They fused American maritime commerce and patriotism with this new marine society, an organization dedicated to supporting the maritime labor force that was fueling the economy of the new republic.

Close inspection of the toasts delivered at these dinners in the first two decades of the nineteenth century reveal a great deal about the East India Marine Society and the country at the time. Beyond the annual toast to

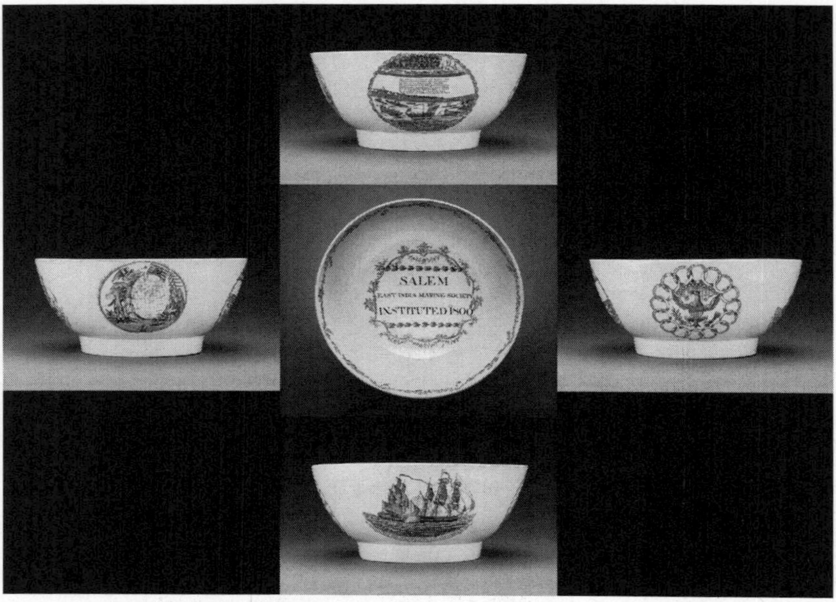

FIGURE 9. One of a pair of East India Marine Society punchbowls, circa 1800–1801. Glazed creamware, 5¾ x 12⅝ in. Peabody Essex Museum Collection, M2.A. © 2013 Peabody Essex Museum, Salem, MA. Photography by Walter Silver.

the Society and its museum, many were given in honor of revered mariners, the maritime experience, American patriotism, commerce linked to overseas trade, and subjects such as "The riches which the arts give, may they find sacred to their support" (1804).[72] To further bind the sea to such themes, the toasts were often sprinkled with maritime metaphors. A toast in 1806 honored "The Salem East India Marine Society—*Improvement* 'ahead,' *Harmony* 'in the beam,' and *Party Spirit* 'astern,' *hull-down*." Sometimes these nautical references were even more overt:

> The enemies of our country—May they be blessed with
> Leaky clumps, Choak'd pumps,
> Sails rent, Grog spent,
> Wormy bread, Wind ahead,
> Cloudy noon, At night no moon,
> Compass lost, Tempest-tost,
> A winter's coast.[73]

To accentuate these sentiments, music was played after each toast was delivered. During one anniversary dinner, a toast to "the memory of Washington" was followed by the "Dead March" from *Saul,* and a toast to the Navy was followed by "Hull's Victory."

Many of the toasts given during the annual dinners of 1804, 1806–11, and 1815–16 addressed the connections between maritime trade and the nation. In 1804, when the United States was profiting in the East Indies trade while Britain and France were at war, Society members toasted both "Commerce with all the nations But the love of our country our best happiness" and "Commerce without violence & no war upon the sea," an allusion to the risks American ships faced during international conflicts. In 1807, a toast linked commerce to agrarianism and a strong nation: "*Commerce and Agriculture*—Their mutual dependence confirms our country's independence." Similarly, in 1809, members honored "Agriculture, Commerce & Manufactures grand Pillars of national existence."

Beyond maritime industry, East India Marine Society members expressed ebullient national pride through toasts to the country, its founding principles, its military heroes, and iconic symbols of the United States. In 1810, the dinner group toasted "Our Country—may it ever be the seat of Liberty, secured by good & wholesome Laws, uprightly & ably administered." Beneath an engraving of *The Apotheosis of Washington,* executed in 1802 by the artist John James Barralet (1747–1815), members offered an 1808 toast to "The Memory of Washington; may his Virtues and Patriotism be followed as well as admired by every American."[74] Two years later, they honored him with "The Memory of Washington—may his undeviating patriotism & integrity be ever imitated by the Rulers, & revered by the People of our nation."

The pillars of the nation were also toasted. In 1807, dinner attendees lifted their glasses to "*Our Constitution*—May she never be '*hove down*' while she is able to swim." The next year, a toast likened the country's "backbone" to a ship's anchor: "The Constitution of the United States of America, may we ever prize it as our principal safeguard from confusion and anarchy, and hold to it as to the sheet Anchor of our political salvation." In 1811, members lauded constitutional principles with "Am. Rights as Freemen—May we be proud in possessing, active in exerting, & zealous in defending them." In an undated toast, possibly delivered in 1817 or 1818, the group celebrated "The American Flag—May the world know that it is not good to insult it." The dearth of toasts related to local issues or organizations emphasizes the power of these national patriotic sentiments.

The sea was a fixture of many toasts. Some offered overt recognitions of water as the medium for enterprise and exchange. In 1806, for instance, the ocean was acknowledged as "The nursery of valour, enterprize, honour and wealth."[75] While many toasts expressed optimism about the sea's ability to create global networks, others honored its capacity to keep America out of international conflicts. As the Napoleonic Wars raged in Europe, the Society members gathered in 1809 toasted "The Atlantic Ocean may it ever separate us from the calamaties [*sic*] *of Europe,*" a sentiment they repeated in subsequent years. Members also praised the sea for its ability to foster knowledge. An undated toast acknowledged the ocean as "The current of information setting the right way, without the undertow of prejudice." This toast was one of the few that alluded to an unbiased way of thinking about the world.

The East India Marine Society often saluted sailors associated with their institution, delivering toasts to deceased or absent members. They honored those who had died overseas—"Our brethren who have fallen in a foreign land, May the sympathy of a brother never be waning for those whose graves are watered by the tears of a stranger" (1806)—and those who were away plying American trade routes—"Our absent Bretheren [*sic*], We wish them happy returns, enrich'd themselves, & enriching their employers" (1811). All American mariners were recognized in 1807 with the toast "*Our Seamen*—May their country ever *deserve* and *find* protection in their bravery." As these examples highlight, the Society acknowledged not only the economic importance of their members' profession but also the principles of brotherhood and support on which all marine societies were founded.

To recognize the accomplishments of past mariners, members delivered toasts to explorers who had paved the way for their own success. The first recorded toast at an anniversary dinner (1804) was delivered to the Portuguese explorer Vasco da Gama (circa 1460–1524), who was praised for opening western trade with the East Indies by being the first European to reach India via the sea. Although no portrait of da Gama hung in the museum, he was toasted at six subsequent dinners and acknowledged as a model for all sailors to follow. One honored "Vasco da Gama, What genius performs may genius immortalize," then adding a maxim that all Society members viewed as a principle goal of their organization: "May each mariner record, so that Enterprise may discover." Other explorers honored at dinners were James Cook and Jean François de Galaup, comte de La Pérouse (1741–88?), both of whom died during voyages of exploration. In 1807, the Society toasted "*Cook and La Perouse*—Martyrs in the cause of science—may a similar *fate* never attend those who shall dare to emulate their *fame*."[76] Christopher Columbus was honored in 1809 with "May the enterprize which directed his steps never be extinguished in the Country he discovered," a sentiment echoed in similar toasts delivered in 1811 and 1815.

Cook, La Pérouse, and Columbus were also immortalized through objects in the museum. The Society owned copies of published volumes on Cook's and La Pérouse's voyages, the first books they acquired; and in 1803, Michele Felice Cornè was commissioned to paint a portrait of Cook for display in the museum.[77] Cornè also painted a version of the artist William Hogarth's (1697–1764) etching *Columbus Breaking the Egg*, which depicts a purported dinner party at which Columbus challenges his critics (see figure 10).[78] After being told that anyone could have discovered the New World, Columbus asks his dinner companions if they can stand an egg up on its smaller end. Following their unsuccessful attempts, Columbus takes his egg and strikes it gently against the table to slightly flatten one end, and the egg stands upright. "Now, gentlemen," he is reputed to have said, "you can all do it!" This painting, along with two bricks from Columbus's house in Genoa (donated in 1822 and 1824), is the most literal encapsulation of a toast from the Society's anniversary dinners. As in the toasts, only a positive view of the explorer was displayed for visitors to see. Thus, the sentiments delivered at annual dinners echoed in the museum for years to come.

Toasts to European mariners reflected one of the founding principles of the East India Marine Society: "promoting a knowledge of navigation and trade to the East Indies" through voyage and discovery.[79] The Society quickly garnered international recognition as an important scientific organization, thanks in part to Nathaniel Bowditch's (1773–1838) involvement in the organization. A veteran of the East India trade as both supercargo and master, Bowditch was, in the words of the mathematician Dirk Struik, "the most famous of early New England scientists."[80] He served as the institution's first caretaker and organizer of its logbooks and journals—in essence, the first librarian for the museum. The Society required all members to carry a separate logbook on their voyages in order

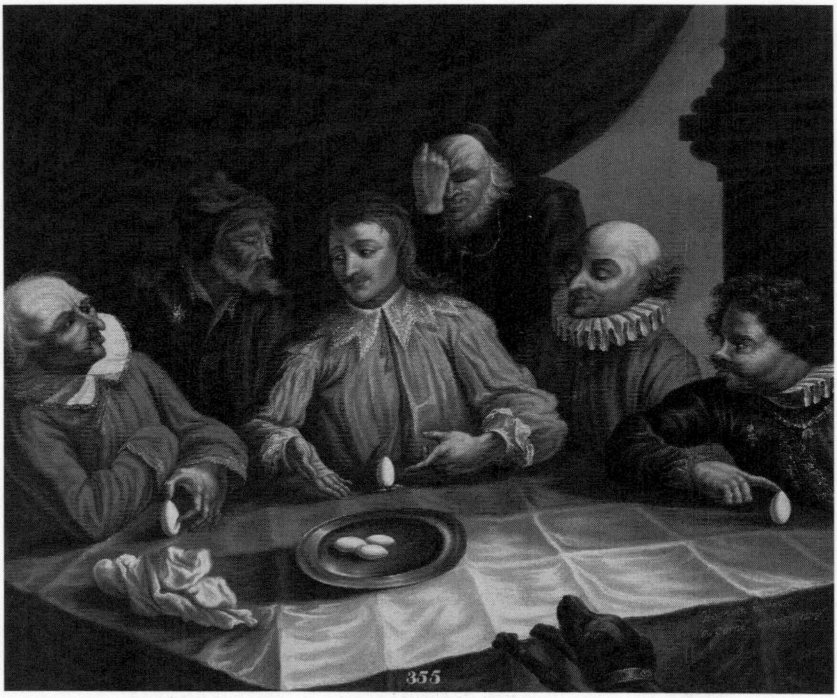

FIGURE 10. Michele Felice Cornè, *Columbus and the Egg,* 1805. Oil on canvas, 38 x 43½ in. Peabody Essex Museum Collection, 108370. © 2016 Peabody Essex Museum, Salem, MA. Photography by Bob Packert. "355" was added to the painting in 1821 when the Society's first superintendent, Seth Bass, labeled objects in the collection with their catalogue numbers.

to "collect such facts and observations as may tend to the improvement and security of navigation," and in this way they created an archive of nautical information that predated any governmental repository and was unsurpassed in the United States in the early nineteenth century.[81] It was also an important resource for the Society members' commercial pursuits, thus blending scientific knowledge with economic gain.

The course of American science would have taken a much different route without the work of Bowditch. He was emblematic of many scientists in the early days of the republic, who were self-taught doctors, lawyers, or clergymen by trade, not the professionals who would characterize the field in the following decades.[82] While Bowditch never developed his own scientific theories, he corrected and improved upon established principles and made them accessible to a wider audience. More than any other figure in the new republic, he helped put the United States, and the East India Marine Society, in the forefront of maritime navigation and mathematics.

Born in Salem on March 26, 1773, Bowditch became proficient in mathematics and science at an early age. Due to family financial troubles, he left school at the age of ten and took an apprenticeship with a Salem ship chandler on Essex Street. Living above the chandlery, he compensated for his lack of formal schooling by immersing himself in reading, studying, and making crude navigational instruments. Edward Holyoke and William Bentley took a keen interest in young Bowditch, allowing him to borrow books from the Salem Philosophical Society Library.[83] Using this collection, he taught himself Latin and French by comparing Bibles written in both languages with their English equivalents. This meant that he was able to read and understand important scientific works of the time. At the age of seventeen, while reading Isaac Newton's *Principia* (1687), Bowditch uncovered a mistake in the calculation of a comet's orbit and informed a Harvard professor of this error. (The professor dismissed Bowditch as a novice.)[84]

In 1795, Bowditch embarked on the first of five voyages to the Far East. His short career at sea contributed greatly to his noted work on navigation. Many mariners at this time used dead reckoning as a navigational tool: that is, they calculated a ship's position based on previously determined points. Bowditch, however, advocated for celestial navigation: taking measurements between the horizon and heavenly bodies. He spent the majority of his free time onboard ship teaching his fellow sailors this more accurate method and reading and correcting John Hamilton Moore's *The Practical Navigator and Seaman's New Daily Assistant* (1772), the leading navigational text of the time.

During his years at sea, Bowditch found more than 8,000 errors in Moore's work, and these corrections became the basis for his own text, *The New American Practical Navigator,* published in 1802. It became an invaluable tool for generations of mariners to come. William Augustus Rogers (1792–1821), who came from a Salem shipowning family filled with East India Marine Society members, consulted the book while onboard the *Tartar* bound for India. In an 1817 journal entry he wrote, "This day employed myself in acquiring a knowledge of practical navigation, which with the class and explicit direction of Mr. Bowditch is easily acquired. . . . [T]his gentleman, who now boasts the highest point of elevation in the mathematical world . . . maintains a security of temper and polite refinement of manners which win the esteem of those who converse with him."[85]

Bowditch received many honors throughout his life. He was elected to every major American and European scientific society, including the American Academy of Arts and Sciences (1799), the American Philosophical Society (1809), and the Royal Societies of London and Edinburgh (1819). In 1823, after his resignation as East India Marine Society president, his fellow members proclaimed he had "elevated the character of his native town and endeared him[self] to his townspeople." At his death, they declared that he was responsible for "much of the usefulness and celebrity to which it [the Society] has attained."[86]

To materially encapsulate their admiration for Bowditch, the Society commissioned Gilbert Stuart (1755–1828), one of America's foremost portraitists, to paint a portrait of him for the museum. However, due to delays and then Stuart's death in 1828, a local artist, Charles Osgood (1809–90), executed the work that was officially presented to the Society on May 6, 1835, and placed "in the most conspicuous & appropriate situation in this Hall" (see figure 11). According to Bowditch's son, Nathaniel Ingersoll Bowditch (1805–61), anyone who entered the Society's "spacious hall . . . [was] arrested by it"; the portrait "invit[ed] the attention of the visitors."[87] According to the *Merchants' Magazine and Commercial Review* of September 1843, the portrait had been hung in "a fitting place for the presence of such a man, amid the trophies of the commerce to which he was a most distinguished benefactor."[88] Bowditch's portrait was the first likeness of a member to be hung on the walls alongside paintings of Captain Cook and Admiral Horatio Nelson (1758–1805). By enshrining his likeness in their museum, the East India Marine Society acknowledged his place, and the Society's, in the international scientific community.

Bowditch's and other members' contributions to navigational science helped elevate the institution and the museum to the national stage in the early nineteenth century. When the first printed catalogue of the museum's collection was published in 1821, copies were sent to former presidents Thomas Jefferson and James Madison (1751–1836). Jefferson saw "with great satisfaction the rich prospect of additions to our science for which we are likely to be indebted to the exertions of such public-minded individuals" as East India Marine Society members. Madison praised the Society as "an Institution which unites with a benevolent object the useful one of

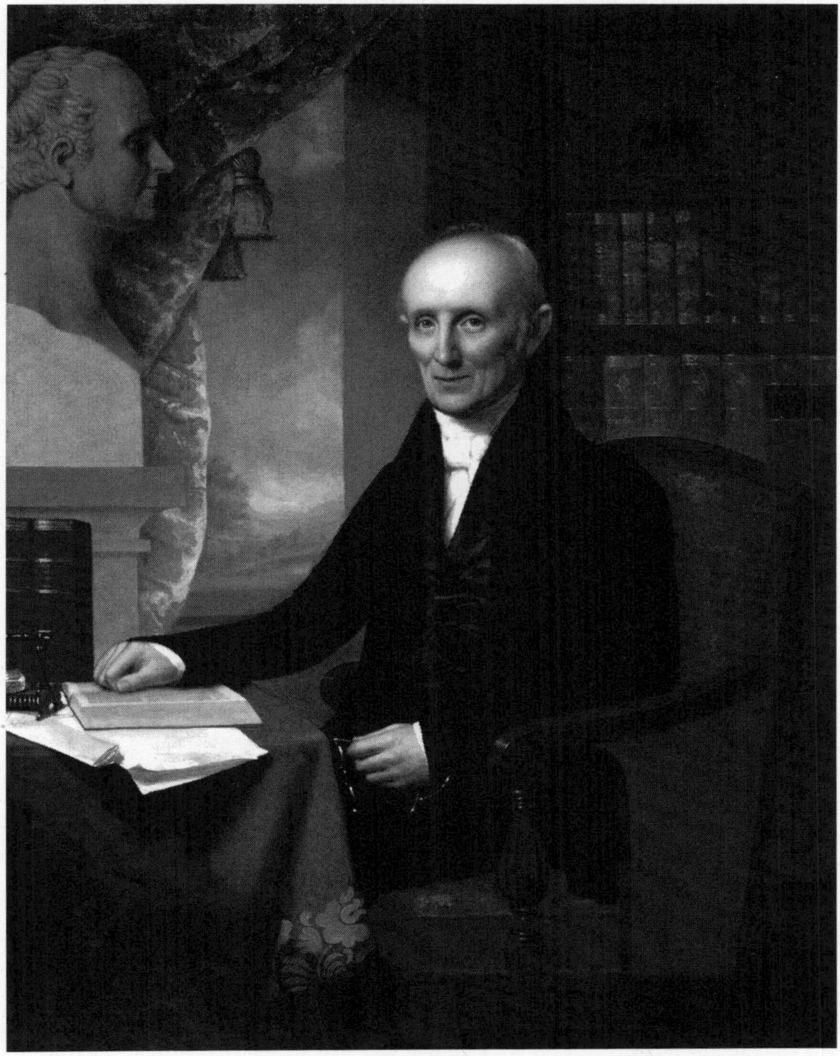

FIGURE 11. Charles Osgood, portrait of Nathaniel Bowditch, 1835. Oil on canvas, 58 x 43½ in. Peabody Essex Museum Collection, M370. © 2006 Peabody Essex Museum, Salem, MA. Photography by Mark Sexton. The bust on the left is of the celebrated astronomer and mathematician Pierre Simon La Place (1749–1827). Below it are two volumes of Bowditch's translation of La Place's most noted work, *Mécanique céleste*. Bowditch was one of only three people in the United States who could read and understand the text, which applied Newton's theory of gravitation to astronomy. He believed that translating it would make it more accessible. The final product, with annotations one and a half times longer than the original work, marked the entrance of American thinkers into celestial mechanics and the end of the Newtonian age in American science.

improving navigation, and another so interesting to all who have a taste for natural and artificial curiosities."[89] Some attributed the link between science and the museum's mission as the reason for its acclaimed status. A Philadelphia newspaper, the *United States Gazette,* declared in April 1824 that "the Salem East India Museum is doubtlessly one of the best institutions, if not the only one, of the kind, in America," a direct result of "the effect of enterprise when directed by science." In the newspaper's opinion, Salem, "by the efforts of her merchants, and the labours of her literary sons," ranked among "the most opulent and most scientific town of our Union."[90]

By the 1830s, the East India Marine Society's reputation as an organization promoting and advancing the science of navigation was strong enough to begin promoting national endeavors. President John Quincy Adams (1767–1848) was attuned to the prospects of nautical and astronomical science and its usefulness to federal policy, and he recognized that astronomy, exploration, national glory, and the improvement of human knowledge were connected.[91] In his first annual address to Congress in 1825, he stated, "One hundred expeditions of circumnavigation like those of Cook and La Perouse would not burden the exchequer of the nation fitting them out so much as the ways and means of defraying a single campaign in war."[92] Adams suggested creating a U.S. voyage of discovery to the northwestern coast of North America. This journey would require passage around Cape Horn and into the South Pacific, an area of great interest to East India Marine Society members and American mariners. In 1828, marine and scientific societies voiced approval of this project in hopes that it would involve charting many of the dangerous reefs and shoals around the South Pacific islands that were damaging American trade ships in these waters.[93] Unfortunately, Congress did not follow through on Adams's ideas. Soon after, he lost the presidency to Andrew Jackson (1767–1845) and, with it, the naval expedition he had fought for.

Nonetheless, Adams's failed attempt at an exploratory venture to the Pacific Northwest laid the groundwork for a larger project. Two months into Jackson's first term, the *New York Mercantile Advertiser* asked, "[W]hy should we, whose destiny is as great as [Europe's], fold our arms in comparative inaction? The annals of our whaling and sealing Ports, and particularly of the Salem East India Marine Society, will shew that we have all the requisites for such enterprises."[94] The newspaper viewed a national geographic expedition as the one accomplishment missing from the fledgling nation's global ascendancy.

In the early 1820s, this call was championed by Jeremiah N. Reynolds (1799–1858), an Ohio newspaper editor who was an advocate for John Cleves Symmes's (1779–1829) hollow earth theory. Reynolds believed that an expedition to the Antarctic would allow explorers to access one of the polar openings that Symmes had theorized. In response to the pleas of American mariners who were trading in the Pacific, he extended his interest to mapping islands in the south seas.[95] During Adams's administration, Reynolds became a special agent to the Navy, and later he made an unsuccessful attempt to privately finance his own expedition. In late 1831, he joined the crew of the U.S.S. *Potomac* on its punitive naval expedition to Sumatra to investigate a major international incident involving inhabitants at Quallah Battoo, who had massacred sailors on the Salem pepper-trading ship *Friendship* captained by Society member Charles Moses Endicott (1793–1863).

On his return to the United States, Reynolds worked on writing a narrative of his voyage on the *Potomac*.[96] No longer an advocate of Symmes's theory, he turned his attention to the South Pacific and promoting an American geographical expedition.[97] He visited the East India Marine Society Museum on November 1, 1834, part of a fact-finding mission for his forthcoming volume, which he hoped would advance support for an exploring expedition. In the book, he mentioned "looking over the record of our mercantile enterprise to the east . . . as preserved in the port-folios of the Salem East India Marine Society," and he looked ahead to the time "when these documents will be referred to, and written up, as interesting items belonging to the history of our country." Reynolds noted that the Society's members, while engaged in commercial enterprise, "were assiduous in gaining a knowledge of the countries they visited, and gathered many curiosities and antiquities of the east, of which they have formed a splendid museum for the benefit of science and the arts, and the gratification of the curious who visit their town."[98]

Reynolds rallied support for an American expedition, petitioning votes from the New England states that were the backbone of the American whaling industry as well from his native Ohio and from renowned scientists such as Benjamin Silliman (1779–1864).[99] The East India Marine Society also entered the fray. In a letter to the *Salem Gazette* in 1834, an unidentified member (likely speaking on behalf of the entire Society) bemoaned the fact that "in a country having such an extended commerce as ours, the keels of whose vessels are daily furrowing over almost every mile of the waters of the navigable globe, . . . so little has heretofore been done either by the government or by individuals in surveys of coasts and harbors, or for the promotion of nautical science generally." The writer believed that the United States lagged behind other maritime nations, that it was "too willing to allow others to pioneer the way" and too reliant on British charts and English and French nautical instruments "by which our ships are guided in their course over the trackless ocean." He declared, "These things ought not to be so," and emphasized that American "facilities in the Pacific Ocean are great and our commerce of as much importance as theirs." The member argued that "something remains yet to be done in that quarter which can be accomplished as well by us, as by any other power." The country, he wrote, is not "deficient in men of science fully competent to conduct an enterprise like the present," but they "are now lying dormant . . . and only need the necessary encouragement to be called forth."[100]

Initially, President Jackson was more interested in internal matters involving banks, public lands, and national surplus than in "John Quincy Adams's lighthouses of the skies" and other scientific pursuits.[101] Yet a growing sense of jingoistic national pride, apparent among many advocates of an exploring expedition, began to align with Jackson's vision of western expansion and conquest. In this changing climate, the East India Marine Society continued to lobby for an American exploring expedition. On December 16, 1834, it submitted a memorial, "Praying that an Expedition be fitted out by the Government to make a Voyage of Discovery and Survey to the South Seas," to the second session of the twenty-third Congress. The memorial was signed by the Society's president, William Fettyplace (1780–1867), and included a list of members.

Following the pattern of a similar memorial submitted by Reynolds a month earlier, the Society advocated for an expedition to chart the Fiji Islands, where many Society members were acquiring resources to trade in China. Reynolds, state representatives, and other organizations had made similar arguments, but Society members were unique in emphasizing that they were the American equivalent of European explorers. Among them were mariners who were "the first to display our national colors in our commerce to the eastern world," "those who have been engaged in trade on coasts and among islands but little known," and those "who have visited the islands in the Pacific as well as those in the east, and have seen and felt the dangers our vessels are exposed to for the want of such protection as an expedition fitted out for the express purpose alone can give." With a vested interest in the South Pacific trading grounds and an understanding of "the losses and . . . painful solicitude" in this region, Society members requested "the protection of their government . . . to point out the position of a dangerous reef." They also asked, in the mold of imperial nationals, for federal defense "against the natives, who had seen nothing of our power to restrain them from unlawful attacks upon their vessels or their lives."[102] In the Society's opinion, a government-sponsored expedition was essential for improved maritime trade, if nothing else.

Two years later, Jackson signed a bill authorizing the United States Exploring Expedition. In 1838, the U.S. Ex. Ex., as it came to be known, left on a four-year mission under the command of Lieutenant Charles Wilkes (1798–1877). It was one of the largest western voyages of discovery in history, and the ethnographic objects and natural history specimens amassed during the expedition were exhibited at the Patent Office Building in Washington, D.C., before becoming part of the Smithsonian Institution's collection.

The Society had an important imprint on the structure of the voyage. Secretary of the Navy Mahlon Dickerson (1770–1853) wrote to members in August 1836 asking for advice on "the formation of a scientific corps for the expedition, & their recommendations of scientific gentlemen of suitable age to be employed as members of this corps"; "recommendations of a philologist to collect vocabularies of the different languages and an Artist to take the portraits of the Natives of the different countries & Islands which may be visited"; "a series of inquiries as to the subjects of natural history"; and "suggestions they may believe calculated to promote the objects of the expedition."[103] A report crafted by Bowditch and other members, along with one from the American Philosophical Society and a communication from the Naval Lyceum of New York, was incorporated into the Navy's instructions for Wilkes and his scientific corps.[104] In addition, two Society members aided the expedition. Benjamin Vanderford (1787–1842), a veteran of trade in Fiji and the Far East, served as a pilot (an experienced mariner who helps guide a ship through congested waterways) and an interpreter, and John Henry Eagleston (1804–84), who was trading in the Fiji Islands at the time, helped pilot one of the expedition's ships, the U.S.S. *Peacock*.[105]

The East India Marine Society's successful advocacy for and involvement in the U.S. Ex. Ex. would be the highwater mark of its national scientific influence. In 1841, members toasted with pride and optimism "*The American Exploring Expedition*—May it safely return, and its success be equal to the efforts of its enterprising conductors, and the great objects for which it was undertaken."[106] The Society's scientific curiosity and achievement undergirded its accumulation of objects for enlightened speculation. Members recognized the fusion of the natural sciences and the collecting of material culture—like the double-ended pipe—as the twin pillars of their organization. Only six years after the English poet and artist William Blake (1757–1827) wrote that "The Foundation of Empire is Art and Science," the Society toasted "Natural History, may commerce never forget its obligations" and "A Cabinet, that every mariner may possess the history of the world" during its festive anniversary dinner in 1804.[107]

Although, like other marine societies, it had been incorporated "for the laudable purpose of affording relief to disabled Seamen, and to the indigent Widows and Families of deceased Members and others," the East India Marine Society distinguished itself from many collecting institutions of the day by instructing members to obtain objects for the museum during their voyages.[108] This unique aspect of the Society's mission was an outgrowth of Salem's commercial maritime trading networks, a rational curiosity that characterized scientific exploration in the new republic and sailors' predisposition to acquire objects from their voyages. While the Society's original bylaws did not directly refer to collecting objects and forming a museum, several articles did allude to these goals. One required "[t]hat a convenient hall, or room to meet in be procured with an adjoining room to deposit the Books, Papers, & charts, or any articles of Curiosity that may be collected or presented to the Society by donation or otherwise." Another directed "[t]hat the most approved books of History, Voyages, Travels and of Navigation and new & correct Charts especially of the East India Seas shall be purchased or procured."[109] By 1821, however, the Society's first published catalogue explicitly named collecting as one of the principle objectives of the organization: "to form a museum of natural and artificial curiosities."[110] In this way, the Society fulfilled "the essential apparatus of the learned gentleman," according to the English philosopher and scientist Francis Bacon (1561–1626): "the collecting of a most perfect and general library" and "a goodly, huge cabinet."[111]

In the nineteenth century, during the height of Salem's maritime clout, the East India Marine Society's membership grew to 140 members, and a vast assortment of objects poured into the museum. During the first few months of the Society's founding in 1801, Jonathan Carnes and other members trading in the Pacific donated thirty-five objects, a number that had more than quintupled by the time William Bentley first visited the museum on August 13 of the same year. Bentley listed "in all 185 articles," which included "several images & paintings of Hindostan, China & Japan, with complete dresses in the Chinese fashion"; "Oyster shells of Sumatra"; "The Albatross"; "Some antiquities . . . curiosities"; and the "foundation for a Library well begun."[112] Three years later, the *Salem Register* noted that "a few years has not extinguished the zeal with which they [the Society members] commenced their labours in collecting and arranging the most important aids to a history of the globe."[113]

Within a decade, the collection grew almost twenty times in size, and it more than doubled during the following ten years, reaching over 2,000 objects by 1821. The museum housed objects that members collected during international trade; that the institution purchased; that Far Eastern merchants offered as friendly tokens of admiration; that interested mariners or individuals donated, often after hearing about the Society via word of mouth or in publications; and that visitors brought to the museum in person. The collection was in many ways akin to earlier European cabinets, containing a vast assortment of natural history specimens and ethnographic material, but it was also a distinctive representation of members' experiences in new lands—tools, weapons, and trade goods from the Pacific Islands; oil paintings and life-size clay figure portraits of the merchants with whom members traded in the East; and an assortment of unusual flora, fauna, and other objects that conjured up memories of life at sea.

Like the double-ended pipe from Sumatra, many of the objects in the collection reflected characteristics of global maritime trade and thus contained multiple meanings. Mariners viewed some objects as symbolic of their trading partners' culture or emblematic of their own maritime experiences. Sailors also purchased other cultural artifacts offered to them, which served as three-dimensional documentations of the encounter between the shipboard community and the native populations.[114] Often, sailors preferred objects that exaggerated physical characteristics they found fascinating, such as a Haida mask of a woman wearing a prominent lip-distending labret donated by Captain Daniel Cross, master of the brig *Rob Roy* during a voyage to the northwestern coast in 1821–25 (see figure 12).[115]

As objects collected from the many ports of call on Salem trade routes passed through multiple hands, their original meaning was altered. Once they were exhibited at the Society's museum, they could be viewed in

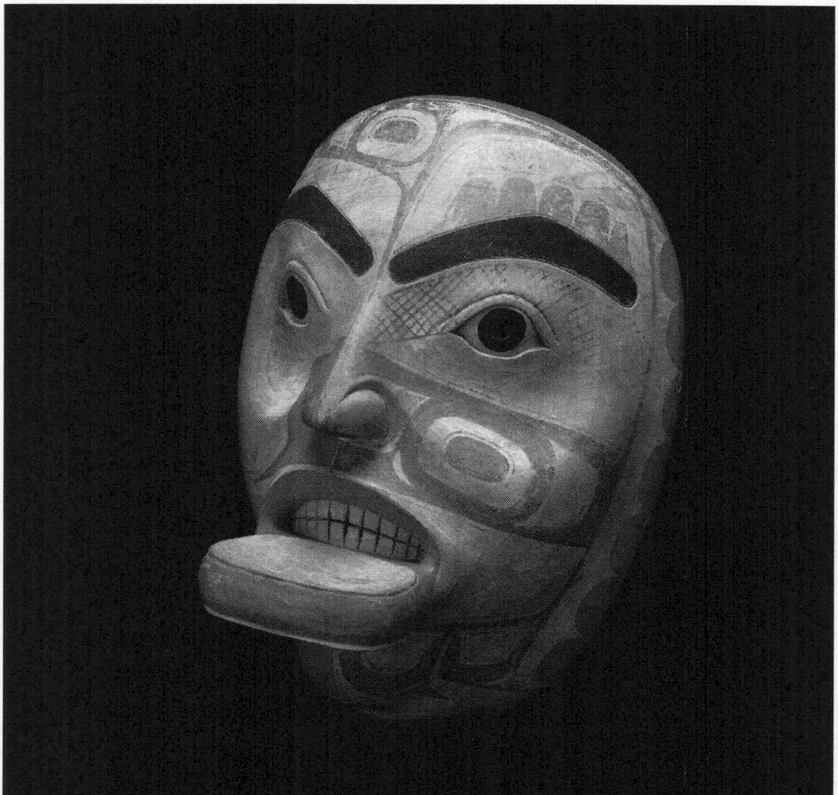

FIGURE 12. Mask carved by a Kaigani Haida artist, circa 1825. Wood, pigment, 10¼ x 7½ x 4 in. Peabody Essex Museum Collection, E3483. © Peabody Essex Museum, Salem, MA. Photography by Mark Sexton and Jeffrey Dykes. This mask from Kasaan, in southeastern Alaska, likely represents Djilakons, a mythical ancestress of the Haida.

multiple ways—as representations of other cultures or as souvenirs of exchange and cultural encounter. Most likely, neither the mariners who acquired these objects nor the Society members and the museum visitors wondered if an object had been made for ceremonial use or trade.[116] In addition, sailors in the early nineteenth century had a limited understanding of indigenous people in other parts of the globe prior to their voyages, apart from published descriptions such as those that appeared in volumes on Cook's voyages to the Pacific. Therefore, American sailors often compared native inhabitants to culturally unrelated people they met at other points of a voyage or at home.[117]

While filled with complexities, the East India Marine Society sought to present visitors with an understanding of the world through the display of objects collected via global exchange. These expressions of cultural identity had a profound impact not only on Salem residents, but also on the diverse American audience that came from across the country to visit the museum, making distant shores as well known as provincial towns. The museum—sometimes referred to as the East India Museum or simply the Salem Museum—was free as long as visitors had an introduction from a member. Writing in the early twentieth century, Salem resident Caroline Howard King (1822–1909) recalled the sense of exotic wonderment she experienced during her visits as a child in the 1830s: "the hours were full of enchantment . . . And indeed in those days the Spice Islands seemed to lie very near our coast."[118] Through the museum and its annual festivities, the Society brought the world back home to its native town.

The East India Marine Society did not collect objects as a means to classify other cultures or races, nor were these objects simply tools for obtaining global knowledge. Rather, this vast array of material culture was displayed as the Society's expression of what it meant to be an American; it denoted both Salem and the new nation's position in the world. In this context, the museum's collection is akin to the letters, journals, and published narratives penned by American expatriates and businessmen in the Far East and other parts of the globe during the same period, which the historian Dane Morrison points to as defining a national character in the new United States: the "true Yankee."[119] The Society used its museum in a similar fashion: to support its vision of an American identity tied to the sea.

The East India Marine Society was immediately recognized as a novel institution in the United States due to its unique attributes. An article in the *Political Repository,* a newspaper centered in Brookfield, Massachusetts, remarked in January 1801 that "the Institution is only in its infancy, yet there is already a very handsome collection. . . . The funds of the society are increasing, . . . which is directed by their constitution to be employed in useful purposes."[120] A year later, the *Monthly Magazine, or, British Register* declared, "The Anglo-Americans looking to the East Indies for the greatest future improvement of their trade and navigation, neglect no means that may contribute to promote their object. A society, under the title of the 'East India Marine Society,' has hence been established, recently, at Salem, with a view to collect charts, maps, and observations, tending to facilitate the navigation of the eastern and southern ocean. Commerce is expected to derive signal benefits from its exertions."[121] The *Boston Weekly Magazine* commented in January 1802 that "[t]he conduct of this Society has been highly honorable to them. . . . They have . . . provided a library for the purpose of mercantile and nautical information; also a very valuable collection in Natural History, coins,' &c."[122]

A couple of years later, an anonymous author, "X," expanded on the Society's growing local and national reputation in a praiseworthy letter to the *Salem Gazette.* "X" distinguished the Society's museum from other American endeavors "with swelling titles and splendid decorations," which "have died soon after their birth." These organizations, according to the author, "injured the reputation and lessened the usefulness of all." In addition, the author pointed to the Society's makeup of members who were "young, curious, and full of enterprise" rather than "men advanced in years, among whom ambition is but a momentary sensation of the soul."[123] Triumphantly, "X" proclaimed:

> Your collection of rare and valuable curiosities surpasses any in New England; and the large additions which are daily made to it induce us to think that it will soon be the first in the United States. Many men of sordid and contracted minds consider a Museum as they do fireworks, that give pleasure only when seen; but it appears different to those who are enlightened by science and refined by taste: They are filled with admiration at every thing which throws light on the history of nations, or exhibits the beauties, or displays the wonders of nature. . . . Your researches, united with the researches of others, will assist the philosopher in discussing that hitherto but partially explored subject, the powers and faculties of the human mind, by showing him the influence of climate, laws, superstition and habit, on society.[124]

The author viewed the Society's museum as the foundation of global knowledge for Salem and ultimately the country, not as a carnival sideshow like many American museums. Finally, "X" boldly predicted that the Society's model would promote similar endeavors at this time and in the future: "Your descendants, in some distant day, will look at what you have done, and while they admire and reverence the indefatigable industry and bold enterprize of their fathers, will feel stimulated to like exertions."[125]

Unfortunately, Salem's maritime fortunes would not be as long-lived as the East India Marine Society's museum. As a result of increasing British and French interference with American commerce during the Napoleonic Wars, President Jefferson prohibited all foreign trade in and out of United States ports in 1807. This Embargo Act had damaging effects on New England's economy, decimating American overseas shipping until it was lifted in March 1809. In Salem, nearly all of the fleet and crews were idle, putting one-fifth of the population out of work. Staying true to its benevolent origins, the East India Marine Society used its prominent position in Salem to offer relief to the town. Despite the opinion of local inhabitants such as William Bentley, who thought the poor "never were better fed in their lives" and "would be glad of an eternal embargo on their labour if they could be better fed for nothing," members organized a Grand Charity Concert held on January 26, "the expense of musick, lights [to] be paid from the funds of this Society."[126] They raised $564 in admission sales. Some of that money was spent on twenty-five cords of wood distributed to forty-seven people in need, and the remaining $452.23 was dispersed to 117 individuals.[127]

In 1809, the embargo was temporarily lifted with all countries except for Britain and France (via the Non-Intercourse Act), but the War of 1812 with Britain resulted in another embargo on foreign trade. By the end of the war, Salem merchants had started to move their businesses to Boston, New York, and other larger harbors.[128] The city never attained its pre-embargo economic prestige, although it remained a busy port until the 1840s. In 1833, a reporter for the *New-York Journal of Commerce* pointed out, "Many of their ships . . . come back loaded with wealth, which they pour into the lap of their country, entering generally either at New York or Boston. Hence there is an *appearance* of far less commerce at Salem than the actual amount." He also noted "that in that small town of only 14,000 inhabitants, there are no less than four or five Marine Insurance Companies, with an agregate [*sic*] capital of $1,000,000," and he believed "by privateering or by commerce, in war or in Peace, Salem . . . will contrive to keep their heads above water,—nay, to get rich, though surrounded as Salem is, by little else than barren rocks."[129] Even as late as 1825, approximately two hundred vessels were sailing out of Salem.

While Salem's commerce between 1815 and 1850 was still linked to the Sumatran pepper trade, the Pacific Islands, the Mediterranean, and the Baltic, trade patterns had changed. Voyages to the East Indies, China, California, and the south seas no longer began and ended in shallow, silting Salem Harbor, which the larger ships that were now dominating overseas trade could not navigate. Because of its railway connections, Boston had absorbed the foreign commerce and shipping of every other Massachusetts seaport.[130] So Salem merchants returned to the Atlantic world, focusing their attention on markets in South America, the West Indies, and the Maritime Provinces of Canada, and they opened new opportunities in East Africa. The goods brought back from these regions were used in nascent Salem industries. Hides and cotton were essential resources for local shoe and textile factories, and gum copal from Zanzibar was processed into a base for varnish. These changes in the dynamics of Salem trade were also reflected in donations to the East India Marine Society Museum, with objects entering the collection from these new trading grounds.

When the banker and philanthropist William Wilson Corcoran (1798–1888) visited the Society's museum on August 29, 1836, he was more than twenty years away from establishing his own Corcoran Museum of American Art in Washington, D.C.[131] Smaller provincial galleries devoted to art as well as lyceums and societies with natural history cabinets opened and closed in the 1820s and 1830s, yet there was still no public national museum, partly due to a lack of cohesion among America's elite social circles.[132] The East India Marine Society Museum filled this void through its national influence and continued to grow. The collection more than doubled by the end of the 1820s, and the highest annual visitation occurred during the next two decades.

The Society's museum inspired similar ventures around the nation. In 1818, the *North American Review*, the oldest literary magazine in the United States, suggested, "Would not the establishment of similar societies in all our commercial towns, having some bond of union among themselves, contribute very much to the advancement of Commerce, and the sciences of Geography and Navigation?"[133] A decade later, Matthew Calbraith Perry (1794–1858), best known for leading an American naval fleet to open up Japan to western interests in 1854, visited the Society's museum twice. In 1833, he helped found the United States Naval Lyceum (1833–89), likely modeled on his experiences at the Society's museum.[134] This lyceum was formed in Brooklyn, New York, "to elevate and adorn the character" of the American Navy through the establishment of a library, a reading room, a bimonthly publication entitled the *Naval Magazine*, and a "Museum of Natural History, Curiosities, &c."[135] Benjamin Silliman, who had visited the East India Marine Society Museum in 1807 and 1834, recognized the similarities between these two collecting institutions and conjectured that the Naval Lyceum might "perhaps, one day emulate the splendid Mariners' Museum at Salem."[136]

Mercantile periodicals and newspapers, which published descriptions of the East India Marine Society Museum, also viewed the institution as a model design for others in the United States. A writer for Freeman Hunt's *Merchant Magazine*, claimed "Numerous opportunities are presented to the mariners of our country, in their successive voyages, to collect materials for similar cabinets, and, by the diffusion of a right spirit among their members, they may be made to subserve important objects, tending to increase the means of intelligence and to improve the condition of those who navigate the ocean."[137] Similarly, the *New-York Journal of Commerce* of August 1841 questioned "Why may not this example be imitated in all our commercial cities? Is the liberality of the arrangement greater than can reasonably be desired and encouraged?" While acknowledging that the public "has no claim on gentlemen to spend their time and money in collecting and preserving the means of entertainment and instruction, for others to use gratis," the *Journal* still felt that the Society's museum was worth emulating. "Still, have not the members of this Society done well? Should they not be honored for it? And would not others deserve honor for following their example?"[138] In an open recommendation "*From the National Gazette To the Masters of vessels in the Port of Philadelphia*," the *Gazette* also concluded "the '*East India Marine Hall*' of Salem is now unequalled by any institution of a similar kind in this country," and a model worth emulating.[139]

In the 1830s, Salem experienced a great intellectual awakening, and the East India Marine Society Museum benefited from the city's transformation with increased attendance from a wide swath of American society.

When the Salem-to-Boston railroad was opened in 1838, George Peabody (1804–92), president of the Eastern Railroad and son of the prosperous Salem shipowner Joseph Peabody, stated, "Few towns can boast of so many solid advantages. . . . Charitable and humane institutions exist nowhere in greater number or on a more respectable footing. The man of literature, science, and taste, may here have access to an Atheneum [*sic*] containing one of the choicest libraries in the country, to an excellent collection of Native Antiquities, and to the fine Cabinets of the Society of Natural History and the East India Museum, the latter of which contains as is well known, a collection of rare and valuable curiosities equal if not superior to any of the kind in Europe or America."[140] Salem continued to reflect national trends, particularly in scientific inquiry, which had evolved since the beginning of the century from an amateurish pursuit to a more professional practice.[141] Academic scientists and school groups visited the Society's museum to study portions of the collection as part of ongoing research.

At this time, though, another museum emerged, due in part to an increasing interest in the study of natural history.[142] In 1848, the Essex Institute was formed through the union of two organizations: the Essex Historical Society (1821) and the Essex County Natural History Society (1833). While focusing on Essex County history, this new institution held a vast library and created a museum of natural history and ethnological objects, often competing with the Society during the 1850s for gifts from a similar pool of donors.[143]

The Salem Lyceum (1830–98) was among the most important of the city's institutions established during this period. Charles W. Upham, who advocated for the establishment of a lyceum in Salem, viewed it as a means of uplifting and educating those individuals affected by the town's economic downturn: "The decline of commerce, and the stagnation of mercantile business, having thrown out of employment a large number of inhabitants of our seaboard town . . . could be engaged in the acquisition and communication of knowledge . . . with a resource most agreeable to their own feelings, and with the means of being useful to others. If their leisure hours were thus occupied, they would be laying up stores of information which would be highly beneficial to them in whatever pursuits they might afterwards be engaged."[144] The lyceum's patrons were discriminating in their assessment of speakers and had high expectations of lectures, wanting "the best of the best" and especially anyone who was lecturing in Boston.[145]

By 1851 the *Salem Register* declared there was a "Lyceum Mania in Salem," noting Salem as "preeminent in the support of Lyceums." All advanced subscription tickets for that year were purchased in less than an hour in a "rush and jam . . . paralleled only by the Jenny Lind excitement" before any lecturer had been announced, leading the paper to conclude that the cause of such commotion "must be that our people are Lyceum-mad."[146] Over the next fifty years, more than eight hundred lectures were delivered by speakers ranging from the authors Ralph Waldo Emerson (1803–82) and Henry David Thoreau (1817–62), to the artist George Catlin (1796–1872), to the inventor Alexander Graham Bell (1847–1922). Many of the lecturers, including Catlin, spent time at the East India Marine Society Museum during their stay in Salem, and thus both organizations fed off each other.

When a local poet, the Reverend Jones Very (1813–30), penned the praiseworthy "The East India Marine Museum" in 1865, he hit upon elements that would help the Society endure to this day. He predicted that its legacy "From age to age might still be handed down, / And distant generations might behold, / And guard the trust, more precious far than gold." Unlike other institutions in the nineteenth century, the East India Marine Society Museum had survived thanks to the work of its members, "that early band, / Who left their homes to sail across the sea."[147]

Chapter Two

"May Resources from the Ambition of Its Members Continue to Accomplish Its Design"

> He, who sails to distant regions of the globe . . . and brings home specimens illustrative of the varied mode of life and climate, is the real benefactor of this country. . . . Who has not remarked the peculiarly interesting conversation of a sagacious, inquisitive and correct sea commander, who narrates what he saw and heard, suffered and acquired?
>
> —obituary of Benjamin Carpenter,
> *Boston Patriot*, September 26, 1823

When the *Boston Patriot* ran its memorial to Benjamin Carpenter (1751–1823), the newspaper recognized that he and his fellow East India Marine Society members were part of a new generation of Salem and U.S. mariners. These intrepid captains saw themselves not provincially as Massachusetts seamen but as American sailors. Although they had been born as British citizens, post–Revolutionary War global trading routes had allowed them to establish a new national identity.[1] The material culture they obtained abroad and through a network of outside donors played a critical part in this ideological exercise, regardless of whether the object acquired was an American print or something from "other hemispheres, where manners, habits, wants, customs and means differ from our own."[2] Subsequent generations of Society members continued to redefine this notion of Americanness through international objects, even as Salem's maritime fortunes changed.

William Story (1774–1864), the half-brother of Supreme Court Justice Joseph Story (1779–1845), joined the East India Marine Society in 1804 as the institution was on the rise and the port of Salem was at its apex.

Officially he was number 95 on the membership roles, and his lifespan almost matched this numerical designation. After commanding merchant vessels to Europe and the Mediterranean in 1797, Story soon made voyages to the East Indies as first officer and then master of the ship *Friendship*, earning the required nautical experience to become a Society member. His career was certainly longer than that of the majority of his brethren, but it mirrored many of their experiences. He served in various capacities on merchant vessels to ports all around the globe, owned ships along with fellow members such as Stephen White (1787–1841)—one of the most influential merchants in Salem in the 1820s and 1830s—and retired to land-based mercantile ventures, operating a general merchandise business in Marblehead.[3]

Like other mariners, though, Story fell on hard times during the War of 1812 and was forced to sell his Marblehead business in 1817 to his brothers-in-law Stephen White and William Fettyplace, both of whom eventually served terms as Society president. Financial hardships forced Story back to the sea in 1821 as master of some of White's ships to Europe and South America, and by 1826 he owned and captained his own vessel, the schooner *Sally*. At fifty-three years old, Story retired from the sea a second time and worked in the Salem Custom House as weigher and gauger until July 4, 1853. When he died at age ninety, the *Salem Register* remarked, "He contributed his full share to the services rendered by that class to the commercial prosperity of this city and the whole country, in the period of his early manhood and during his prime."[4]

From 1802 to 1804, Story was master and part owner of the *Friendship* on a twenty-six-month-long voyage to Sumatra and Canton. Like the captain's, the *Friendship*'s career was long and multifaceted. It was built in Salem by Enos Briggs and launched on May 28, 1797, the same year Story commanded his first ship. The *Friendship* made seventeen voyages from 1797 until 1812, when it was captured and condemned by the British. Over the course of those voyages it reached ports in the East Indies and Europe and earned its various owners $141,394.33 in profit.[5]

During Story's voyage, the ship's second mate, Thomas Russell (1780–1817), and the carpenter, Mr. Odell, built a model of the vessel (purportedly for Story's son, William, Jr.) (see figure 13). It was, and still is, very common for sailors to commemorate a voyage through artwork such as ship models, and many are accurate depictions of sailing vessels since mariner modelers know their ships from stem to stern. This example, however, is distinct in many ways. Russell and Odell spared no effort in creating a model that was nine feet long, much bigger than most ship models of the time. The scale and the level of craftsmanship are all the more remarkable because the two worked on the project in the confined area between the vessel's decks while at sea.[6]

As this model was too large to display in Story's home, he donated it to the East India Marine Society Museum soon after arriving back in Salem. Like Story and the vessel he commanded, the model had a multidimensional history. It was a fixture in the museum as the most accurate depiction of a Salem trading ship during the port's golden age, and it was later used in the last vestiges of the Society's parades.[7] Any mariners who viewed the model would instantaneously recall moments from their own careers: voyages to the far corners of the globe that were simultaneously exciting

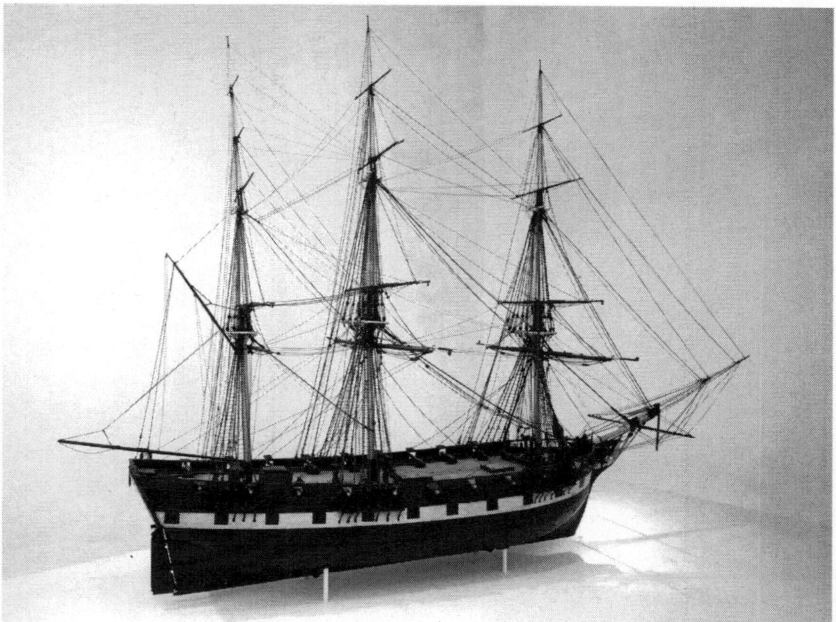

FIGURE 13. Model of the ship *Friendship* made by Thomas Russell and Mr. Odell on board the ship, 1804. Wood, cordage, paint, 96 x 140 x 55 in. Peabody Essex Museum Collection, M48. © Peabody Essex Museum, Salem, MA. Photography by Jeffrey R. Dykes.

ventures and long arduous trips spent in cramped quarters. This object likely triggered synesthetic associations, from an "atmosphere redolent with the perfumes from the east, warm and fragrant and silent," to the fetid and putrid smells associated with life on board a ship.[8]

The fathers and grandfathers of East India Marine Society members grew up in a town bound to the sea. Colonial-era Salem men who worked on coastal and Atlantic voyages had grown up together and comprised 66 to 80 percent of a ship's crew.[9] These men were not away from home for years on end, as the next generation would be when voyages ventured to the far side of the globe, and they retired to a life ashore once their sailing days were done. As Nathaniel Hawthorne wrote in his introduction to *The Scarlet Letter* (1850), "From father to son, for above a hundred years, they followed the sea; a grey-headed shipmaster, in each generation, retiring from the quarter-deck to the homestead, while a boy of fourteen took the hereditary place before the mast, confronting the salt spray and the gale, which had blustered against his sire and grandsire."[10]

The men who signed the Society's founding articles in October 1799 represented a transitional generation. They were a mix of Salem's rising merchant elite in the new republic. With an average age of thirty-seven, they were seasoned mariners who had gone to sea in their teenage years.[11] Many had cut their teeth in the Atlantic trade, such as Ichabod Nichols (1749–1839), who was a captain by age twenty and made several successful voyages to the West Indies before entering the colonial militia in 1776. Others, like Jonathan Carnes and Benjamin Carpenter, who commanded the first vessel to carry "the thirteen stripes around the Cape of Good Hope after the peace of 1783," ventured to the East Indies in the early years of the new United States.[12]

Some Society members were well off, born into the most powerful shipping families of the day—the Derbys and the Crowninshields. Others, like Nathaniel Bowditch, had little formal education and worked at an early age to support their families but ultimately became successful merchants themselves. Many served on board other members' ships, eventually transitioning to life after sea as merchant shipowners, landowners outside Salem, or, like Nathaniel Silsbee, politicians. Some, like Carpenter and Carnes, served a full life bound to the mast.

While the dynamics of Salem's trade changed during the course of the nineteenth century, with some prosperous merchants moving to Boston, the complexion of the East India Marine Society did not. The multidimensional characteristics of the first thirty members remained true throughout most of the antebellum period. James Buffington Briggs (1790–1857), who became a member in 1821, was a career sailor, only retiring in his fifties. Stephen White spent most of his career financing voyages rather than commanding them and later served in the Massachusetts state legislature. In addition to working with each other (such as co-owning vessels), many members were related as fathers and sons and brothers, either by birth or through marriage. This was not unusual, given Salem's close-knit maritime community.[13]

Regardless of their upbringing, these mariners relied on the advice of veterans within the maritime industry, especially those who had sailed on Salem's first global trading ships. For many, relatives and friends provided invaluable "nautical coaching," and instilled within these greenhands the importance of observation, recording, and collecting. When George Nichols (1778–1865) was preparing for his first voyage in 1795 on the barque *Essex*, his father, Ichabod, imparted worldly advice and guidance to his son on the proper decorum to keep on board ship and the principles to adhere to when dealing with fellow sailors, officers, and trading partners, among many other things. Ichabod told George to make himself "agreeable" to others on the ship and to follow orders. "Don't think yourself above doing any thing that Captn Green or the mates may order, for you maybe assured that they will not order you to do what is out of Character to be done onboard," he instructed. Most importantly, Ichabod stressed the importance of observing and recording: "You had best Keep a Journal of the Ships way and also the most important occurrences that may happen on the Voyage."[14]

Two decades later, Joseph Gilbert Waters (1796–1878) conveyed similar advice to his younger brother William Dean Waters (1798–1880)—who became a Society member in 1821—before his first voyage. In a letter sent to the ship *Caroline* in Sumatra, Joseph commented, "I did not expect, when I parted with you in Salem, that you would have so soon have followed my example, in seeking the road to fortune. But we are now alike wanderers in pursuit of the means of our future subsistence, we must now depend on ourselves." Joseph emphasized character and morality; and as William had trained as a lawyer prior to going to sea, he noted, "[t]hese good qualities are essential to the character of every honest man, and of course not excluded from a Lawyers code of morality." Joseph supported his brother's decision to choose a career at sea, as he believed it "will not fail of rewarding you in a few years if not with a fortune, at least a competency." Above all, he advised William to use his time on board ship for "the improvement of your mind"—studying financial markets at trading ports; reading books on history and science; and, most importantly, observing and recording "the motives, which operate to produce particular casts of character" in order to obtain "another kind of knowledge very useful . . . that of the world."[15]

Instilled with a passion for learning, these sailors used their journals and diaries to record nautical, natural, and ethnographic observations. In addition, they sometimes made personal reflections about their experiences at sea that, like the model of the *Friendship*, would be understood by any mariner. These written observations provide a window into the minds of nineteenth-century sailors venturing across the globe: their thoughts on the maritime experience, the contact zones negotiated abroad, and their notions of what it was to be an American. They also reveal the diversity of East India Marine Society members and their attitudes toward the indigenous communities living in the far reaches of the world, which can be used to contextualize the objects they collected from their voyages.

Many mariners who were embarking on a voyage for the first time reflected on the great unknown before them. When seventeen-year-old Benjamin Hodges, Jr.—the son of Benjamin Hodges—left for Europe onboard the ship *Union* in 1803, he wrote in his journal that he "commences a course of life entirely new," one where "Imagination must . . . be employed" to paint a scene "with the most brilliant colors." Hodges understood that he was leaving the company of friends whom he had known all his life to "enter upon a state, of which at present I can form little idea." "Instead of strangers," Hodges wrote, he "must fancy the most valued of my acquaintances to hold conversations with me, and bring them to my presence by contemplation." He realized that there would be high and low points during the voyage but trusted that "the great design will be accomplished[,] that knowledge of men and manners Will be acquired, which ride under life so much more pleasant as to counterbalance away evil. That self-knowledge which constitutes true wisdom can only be acquired by a knowledge of human nature."[16]

Sometimes sailors were filled with patriotic sentiment when leaving the United States for the first time. William Augustus Rogers recounted a sense of pride for his country when he departed from the shores of Nahant and Marblehead. He beheld "the setting sun covering with his golden mantle the freest 'of all the lands he shines upon,' the land of peace and rational liberty, uncontaminated with licentiousness, and unrestrained by tyranny, the asylum of oppressed humanity, the refuge of itenerant [*sic*] men." He viewed the United States as a "Western star shone with honor's purest light, to guide the oppressed emigrant to the cradle of freedom, and the sea worn mariner to the land of his home." He believed that the nation would continue to augment these virtues while he was away at sea, and he would return home to "find thy sons as wise, as brave, as free and as virtuous as they now are."[17]

Beyond their personal feelings and beliefs connected to life at sea, mariners reflected on other cultures. East India Marine Society member George Cleveland (1781–1840), looking back at his life and career in 1838, believed that "[e]very individual of the human race is different from every other, in feelings, sentiment, knowledge and temper,—and hence the difference of action which constantly occurs among mankind. This infinite diversity in man, is one of the wonders of creation."[18] Benjamin Crowninshield, master of the brig *Henry* during a voyage to Calcutta in 1789, wrote a very detailed description of a *sati*, the ritual suicide of a widow on her husband's funeral pyre. At the end of his lengthy account, Crowninshield concluded, "Thus ended a most horrid sight, and whether it is right or wrong, I leave it for other people to determine. There is this in it, it appeared very solemn to me. I did not think it was in the power of a human person to meet death in such a manner."[19] The objectivity of his account is uncharacteristic in comparison to those of other westerners at this time.

The Society's mission, its guidelines for collecting, and the activities of its members not only reinforced the unconscious act of collecting that sailors already possessed but also influenced non-members to support the Society's endeavors. William Augustus Rogers noted in his journal while on board the ship *Tartar*, "I caught a large grey Albatross, which measured from tip to tip 10 ft. 3 inch. It is the first we have caught on our passage. I have taken off his skin whole and endeavor to preserve him for the E.I.M.S."[20] Unlike the characters in Samuel Taylor Coleridge's (1772–1834) "The Rime of the Ancient Mariner," American sailors in the late eighteenth and nineteenth centuries did not let superstition hold them back from killing this species of bird, or any creature for that matter. Rogers's account is one of many instances of similar shipboard collecting of natural specimens.

On rare occasions, East India Marine Society members reminisced about the objects collected during their voyages, some relating unusual events from American trading ventures. John Henry Eagleston, while commanding the ship *Mermaid* to Fiji in 1838, recounted that he "made prisoner one of the crew who massacred the officers of the Manila Brig mentioned in a former voyage." This man, noted as a Spaniard but dressed as a Fijian and accompanied by local inhabitants, had attempted to capture Eagleston's ship under the guise of friendly bartering for goods. Eagleston knew his true identity and plan and had him "put him in double irons" once he stepped onto the deck. The prisoner was kept below and watched by the ship's carpenter, who informed Eagleston the next morning that the prisoner had a spare head! Eagleston recounted, "Going below I found the head had disappeared & at once suspecting the devil wore a Wig, I gave it a kick and sent it flying across the deck, leaving him With his hair drawn up and tied in a knot on his head. The frame of the Wig was light basket work and well filled with Fiji hair & dressed as in life. It being the first I ever saw of the kind, I called it mine & it is to be seen in the East India Museum."[21] Eagleston donated this object to the Society in 1839, and the story was recorded in its internal catalogue. Eagleston's account is one of the few that bind together American mariners' written reflections of life at sea with the material culture that encapsulated those experiences.

More often, like the model of the *Friendship*, the objects mariners collected were silent symbols of their voyages and other cultures encountered across the globe. This model is a multicultural artistic venture: the combined efforts of American and Indonesian craftsmen. Its eighteen brass cannons, each with bored barrels, were cast by indigenous people in the port of Palembang, Sumatra, for fifty dollars. These Indonesian artisans were used to producing full-scale versions for defense in a region filled with rival trading nations, Malay pirates, and adverse political factions. The cannons evoked further associations related to American mariners' experiences in ports around the world. For instance, Story, while trading in Sumatra as master of the ship *Marquis De Someruelas* in 1806, was attacked in one of the branches of the Great Salt River. While Society members created friendly trading relationships, the dangers of international trade were palpable and often tied to the objects they brought back home.

Along with the influence of other mariners and travel narratives, American sailors had developed a desire to collect objects of all types. As global traders aboard vessels such as the *Friendship* during an era of unfettered trade in the early nineteenth century, East India Marine Society members were uniquely positioned to create an international collection in the antebellum United States. This inclination to collect grew out of sailors' almost genetic tendency to bring back souvenirs from their voyages that were a reflection of both the far-reaching networks of trade and the sailors themselves.[22] The Society was also cognizant of the recent European drive toward global geographic exploration and the call to obtain objects from around the globe for national collections.

Scientific discovery was also explicitly and implicitly woven into the fabric of the Society. In the early days of the new republic, nautical prowess was instrumental to mercantile success, and accurate aids for navigation were a necessity. Yankee sailors needed precise sea charts and reliable journals and logs to steer a true course through newly established trading grounds. The United States was at a disadvantage in these early years in comparison to Britain, which kept its routes and sources for obtaining goods a secret or had established trading companies (such as the British East India Company) that provided their ships with professionally made charts and accurate sailing directions.[23] Unlike the dominant maritime powers of Europe, the United States had no governmental body devoted to amassing pertinent nautical information or charting oceans for the nation's merchants and its fledgling Navy until 1807, when President Thomas Jefferson authorized the coast survey.[24] Late eighteenth- and early nineteenth-century American captains sailing around the globe, therefore, used both English and Dutch charts and published texts.[25]

The East India Marine Society knew that works related to navigation were worth their weight in gold. Like other marine societies, they required that members communicate in writing to the committee of observation "the bearings and distances of all Capes and Head Lands, of the Latitudes and Longitude of Islands, rocks and shoals, of soundings, tides and currents, of unusual occurrences, storms and accidents."[26] In order to aid their members' business interests in the Far East, the Society had been founded to promote obtaining nautical information beyond the confines of the Atlantic world. In the introduction to the "Act of Incorporation" of the East India Marine Society in 1801, the organization is officially labeled as one "promoting a knowledge of navigation and trade to the East Indies."[27] Unlike other marine societies, the East India Marine Society's articles required its committee of observation to acquire "all approved Books of History of Voyages and Travels and of Navigation," and members were instructed to aid in "collecting all valuable publications in every Language either as donations to the Society or to be held in their own private right, for the temporary use of the Society under such terms."[28]

Of the approximately two hundred volumes the Society amassed during the antebellum period—including members' journals, the nucleus of its library—three-quarters relate to maritime matters. It purchased and was given several rare and valuable illustrated editions related to Captain Cook, La Pérouse, and George Vancouver's famed voyages of discovery; books devoted to ship design such as *Elements of Rigging and Seamanship* published in London in 1794 and the *Shipwright's Vade Mecum* from 1805; and standard nautical references such as William Falconer's *Universal Dictionary of the Marine* (first published in London in 1769). By 1818, the library had already received public attention. The *Boston Intelligencer and Evening Gazette* reported that the Society "has the elements of a Library, which already contains the best modern voyages, and the best books on shipbuilding, in aid of Navigation, and respecting the Commerce of the Globe."[29]

To buttress this collection, the Society collected thirty-five maps and charts of local and overseas waters. As the cartographic historian Lloyd A. Brown has noted, charts were "the key to empire, the way to wealth."[30] The most important set in the collection was a complete run of *The Atlantic Neptune*. This series, created under the direction of the Swiss Huguenot cartographer Joseph Frederick Wallet DesBarres (1721–1824)—who served in the Seven Years' War and was later the governor of Cape Breton Island and Prince Edward Island—was the culmination of an extensive British surveying project of the eastern seaboard of North America during the 1760s and 1770s. The British navy considered these charts a military secret, and they were used extensively during the American Revolutionary War.[31]

The East India Marine Society's library was one the most important collections of books, manuscripts, and charts related to maritime endeavors in the United States in the first quarter of the nineteenth century.[32] These valuable printed aids to maritime trade were not static collections, though, but were used by members engaged in global pursuits. Starting in July 1801, the secretary of the Society was "authorised to furnish any member with one of Mr. Churchmans Variation Charts that may apply and record the persons name," and the treasurer was ordered to "purchase Vancouvers Voyages, with the Charts and annexed."[33] In addition, the Society voted that "no member be allowed to keep any book from the hall, exceeding three weeks . . . without application to the secretary." Almost immediately, members borrowed material from the collection, as the minutes for this meeting note: "Capt. Benjamin Crowninnshield [*sic*] has taken out one of Churchmans Variation Charts."[34] In addition to members, mariners outside the institution were granted access to the collection for research purposes. The Society, therefore, took on the role of national promoter of American maritime trade when there was no established federal body.

The Society's efforts to accumulate firsthand nautical knowledge were codified early on. All members returning from sea were instructed "to present a Journal of their Voyages to the President for the inspection of the Committee."[35] Two years later, they refined this article of the bylaws, voting that "a committee [John Osgood, Jonathan Mason, and Nathaniel Bowditch] be appointed to prepare blank forms and printed directions to be furnished [to] members going abroad, for the purpose of collecting nautical information and procuring natural curiosities."[36] These printed directions were not only an organizational means to fulfill one of their objectives but also contained useful information illuminating the Society's larger collecting goals.

On the front page of the "*Blank Journals* for the use of the Society" provided to every member "bound to sea . . . to be returned at the end of his voyage" was a lengthy set of directions for filling out the journal: recording latitude and longitude and the methods to use for observing variation, winds, weather, currents, and bearings on capes and islands with estimated distances. At the end of this section were instructions of a mercantile nature: "A blank page is also assigned for an account of the coin, weights and measures of the several places touched at in the voyage; and it is hoped that care will be taken in acquiring information on these subjects. Any remarks on the commerce of the different places touched at in the voyage, with the imports, exports, and manner of transacting business, will be of public utility."[37] While these types of observations were normally scattered throughout a captain's journal or a ship's logbook, the Society explicitly required members to record this information in a more organized fashion. Further, by incorporating business-related interests within the guidelines for filling out journals, the Society fused commercial interests with scientific observation.

To aid in the precise collection and organization of members' journals, the East India Marine Society created a new officer: inspector of journals. This officer arranged the journals and deposited them in the Society's library "for the use of the members" as well as recorded, "in Books to be kept for the purpose, such communications as the President and Committee may think useful to Navigation."[38] Bowditch was the first member elected to this new office in January 1804, only ten days removed from his last voyage. He was meticulous in his arrangement, analysis, and binding of the journals brought back by members during his tenure as inspector—a post he held until 1820, when he became president of the Society—and made sure that members adhered to the written articles and instructions. The large quarto volumes bound during Bowditch's tenure in this position contain the logs of more than a hundred voyages from Salem or Boston to the Indian Ocean, China Sea, or the Pacific. Throughout them, his hand is readily apparent in the form of lengthy synopses of every voyage written at the beginning of each volume.[39]

The journals brought back by Society members—with some donated by non-members—reflect a conscious effort to promote the institution's mission. These logs are filled with nautical experimentation, discovery, and occasional reflections on areas of the globe visited during a voyage. Many are embellished, here and there, with diagrams, maps, drawings of coasts, sketches of indigenous craft, and depictions of natural history specimens caught and preserved by sailors. Some drawings literally connect the maritime experience to American identity, such as William Haswell's frontispiece to his *Remarks on a Voyage to the Marianna Islands,* an account of his experiences on the barque *Lydia* (the first American ship to reach Guam) (see figure 14). In this illustration, Neptune rides his chariot and extends his arm toward a rocky coast where the American flag stands in front of a putto. This portly figure holds a shield with the word "Liberty" below an eagle with anchor. Above the scene are the words "Todo El Mundo Ver Estrellas Americano," which translates as "All the World Sees American Stars."[40] These words, combined with the figures and symbols below them, may be a reference to the early accomplishments of Yankee sailors in the new republic.

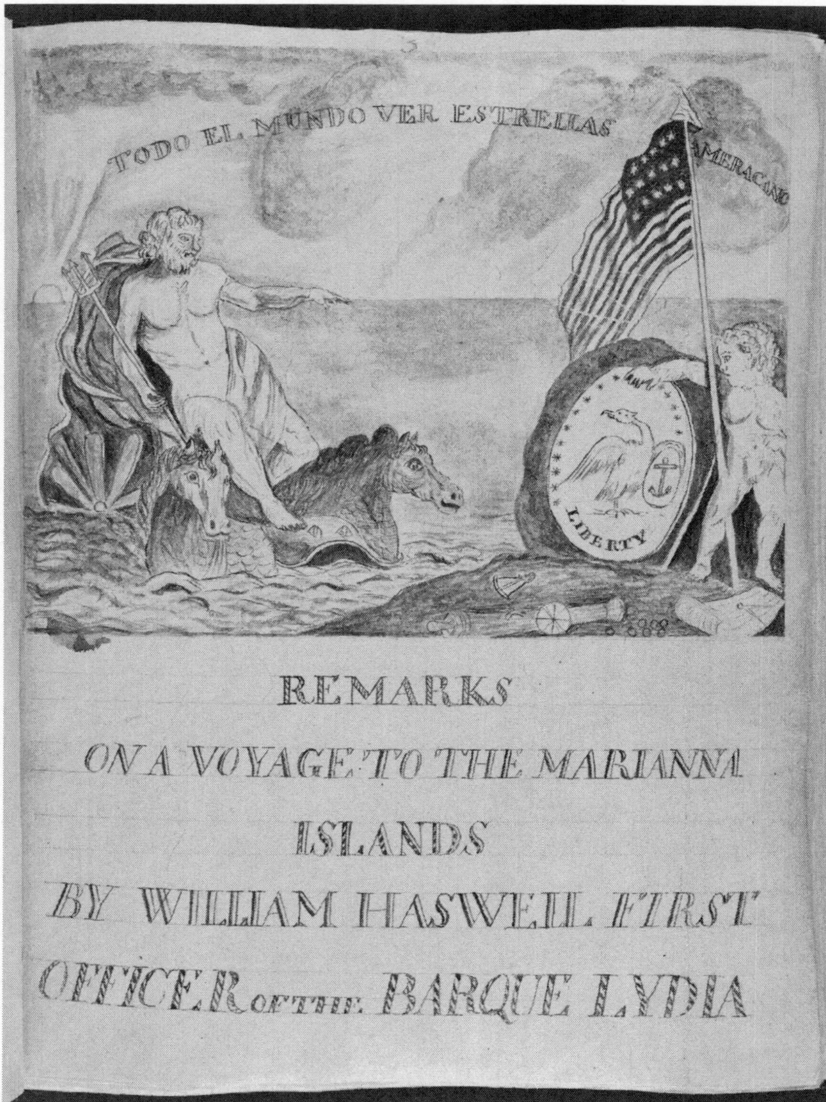

FIGURE 14. William Haswell, *Todo El Mundo Ver Estrellas Americano,* 1802. Pencil on paper, 9 1/8 x 7 in. Peabody Essex Museum Collection, LIBMH-88-VOL13-IT91 © 2012 Peabody Essex Museum, Salem, MA. Photography by Kathy Tarantola.

Recording unusual observations was probably a welcome task for some mariners as there were long stretches of voyages filled with tedium and inactivity. Timothy Ropes, Jr., a supercargo on board the brig *Herald* in 1823, bemoaned the fact that "[a]s usual in a passage at Sea, day after day passes and furnishes that little for one to record.—No Neptune skimming the surface of the ocean, No Sea Serpent or other fabled monsters of the deep, no Mermaids nor Whales and but now and then a Porpoise or a Flying fish makes a visit." A few days later, he finally observed "one 'wonder of the deep' . . . A Water Spout . . . the first I had ever seen."[41]

Because they carried formal East India Marine Society journals, members felt an additional sense of duty to record observations for their brother mariners. Dudley Leavitt Pickman (1779–1846), on a voyage to Sumatra aboard the ship *Anna*, corrected the latitude of certain islands, noting, "These Places are laid down very erroneously in the charts." On this same voyage, he tested two of Gould's patent logs (a torpedo-shaped device with rotary fins dragged from a ship's stern to determine speed and distance traveled) and was obviously unimpressed with these new devices: "The result of the observations proved that no dependence could be placed in the log and they were gross impositions."[42] Some captains extended their interest in recording information for fellow Society members to their personal journals. James Stuart, in his journal kept on the ship *Cordelia* during a voyage to Callao, Lima, and Guayaquil in 1803, opened with a note directed "To the President, Directors and Members of the East India Marine Society, Salem, Massachusetts." He offered his journal for their inspection, "as this may afford some information to future Navigators . . . having no other motive than information; which if in any degree I have or can be instrumental in communicating, their approbation will be the highest reward that can be bestowed."[43]

At the same time that Society members were accumulating nautical information, Bowditch was putting his stamp on navigational science across the globe. As first mate and clerk onboard the ship *Henry* in 1795 and 1796, he uncovered many mistakes in Moore's *Practical Navigator*. Edmund Blunt (1770–1862), a publisher of nautical works in Newburyport, Massachusetts, learned of Bowditch's corrections to Moore's volume and asked him to formally edit it while on his next voyage.[44] In 1799, a new edition of *The Practical Navigator* was published with all of Bowditch's corrections. He was acknowledged in the book for his efforts and subsequently elected to the American Academy of Arts and Sciences. By the time a third edition was slated for publication, Bowditch had found more than 8,000 errors, and Blunt believed that Bowditch should rewrite the book. In 1802, the first edition of *The New American Practical Navigator* was published under Bowditch's name.

Almost immediately, Bowditch's *Practical Navigator* became the most important and complete navigational handbook written. At this time, most ships could not afford a marine chronometer, the timepiece perfected by the Englishman John Harrison (1693–1776) in the 1760s and 1770s and used to determine a vessel's longitude at sea. Instead, sailors relied upon compasses, logs, sextants, and lead lines to determine their position at sea. Although many sailors who traveled with Bowditch first questioned his methods, *The New American Practical Navigator* quickly eliminated their concerns and provided them with a more reliable method of navigation. His ability to simplify complex methods became so revered among his contemporaries that sailors could obtain an officer's berth simply by stating that they had sailed with Bowditch. Robert Bennett Forbes (1804–89), a noted China trade merchant and mariner from Boston, said he went to sea at the age of thirteen with a "Testament, a Bowditch, a quadrant, a chest of sea clothes, and a mother's blessing."[45] *The New American Practical Navigator* is still published and is standard equipment for professional mariners and U.S. Navy seamen.

In 1801, Bowditch submitted the final draft of his text to the East India Marine Society to review "and give such certificate as they may think proper." They scrutinized this new edition and determined that he had "corrected the best volume on navigation . . . and also considerably improved the old methods of calculation and added new ones of his own."[46] The first edition of Bowditch's *Practical Navigator* included the title page "Report of the Committee, appointed by the East India Marine Society of Salem, at their meeting on the 6th of May 1801." Members believed that the new book was "highly deserving of the approbation and encouragement of the society, not only as being the most correct and ample now extant, but as being a genuine American production; and as such they hesitate not to recommend it to the attention of Navigators, and of the public at large."[47] This preface was printed in subsequent editions, and the Society toasted Bowditch's work in 1804: "The Practical Navigator. Facts first, then theories."[48] Bowditch and the East India Marine Society legitimized each other's pursuits in one volume, and from this point on, the Society's seal of approval was sought for other important American navigational works.[49]

The East India Marine Society built upon a maritime culture of recording and collecting by codifying the practice for its members. On the frontispiece of blank Society journals, after the instructions for documenting nautical details and commercial observations, were directions to note "[w]hatever is singular in the manners, customs, dress, ornaments, &c. of any people . . . deserving of notice." At the bottom of the page were guidelines for collecting natural history objects: "There should be collected, for the Museum, specimens of various kinds of vegetable substances, earths, minerals, ores, metals, volcanic substances, &c. There should also be preserved such parts of birds, insects, fish, &c. as serve most easily to distinguish them, and if no part can be preserved, a description of any that are remarkable, may be given."[50] These directions—the first printed evidence of the Society's interest in creating a museum—were common parlance for European naturalists on voyages of discovery in the nineteenth century but were unusual for American commercial voyages. In turn, Society members, like the Peales and later P. T. Barnum, collected natural specimens of interest to scientists as well as items that bordered on the unusual, such as a "ball of hair from the stomach of a cow from Madagascar."[51]

The last section of instructions to Society members contained specific directions for collecting ethnological objects for a museum collection: "Inquiry should be made for any remarkable books in use among any of the eastern nations, with their subjects, dates, and titles. Articles of the dress and ornaments of any nation, with the images and objects of religious devotion, should be procured."[52] This final passage, among the earliest American museum collecting strategies, aided members in building an institution reflecting their global trading networks.

In Benjamin Carpenter's obituary, the *Boston Patriot* noted that his "exertions were not confined to the planks of a ship." It acknowledged his role as an early member of the East India Marine Society "who founded that beautiful museum, which adorns the town of Salem." The obituary stated, "The idea of depositing curious articles, brought from abroad in one place, instead of scattering them here and there, as heretofore, arose in a small club. . . . Hence originated that neat collection of curiosities in nature and art in Salem."[53] Though the majority of Society members were not academically trained scientists such as Bowditch, in the early days of the new republic their maritime prowess made up for this deficiency at a time when most scientific minds did not receive a formal education. As the century progressed, and the landscape of American and European science demanded professionalization, East India Marine Society members were no longer on the cutting edge and their efforts were considered amateur. Still, their collections and accomplishments related to discovery were recognized as American endeavors at the highest scale, and the museum became "[t]he chief object of attraction to most strangers in Salem."[54]

Chapter Three

"GATHERED, WITH COST AND PAINS, FROM EVERY CLIME"

> It is proposed by the New Marine Society, called the East India Marine Society, to make a Cabinet.
>
> —*The Diary of William Bentley*, October 22, 1799

A few weeks after documenting the Society's inception, William Bentley recorded that "Mr. Carnes has presented his curiosities to the new formed East India Marine Society & they are providing a Museum & Cabinet." This first donation of "various specimens of shells . . . the tooth of an Elephant, a pipe with two stems, a petrified mushroom cap & stem, & two specimens of boxes in gold" initiated a collection that grew exponentially in the following three decades. While the Society promoted objects "found beyond the Cape of Good Hope and Cape Horn," the scope of the collection was truly global.[1] Of the over 6,400 objects acquired during sixty-eight years of collecting, approximately one-third were from regions other than those beyond the capes. They included western paintings and sculptures, objects from native North and South American cultures, Near Eastern antiquities, and American and European coins and paper bills.

The East India Marine Society amassed a wealth of material culture during the years before the Civil War, but not solely through the work of its members. While Carnes and many others helped establish an internal impetus to collect for the museum, almost half of the objects accumulated between 1799 and 1867 were donated by mariners who were not members, trading partners abroad, the lay public, and many others who were "friendly to the institution"—attesting to the international networks formed by American maritime trade.[2] Like the *Friendship* model, the act of collecting was a communal effort and represented a vast acquisition network. In this way the museum was unlike any other in the antebellum United States.

Salem mariners' pioneering voyages to the Pacific Islands and the East Indies in the early days of the new republic—during which they reached ports on all of the continents except for Antarctica—provided the means for acquiring most of the objects in the museum. Thus, in the first decades of the nineteenth century, the collection reflected both Salem and U.S. overseas trade. In regions where Europeans had already established business relations, such as China and India, the objects brought back for the museum were mostly premade or commissioned souvenirs, markers of trading relationships, or emblems of the local cultures. In places unaccustomed to westerners or new to western contact, such as the Pacific Islands and the northwestern coast of North America, the objects sent back to the Society were more reflective of indigenous societies. In Europe and the Near East, an established antiquities and art market in ports or at ancient sites supplied American mariners with artifacts and western art to symbolize an American enlightenment. In the United States, military expeditions obtained emblems of Native Americans who were being removed from their lands. Objects commissioned by the Society and other outside donations filled in gaps pertaining to these and other established narratives linked to the maritime experience. By the 1830s and 1840s, however, a dwindling number of donations reflected changes in American maritime ventures abroad and a shift away from the East India Marine Society as Salem's premier collecting institution.

Early nineteenth-century Salem was a center of the China and pepper trades, but the largest collections of "artificial curiosities" in the museum at this time came from the South Pacific islands and the Pacific Northwest region of the modern-day United States and British Columbia.[3] In these locations Americans discovered marketable trade items to use when obtaining tea, silks, and other goods from the Far East. American mariners dominated the trade in the area known as Oceania, a vast region of the central and southern Pacific Ocean dotted with thousands of islands. Yankee merchants' greatest influence was in Polynesia—a triangle extending 5,000 miles from Easter Island to Fiji and 500 miles from Honolulu to southern New Zealand, including the island groups of the Marquesas, the Societies, the Tuamotus, the Cooks, the Australs, Samoa, and Tonga.[4] They also touched Australia, Micronesia, and Melanesia on the western periphery of Polynesia. Until the 1840s New England was at the forefront of American contact in this expansive region, a result of commercial maritime pursuits of natural resources for trade in the Far East rather than the geographical exploration that characterized European endeavors in this area.

The origins of American interest in the Pacific lie in the narrative of the first Yankee in that region, John Ledyard (1751–89). The son of a sea captain from Groton, Connecticut, Ledyard volunteered for Captain James Cook's third and final voyage of exploration in 1776 and "surreptitiously" published his account of the voyage in 1783. In this volume, he goes into depth about the large profits made in buying sea otter skins "for trifles on the Northwest Coast and sold at Canton."[5] Ledyard encouraged his fellow American mariners to venture to this region because native New England resources such as timber and fish did not appeal to Chinese merchants. Following Cook's and Ledyard's lead, the *Columbia*, the first American ship to enter the Pacific Northwest fur trade, left Boston in 1787 with Salem mariner John Derby (1741–1812) as a crewmember. When the vessel returned in 1790, it had earned the distinction of being the first American ship to circumnavigate the globe, reaching Hawai'i, Tahiti, and China. En route Derby had collected many objects that reflected this new American trade route. In March 1800, he donated thirty-two items to the East India Marine Society, including tapa cloth from Hawai'i; fishhooks and bows and arrows from the Pacific Northwest; and a joiner's plane, a tinderbox, and smoking pipes from China.

When American mariners first reached the Pacific Northwest, they encountered local inhabitants accustomed to trading with Europeans. For these voyages, collecting indigenous objects as souvenirs was secondary to acquiring important trading items, but it was pursued nonetheless.[6] Native inhabitants recognized that Europeans and Americans desired their cultural objects, and they became savvy traders. During Cook's third expedition to the Pacific on the H.M.S. *Discovery*, a crewmember noted, "One clever Nootkan put on a bird's mask and offered it for sale, while another sitting next to him stealthily used a whistle to imitate a bird call so effectively that the sound seemed to come from the mask itself."[7]

Of the 106 objects the East India Marine Society collected from the Pacific Northwest in the antebellum period, the majority related to indigenous fishing: canoe models, paddles, fishhooks, and waterproof clothing.[8]

Some called into question the happy trading relationship between western merchants and native communities. For instance, in 1830 one Society member, William Osgood (1784–1834), donated a double-ended dagger, recorded in the museum catalogue as "Bayonets bound together & used as a dagger by the natives of Nootka Sound, supposed to be a remnant of the arms of the ship *Boston* which was taken by surprise & the crew murdered by the celebrated chief Maquina [*sic*]. See Jewett's [*sic*] Narrative."[9]

The reference was to John Rodgers Jewitt (1783–1819), the *Boston*'s blacksmith and one of two survivors of an attack on the fur-trading ship at Yuquot (Friendly Cove) in British Columbia. These men were members of the Mowachaht First Nations, who became incensed after the ship's Captain Salter insulted the chief Maquinna. The affront had reignited ill feelings among the Mowachaht traders, who had already had negative experiences with western trading vessels in the region. Jewitt was spared because his metalworking skills were deemed useful. On board the *Boston* he had made "daggers, knives, and small hatchets for the Indian trade," and during his two-year captivity (1803–5) he produced the Society's dagger and others.[10] Raw steel and steel bayonets were prize goods for Native Americans in the region, so Jewitt incorporated both western and indigenous materials and techniques when making the dagger, whose form is reminiscent of pre-contact examples.

The dagger illuminates several connections within the complex world of the fur trade in the Pacific Northwest. Given that Maquinna's reputation was greatly enhanced by Jewitt's service to him, the dagger represents a reversal of power: an indigenous culture using Euro-Americans for its own benefit. Jewitt subsequently exploited the native community for his personal gain by publishing a narrative of his experiences and performing a play based on it. Within the object's social biography, this dagger was decontextualized and collected by an American ship captain as an example of native craft, illustrating how the cultural perception and meaning of objects can transform over time through exchange and interaction among different people. This process altered the meaning of objects from their indigenous contexts, particularly when they were put on display in museums. Thus, the double-ended dagger—like the Sumatran pipe and many other pieces from other parts of the globe—had multiple meanings.

Other objects in the East India Marine Society collection reveal larger changes in the China trade that was developing in the early nineteenth century. The majority of Pacific Northwest material culture donated to the Society was acquired secondhand by members and other mariners who never reached the shores of the region. Osgood, for example, was master of several voyages to Hawai'i but never sailed to the Pacific Northwest. Instead, he was a courier for objects from other captains in the Pacific. In 1799, the ship *Minerva* of Salem, captained by Nantucket-born Mayhew Folger (1774–1828)—a cousin of Benjamin Franklin—collected more than forty objects from the northwestern coast and the South Pacific. It was the first Salem vessel to circumnavigate the globe; and the objects Folger obtained (such as a Tlingit anthropomorphic fishhook imbued with supernatural powers to aid a fisherman) were purchased from Society member Clifford Crowninshield (*Minerva*'s co-owner) for the museum. Yet the *Minerva* never reached the Pacific Northwest, so Folger likely obtained these objects from other vessels in the South Pacific that had recently traded in that region.[11]

As sea otter pelts became harder to obtain, Salem captains were at the forefront of finding and exploiting new resources to trade for goods in China. At first, American mariners stopped in Hawai'i and filled their ships' holds with another valuable trade commodity on the Canton market: sandalwood. This fragrant wood, procured almost entirely from India in the late eighteenth century, was used to make bureaus, chests, fans, and combs. In the early nineteenth century, when the Hawaiian islands were controlled by Kamehameha I and Kamehameha II (circa 1797–1824), Yankee traders exchanged wine, axes, fancy clothing, and even ships for this wood.[12]

Sandalwood was quickly overexploited, and mariners moved farther into the South Pacific to procure it—reaching the Societies, Samoa, Tonga, and especially Fiji. In doing so, they discovered another natural commodity of value in the China trade: the marine invertebrate known as trepang, also called sea cucumber or bêche-de-mer. The Chinese had a fondness for trepang soup, and the animal garnered high prices in Canton and Manila. Salem captains Benjamin Vanderford and William Driver (1803–86), discovered great quantities of the creature in the shallow waters off Fiji and learned from Malay traders how to procure and cure it for trade. (Driver also coined the moniker "Old Glory" for the American flag.)

Venturing further into the Pacific for these natural resources, nineteen East India Marine Society members donated more than a hundred objects from Aotearoa (modern-day New Zealand), Hawai'i, the Marquesas, Tahiti, Fiji, Samoa, the Cooks, and the Australs in the first two decades of the nineteenth century. These gifts include tapa cloth, fishing equipment, paddles, weapons, articles for personal adornment, household objects, musical instruments, tools, and religious and ceremonial objects. The growth of the Pacific collection was aided early on by mariners who were not Society members. In 1802, for example, Salem captain and China trader Daniel Ward (1782–1813) donated objects from his travels to Tahiti, Tonga, Hawai'i, and Aotearoa: a greenstone pendant, or *hei-tiki*; a fishhook and a parrot ring from Aotearoa (the first Maori objects to enter a museum collection); and two Tahitian tattooing instruments.

The same year, the English mariner John Fitzpatrick Jeffrie (dates unknown), who was purser on board the British ship *Earl Cornwallis*, gave Pacific Islands objects to the Society. Jeffrie had heard about the museum through member John Holman (1769–1852); and while in the "Isle of France" (Mauritius), he sent along eighteen objects including "Otaheitan" fishhooks, a spear, bows, arrows, and a mourning mask. In a letter accompanying the objects—"trifles scarcely worthy [of] your acceptance"—Jeffrie expressed his admiration for both the Society and Salem. He acknowledged that the "great character gain'd by the town of Salem, for her spirited and disinterested support of Boston, while the latter was suffering under the lash of British power," had never diminished and that "every honest citizen of the world must feel anxious that it never may!" Jeffrie extended his praise to America, stating that while war raged on around the globe "we have witness'd AMERICA . . . smiling in the midst of plentiful harvests and domestic comforts,—while every sea has been cover'd and every port and harbor fill'd by her shipping . . . and at once pouring wealth and infamtion [*sic*] into her lap." Jeffrie specifically admired Salem merchants' "good exertions . . . for the increase of a knowledge of nature, which they did not fail to unite with the advance of their fortunes," and believed they looked beyond business ventures and "made it their pride to collect all those productions which excite curiosity and the great, tho' pleasing study of the beauties of nature!"[13] For Jeffrie, Salem mariners were representative of the country's learned desire to use maritime trade as a means to collect objects for enlightened speculation.

The material culture collected by the East India Marine Society from these islands mirror images published in its volume of Captain Cook's voyages (see figure 15, left). The Society's three-dimensional version, equally as static as the book illustrations, painted a multifaceted picture of Pacific islanders. The canoe models, paddles, and fishing gear highlighted the maritime nature of these cultures, as did similar objects from the Pacific Northwest. Yet certain articles of dress and personal adornment denoted the Society's view of indigenous people as curious objects in and of themselves. The plethora of clubs, the largest category of material from the region, reflected a vision of Pacific islanders as violent and savage while also noting the tense trading climate (see figure 15, right).

In Fiji, Yankee mariners hired workers from local chiefs for collecting bêche-de-mer, building drying sheds, and smoking and packing the sea cucumbers. In addition, they gathered other important local trade goods, primarily pearls and tortoiseshell. The Fijians who harvested bêche-de-mer could be aggressive to westerners and hostile to sailors. Society member

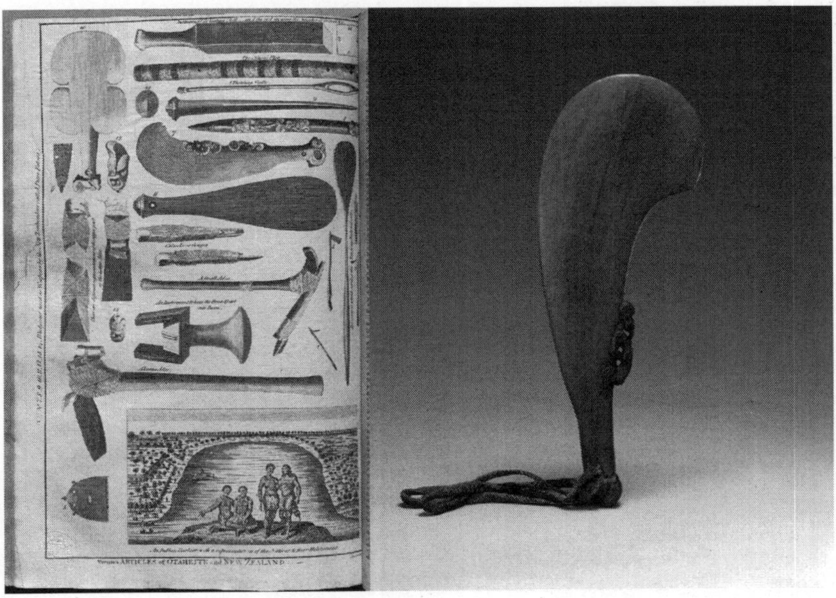

FIGURE 15. Left: "Various Articles of Otaheite and New Zealand," in George William Anderson, *A New, Authentic, and Complete Collection of Voyages Round the World*, 1784. Peabody Essex Museum Collection, LIBG420.C62-A5–1784-C.1. © 2016 Peabody Essex Museum, Salem, MA. Photography by Kathy Tarantola. Right: *Wahaika* (club) made by a Maori artist in Aotearoa (New Zealand), circa 1800–6. Wood, flax, fiber, 17½ x 6½ x 1 in. Peabody Essex Museum Collection, E5533. © Peabody Essex Museum, Salem, MA.

William Endicott (1803–88), third mate on the ship *Glide,* which was wrecked during a trading venture to Fiji in 1829, noted that indigenous men not controlled by chiefs often destroyed drying huts. He recounted instances when Yankee mariners' lives were at risk and times when Fijian men killed members of a ship's crew. One day, he recalled, the ship's carpenter "was employed in cutting the anchor stocks and the men were guarding him from the natives" when a group of local Fijians suddenly "rushed down from the mountains and attacked" the men, killing Edmund Knight and Joshua B. Derby of Salem "with their clubs."[14]

These incidents clouded Endicott's view of Fijians as "a race of people who differ very much from the other uncivilized nations in the South Pacific Ocean, in customs, language and particularly their complexion." He believed they were "extremely fierce and savage, frequently at war with each other and are addicted to the horrid practice of eating their enemies when killed in battle."[15] Two Fijian sailing needles in the Society's collection, made from the thigh or shinbone of an enemy who had been cooked and eaten, echo Endicott's reference to cannibalism.[16]

In this tense climate, New England merchants, whalers, and missionaries from England all tried to do business. Salem captains such as Vanderford, Driver, Eagleston, and others annually returned to Fiji and formed mutual trading partnerships. Through this trade network, Salem mariners touched upon other islands in the South Pacific and both acquired and traded specific objects. East India Marine Society members' logbooks and journals reveal why certain pieces of material culture were obtained and traded in these different regions. In the Marquesas on the eastern edge of Polynesia, where American vessels rounding Cape Horn often stopped for provisions, indigenous communities sought sperm whale teeth in exchange for sandalwood. These teeth were considered to be important cultural objects (*tabua*), markers of status and authority, and they were exchanged with other chiefs to maintain and solidify strong relationships. In 1801, Society member Nathaniel Appleton (1778–1809) recorded in his journal on board the ship *Concord* that the only thing the crew could exchange for provisions from local traders in Resolution Bay "was spermacetti [*sic*] whales teeth." He wrote that the crew "had eight or ten which the whalers gave us, for which we got a hog a piece."[17]

Fifteen years later Charles Forbes (1791–1821), ship's clerk on board the *Indus* during a voyage to the South Seas islands from 1815 to 1817, wrote in his journal that he was "forming whale's teeth from ivory & preparing other articles of the ship's trade." When the *Indus* was in the Marquesas a few months later, Forbes noted in a long passage of observations and recommendations on trading with native inhabitants that "a few whale's teeth (the longer the size the better) may sometimes produce sandal wood and generally prove a good article for purchasing hogs & other provisions."[18] In addition to *tabua*, Marquesan craftsmen carved whales' teeth into objects such as ear ornaments (*ha'akai*).[19] Two decades later, John Eagleston noted that sperm whale teeth were valued trade goods in other areas of the Pacific. Several undecorated whales' teeth were donated to the East India Marine Society just as American whalers were starting to use these cetacean canvases for shipboard art. In 1831, Society members William Osgood, George Pierce (1809–58), and James W. Cheever (1791–1857) donated sperm whales' teeth that were recorded in the museum catalogue as "curiously carved," the first examples of scrimshaw to enter an American museum collection.[20]

With a cargo hold full of valuable pelts, sandalwood, or trepang, ships sailed on to China. The development and growth of the United States–China trade began when the ship *Empress of China* left New York in 1784 bound for the east, followed a year later by Salem's *Grand Turk*. During the next decade, American vessels were often as numerous as British ships in China, and by 1803, they outnumbered the British and all other nations combined.[21] After the War of 1812, the nature of this trade changed. The American home market had grown with more capital and more specie, and trade in China shifted away from individual investors and small partnerships to concentrate in the hands of a few large companies in bigger ports such as New York, Boston, and Philadelphia.[22]

The desire for tea, silk, and other products came from the west, but the Chinese controlled and delineated the terms of exchange during the height of this trade. Unlike the Pacific Northwest and the south sea islands, where European and American merchants had direct access to goods, foreign traders were never allowed into the interior of China. In Canton, they were sequestered to the Foreign Factories, a complex of warehouses reserved for western traders on the Pearl River, within Canton Harbor but outside the city walls. Between 1760 and 1840, the Chinese also placed numerous restrictions on all trade in Canton: "No foreign warships may sail inside the Bogue [the harbor approach to the city]. Neither foreign women nor firearms may be brought into the factories. . . . [F]oreign ships must not enter into direct communication with the Chinese people and merchants without the immediate supervision (of a native Chinese). Each factory is restricted for its service to 8 Chinese."[23] European traders, referred to as "foreign barbarians," constantly complained about these restrictions as well as the requirement that trade be conducted only at Canton. Starting in 1839, however, the relations between China and the west were transformed with the outbreak of the Opium Wars. The powerful British military forced China to cede territory (Hong Kong) and level trade relations with the west.

In spite of trade restrictions, American merchants were able to acquire a variety of material culture from China. Porcelain ceramics, furniture, and other decorative objects made specifically for export (known as export art) filled the hold of many western ships. In 1800, Elias Hasket Derby, Jr., gave the East India Marine Society a porcelain punchbowl with a depiction of a ship labeled "Ship Grand Turk at Canton 1786," a gift from the Hong merchant Pinqua; and in 1806, a member, Ward Blackler (1780–1815), presented the Society with two soup tureens in the form of geese.[24]

In the antebellum period before the California gold rush, Americans used objects obtained from China to construct an image of Chinese people as exotic representations of the Orient. This cultural construct was forged in popular culture institutions like museums. Charles Willson Peale's museum in Philadelphia opened the same year that the *Empress of China* reached the Far East, and thus the museum contained one of the earliest exhibitions of Chinese materials: utensils, weapons, and the wrappings used to bind Chinese women's feet. In 1805, Peale exhibited objects and life-sized figures in a diorama next to models of Native Americans and other "exotic" peoples.[25]

The East India Marine Society's collection was a carefully constructed view of the Orient made by both Chinese and western manufacturers. One of the earliest objects donated to the museum was the dress of the Canton Hong merchant Yamqua (active 1776–1804), given by Benjamin Hodges. The Society transformed this simple garment into a figure of the merchant himself, commissioning Salem's foremost architect and woodcarver Samuel McIntire (1757–1811) to carve the head and hands (see figure 16). McIntire made them as realistic as possible, perhaps working off an account from Hodges, carving indentations to indicate scars caused by smallpox and using human hair for the figure's mustache and braided pigtail.[26] Michele Felice Cornè then painted the carving, adeptly augmenting the life-like qualities of the sculpture by applying light traces of blue paint to the protruding veins on the forearms and hands. Another Mandarin dress, this one donated a year earlier by William Ward (1761–1827) and worn by members in the Society's annual parades in the early nineteenth century, was also put onto a carved figure.

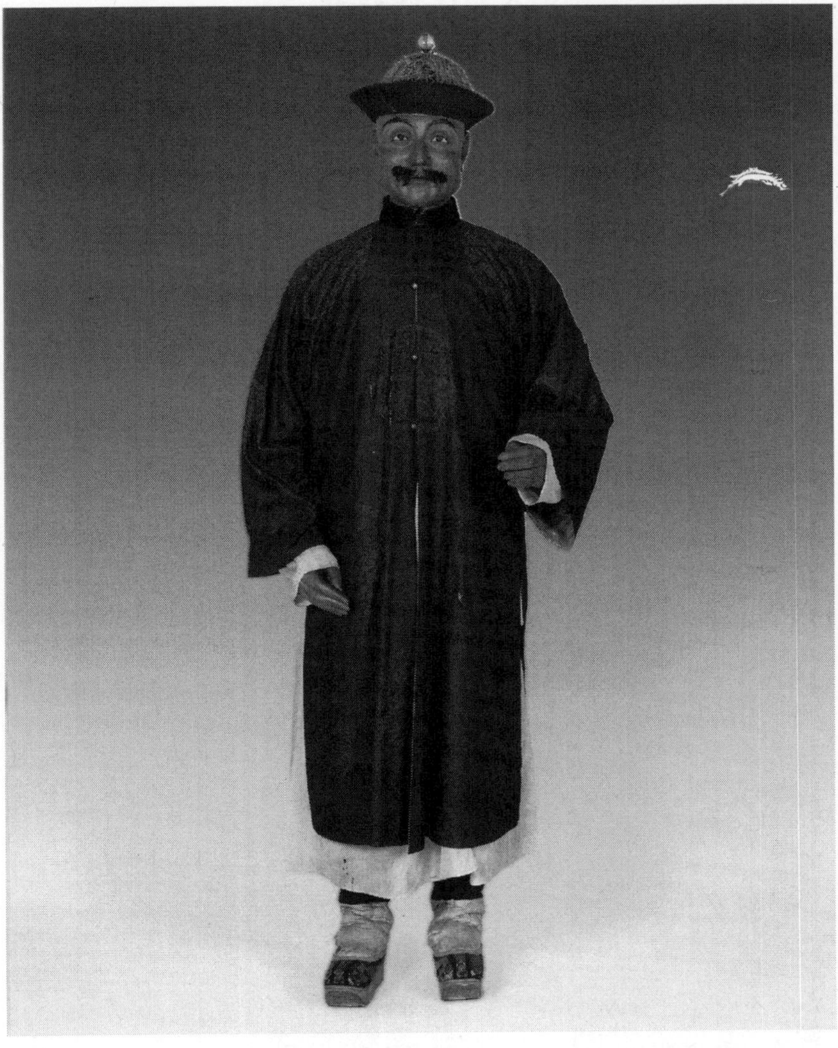

FIGURE 16. Figure of Yamqua by multiple artists, 1801. Mixed media, 72 x 20 x 20 in. Peabody Essex Museum Collection, E7161.1–4. © Peabody Essex Museum, Salem, MA. Photography by Mark Sexton.

These figures, along with others given to the Society in the following years, became mainstays of the museum—gazed upon by many nineteenth- and twentieth-century visitors. Early on they were considered a means for attracting visitors and possibly for eliciting money to support the Society's charitable endeavors. In November 1803, a committee formed "to examine the state of the Society" brought forth an idea to use the museum to increase funds for charitable ventures:

> [T]he museum of the Society might be made an object of Profit for charitable Purposes, were attention paid to collecting from the different parts of the East Indies, the dresses of the several classes of Natives to be placed on figures made for the purpose, and by procuring such other articles as would serve to attract attention, without incurring a greater expense than the Society could afford. . . . [W]henever this shall be the case, the whole net Profits shall be appropriated for such charitable uses as the Society may then direct, and no part thereof be applied to increasing the funds of the Society.[27]

While the Society officers did not follow through with the committee's recommendation, the link between collecting and the display of popular objects for charitable purposes adds another layer of meaning to the figures.

Chinese artists, too, crafted porcelain figurines for export to the west. Many depicted nobility and everyday people, reflecting an American interest in the dress and customs of this culture. A few of these unfired figurines, some with nodding heads or moving hands, were donated to the Society. Captain Richard Wheatland presented four in 1803: a purported Mandarin husband and wife, a laborer packing tea, and a porter carrying two chests of tea. The latter two reveal western interest in objects illustrating the procurement and processing of this popular commodity.[28]

To enhance what Caroline Howard King has called the museum's "Eastern flavor," Society member Thomas Wren Ward (1786–1858) donated a portrait of the Canton silk merchant Eshing in 1809. It was painted by the Chinese artist Guan Zuolin (active 1785–1810), better known as Spoilum (see figure 6, no. 11). Ward likely traded with Eshing while captaining the *Minerva* in Canton in the fall of 1809; he was well respected by many Yankee mariners. Benjamin Shreve, an officer on the ship, believed that, "[o]f outside Merchants Eshing is the first. He . . . always has supported the Character of an honest man, and many purchase of him without ever seeing their Goods. He is the most Candid man in Canton—his goods will pass in the United States without opening."[29]

To complete this Cantonese mercantile tableau, the East India Marine Society commissioned Cornè to paint a fireboard of the Foreign Factories at Canton (see figure 6, no. 24). Cornè never visited China, so this work was based on a published image that he likely saw in Salem.[30] Alongside the European flags that stand in front of each warehouse in the painting is the American flag signifying the U.S. presence in this region. The subject matter, though, depicting the only portion of the port accessible to overseas merchants, denotes eastern control of western mercantile interests.

In addition to export art, the Society's collection of Chinese objects included indigenous material culture similar to examples in Peale's museum. Six shoes and two models of women's feet donated between 1800 and 1826 indicate a fascination with the Chinese process of foot binding, and an equal number of opium pipes given during this period relate a similar obsession with the clandestine American trade of this drug. Scientific and spiritual objects were part of the collection as well, from an abacus to a 5⅝-inch soapstone figure of a maitreya Buddha, a popular piece among museum visitors in later years. A book titled *The Chinese Art of Curing Diseases* also attracted viewers. Bound between two carved and stained pieces of wood, this seventeenth-century volume contains twenty-four hand-painted figures with captions in Chinese, accompanied by a Jesuit priest's Latin translation of the work. Any visitor who went through this volume without knowledge of either language would have had little interpretive information about the book beyond the brief catalogue entry. Most likely, a visitor would form an understanding of this object, and many others, through a distorted lens—preconceived notions of Chinese culture mixed with their own imaginings.

Americans trading in India also entered an already established east-west contact zone involving a significant European presence in the country. U.S. voyages to India commenced as soon as the ink was dry on the Treaty of Paris in 1783, and Salem mariners were at the forefront of the new trade route. George Cleveland recalled that American traders initially did not know what products would sell in India. When his father sailed to India on the ship *Sally* of Boston in 1788, "the cargo sent out, (owing to the ignorance which prevailed at that time, respecting the trade of India) was entirely unsuited to the market."[31]

European merchants, primarily British, were uneasy with Yankee traders in India. While they did not want this upstart nation to interfere with their business, they did want American silver specie to aid in funding their military.[32] In order to exert control over U.S. trade in India, the British negotiated the Jay Treaty in 1794. This agreement allowed American vessels to trade in British-controlled ports as long as they then sailed directly home and did not exchange acquired goods in other Indian ports or in Europe. This stipulation irked many American mariners because they were used to profiting from moving goods within Indian ports for freight charges and supplying commodities where they were most in demand.[33]

During the Napoleonic Wars, however, control tipped in favor of America. From 1795 to 1805, U.S. trade with India surpassed India's trade with the entire European continent, bringing in valuable cotton and silk textiles as well as sugar, ginger, indigo, and opium. The Non-Intercourse Act of 1809 and the War of 1812 altered the situation as raw materials rather than finished textiles were imported to fuel American industrialization. The trade waned in the 1820s but rose again in the 1840s and 1850s.[34] American-Indian connections therefore spanned the antebellum period; and as with China, travel narratives, prints, and export goods filled American minds with visual images and a negotiated understanding of this eastern land.

American voyages to India in the late eighteenth century were not always well-calculated affairs, but they still inspired young Salem mariners who were instrumental in this burgeoning exchange network. George Cleveland made his first trip to the region in 1798, at the age of eighteen, on the brig *Hannah*, which reached India after being at sea for more than five months. He remarked that when entering Calcutta, the first piece of land he had seen since the ship had left Cape Ann, Massachusetts, "the beauty of the scenery . . . after being so long at sea, [was] more delightful, than I can possibly describe; indeed it seemed almost like enchantment."[35] Cleveland listed the ship's cargo as "the money on freight, Fifty Thous and Spanish Dollars, which were invested in Calcutta, in sugar and Piece goods."[36]

Once in India, Salem merchants had to navigate through an established trading network. As in the Chinese port of Canton, all business required the mediation of local agents to obtain desired goods. In Calcutta they were *banians*, in Madras *dubashes*. Regardless of their regional names, these men had forged a place in an Indian marketplace teeming with European traders. With a burgeoning American presence in the country, a few of these indigenous agents started to specialize in trade with Yankee merchants.

Their knowledge of the markets was invaluable, and they also extended credit to American clients. Benjamin Carpenter commented, "The dubash is useful when you are at loss for a market and will frequently dispose of your articles, when you have made every effort without success."[37] Because American masters and supercargoes were indebted to these agents, especially in Calcutta, they formed strong bonds and even friendships.

American mariners' understanding of Indian society was negotiated in these ports where they learned about not only the local culture but also their new national identity as citizens of the United States. Until they landed on Indian shores, their only exposure to this country had been through late-eighteenth-century travel narratives, gazetteers, and navigational charts, often acquired in London.[38] Unlike in China, westerners were not sequestered to one area outside a port but could fully immerse themselves in the region.

In this early exchange, both cultures formed opinions of each other. Indians, through direct interactions with Yankee traders, identified them as a people distinct from the British. Back home, an American understanding of Indian culture came through commodities and curiosities. Indian cloth, principally inexpensive cotton, was the chief import from the region in the early nineteenth century, and many notices for sale were frequently published in U.S. newspapers.[39] The objects collected by East India Marine Society members and other donors to the collection, therefore, reflected what Americans viewed as Indian material culture and representations of Indian inhabitants. Of the approximately ninety objects given to the museum in the antebellum period, the majority were sculpted portrait figures of nineteenth-century Indians; smoking devices such as hookahs, or "hubble-bubbles"; and religious sculptures. Other portions of this collection, the third largest group of "artificial curiosities" in the museum, were fans, weapons, and the palanquin used in the Society's annual parades.

Among the first donations from India to the museum were objects associated with the markets of trade that cemented American-Indian relationships. Principal among the Indian agents specializing in the American trade in Bombay was Nusserwanjee Maneckjee Wadia, who came from a prominent Parsi family. He developed a strong relationship with Society member George Nichols and helped him purchase "a beautiful striped muslin . . . made in Bombay for some distinguished person" to use for his fiancée's dress. He also gave him a "camel's shawl" for his bride-to-be.[40]

In Calcutta, Ramdulal Dey (1752–1825), the most prominent and wealthiest banian specializing in the American trade, was also one of the most respected among Yankee mariners. Dey, like some of his new trading partners, came from modest means and built his fortune with keen business acumen to become the wealthiest man in Calcutta. In 1801, some merchants presented him with a life-sized portrait of George Washington painted in the style of Gilbert Stuart.[41] As the most iconic figure in American history, Washington's likeness had been appropriated around the globe as a means of memorial or unification since his death. In this instance, the portrait given to Dey was a reflection of a new American presence in India: a republic free from British rule.

These Indian agents made some of the earliest donations to the East India Marine Society's collection through their American business partners. In 1805, Nusserwanjee gave "a complete Parsee dress"—consisting of shoes, a robe, shawl, and turban—(see figure 6, no. 23) and his portrait through member John R. Dalling (1779–1808) (see figure 17).[42] As with the figure of Yamqua, the Society made a mannequin in Nusserwanjee's likeness modeled after his portrait to display this outfit. Two years earlier, Calcutta banian Durgaprasad Ghose donated two musical instruments—a *dholak* (drum) and *tambura* (stringed drone)—and a *kittishal* (a parasol used for sheltering a palanquin). Ghose had a good relationship with many Salem merchants who were Society members, and his gifts were intended for their annual parades, adding yet another level of complexity to these performances. The donations from these Indian merchants were not merely indicative of friendly business exchange. Because the two agents knew about the museum and its mission, they symbolized a conscious desire to represent Indian culture in this new American institution.[43]

The figure of Nusserwanjee was the first of forty large and small figural sculptures of Indian people that the East India Marine Society collected. In 1823, James Buffington Briggs (1790–1857), who went to India under the employ of Joseph Peabody, acquired seven life-sized clay figures "copied from nature by a distinguished native artist of Calcutta" for the museum while he was master of the ship *Emerald*.[44] Samuel Barton (1804–40), another Society member, employed by Peabody as supercargo on the ship *George* during a voyage to Calcutta in 1834, donated twenty-one smaller-scale figures, "Idols at the Bazar price," acquired through Indian agent Sri Goundhun Ghose.[45] Both sets represent the servants, religious devotees, and entertainers familiar to Americans in Calcutta, which Indian agents

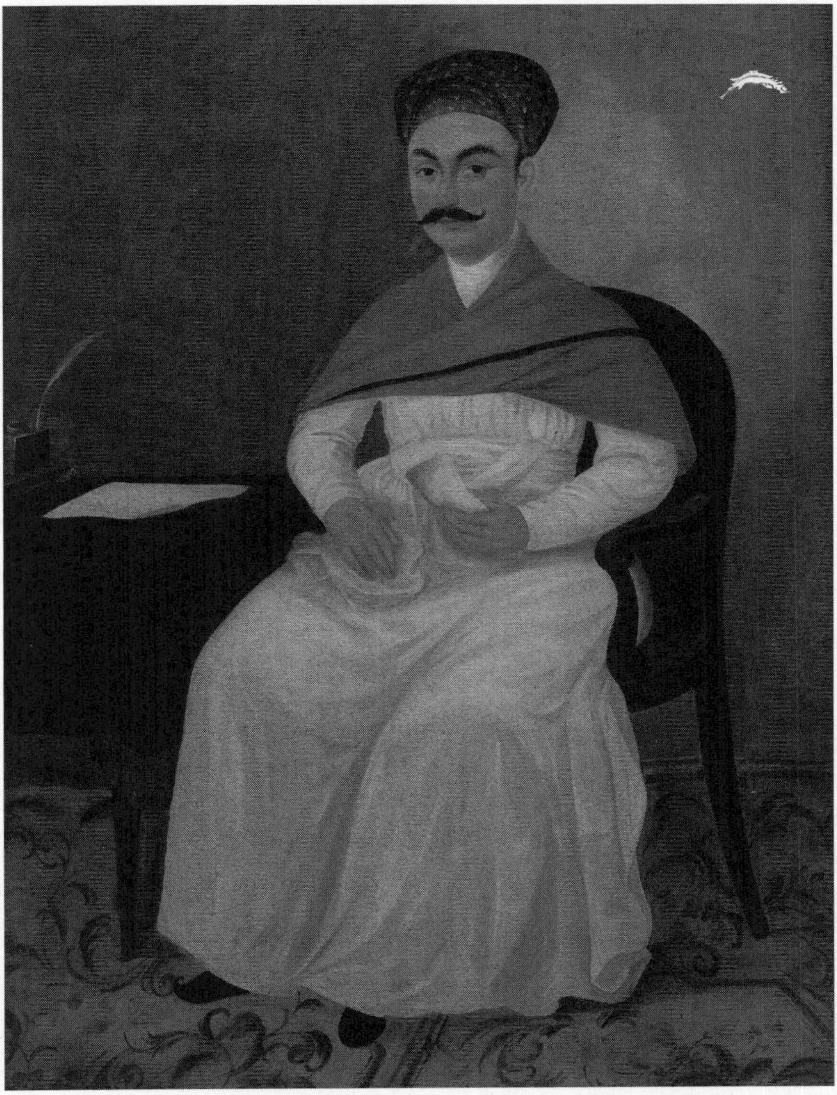

FIGURE 17. Portrait of Nusserwanjee Maneckjee Wadia, by an unknown artist in India, circa 1802. Oil on canvas, 39 x 29 in. Peabody Essex Museum Collection, M245. © Peabody Essex Museum, Salem, MA. Photography by Jeffrey R. Dykes.

like Ghose believed westerners wanted as souvenirs.[46] These figures, like those constructed by the Society, were intentionally made for western display and were often "types" of people rather than representations of actual individuals.[47]

In the 1840s, the most prominent Indian agents, Raj Kissen Mitter and Rajinder Dutt, cemented their relationship with Yankee mariners through visual arts. Each had life-sized portrait figures made for American clients to bring back home (see figure 5, nos. 12 and 13).[48] When they were donated to the Society, this new generation of Indian businessmen joined their brethren in East India Marine Hall, subject to a western gaze. The entire ensemble replicated American mariners' real and exoticized experiences in India for museum visitors.

Salem merchants were equally influential in trade with other ports in the east, and objects acquired in these regions enhanced the American global narrative on display in the museum. Four Society members were part of the earliest U.S. voyages to Japan. The connections between these two nations began at the end of the eighteenth century, 160 years into Japan's *sakoku,* or "closed country" policy, and long before the voyage of Commodore Matthew Perry's "Black Fleet" in 1853. The only people allowed into the country during this period were Chinese and Dutch merchants, who were sequestered on the man-made island of Deshima in Nagasaki Harbor. At the close of the eighteenth century, the Napoleonic Wars disrupted Dutch maritime commerce in the Pacific. Because English privateers were capturing their ships, Dutch officers in Batavia chartered neutral ships from other nations to make official voyages to Japan under the Dutch flag.[49] Following the monsoon pattern, vessels would leave Batavia in June and return in December. The chartered ships were required to follow exact protocols laid out by the Dutch so as not to incur suspicion, though it is likely the Japanese were not blind to what was going on and allowed this digression in order to continue trade.

The Salem ship *Franklin*, captained by James Devereux (1766–1846), was the second American vessel to undertake a Dutch charter. When the vessel returned to its homeport in 1800, it was the first to arrive in the United States with a cargo from Japan. For this feat, Devereux was made a member of the East India Marine Society. In return for his induction, he gave it Japanese objects obtained on the voyage, the first to enter an American collection. This donation included his logbook containing the specific orders and decorum Dutch merchants required Americans to follow when in Japan and five multicolored Japanese wood-block prints dating from the mid- to late 1790s—four of female courtesans and one of a domestic scene.[50] Unlike the export art produced for western clients, the objects

Devereux brought back were acquired in a native context, purchased on the main island of Kyushu rather than on the free-trading island of Fapenberg, where the other sailors bought personal keepsakes.[51]

During the next three years, more Japanese objects entered the collection, roughly two-thirds of the material the Society collected from this country in the antebellum period. Though only representing a short moment in Japanese-American relations, the objects, like the prints, were more representative of native Japanese culture than were those acquired in China.

The next vessel to take on a Dutch charter was the Boston ship *Massachusetts*. On board was twenty-three-year-old William Cleveland (1777–1842), who served as captain's clerk and would become a Society member in 1821. Cleveland's journal provided greater detail on Japanese culture than Devereux's formulaic logbook did, depicting changing attitudes toward Japanese people and eastern views of the west. Cleveland came to Japan as a young man "who had crammed into his head prejudices about stereotyped Japan" before entering this new land, a result of the "repeated cautions" of the Dutch agents on board the ship. Very quickly, though, he acknowledged that "many of the Japanese are assiduous in their endeavores [*sic*] . . . respectful & engaging," and stated that the Dutch had told the ship's crew to "look upon the Japanders as a Cruel people before coming in." Cleveland and his fellow sailors realized that "[m]any stories we now think exaggered [*sic*] and some intirely [*sic*] unfounded."[52]

While initially taken aback by the "low opinion the Japanders have of America," Cleveland and his fellow crewmen worked to alter this perceived misconception. He wrote, "[S]ome of them enquired to-day whether America was as large as Nangassacky [*sic*] & on being shown a Map of the World were astonished at the extent of America & the diminutive appearance of the Dutch dominions. Cliné! Cliné! said one, who at the same time express'd a wish to go to America, but said it was impossible." Cleveland also contextualized many observations made in Japan with his experiences back in the United States. During his second day in Nagasaki he commented, "[T]he houses are built of Wood & have much the appearance of American buildings," and reflected, "The deep tones of Bells which appeared to something like the tolling of Bells in America, with about half a minutes [*sic*] pause between the strokes rendered the scene solemn as well as beautiful. Oh! home how I Love Thee!"[53]

Cleveland provided some of the earliest American descriptions of Japanese people. When some Japanese inspectors came on board the ship on July 18, 1800, he wrote a lengthy sketch on their "neat, simple & not inelegant" dress. He observed their "long loose gown of stripped [*sic*] Cotton, secure[d] together by a sash, where they affix their swords," and "skirts like the Women of Europe or America." He also commented on their "shoes . . . made of straw," which "have no Tops to them except a piece of Rattan to go across the Foot, with another piece from the first to the soul [*sic*], between the great & second Toe."[54] As a physical encapsulation of this description, Cleveland obtained "a Japanese sandal"—what we would describe today as a flip-flop—and donated it to the East India Marine Society in 1803.

Because many Salem traders sailed beyond the Cape of Good Hope on their way to the Far East, Society members obtained a number of objects from Africa for the museum. Most of the early acquisitions were weapons—some from northern Africa, which was patrolled by hostile Barbary pirates; others from central and southern Africa, where New Englanders traded for gum copal, ivory, gold, and beeswax.[55] As the century progressed, American mariners ventured to the eastern side of the continent. One of their centers of trade was Zanzibar, a junction for inland caravan routes and trading ships from the Indian Ocean. Sayyid Said (1804–56), the Imam of Muscat, was transforming Zanzibar in the second quarter of the nineteenth century into a locus for obtaining cloves, ivory, and slaves.[56] After American-Zanzibar trade relations were formalized with a commercial treaty in 1835, an American consulate was created there, with Society member Richard Palmer Waters (1807–87) appointed as the first consul.[57] Salem dominated American trade for the region's ivory, hides, gum copal, and peanuts into the 1860s.[58]

The Society's African collection, while small, still contributed to the global narrative of the museum. Member Henry Leavitt (1803–30), who made several voyages to the east coast of Africa, donated boat models, books, and natural history specimens from Zanzibar and Madagascar.[59] Other utilitarian objects and weapons entered the collection in the following years. To enhance the maritime aspects of this region, Cornè was commissioned in 1804 to paint a fireboard of Cape Town, South Africa, a frequent stopping point for American mariners who needed to acquire provisions and conduct repairs on their ships (see figure 6, no. 22).

Collectively, this random assortment of material culture—which included an Ashanti stool from Ghana and a drum in the form of a European sailor from Loango—either educated or confused visitors about the diverse cultural makeup of the continent.

Throughout the antebellum period, Atlantic trade routes in the new republic and East Indies voyages brought Society members to South American ports, which became part of an extensive trade network. Peru was a source of silver specie used to obtain goods from the Far East; and as the decades progressed and Salem's trade diversified, the country was also a source for guano, a natural fertilizer. During the late antebellum period, the rubber trade brought Salem captains into contact with indigenous people in the Amazon River basin. To Society members and other tourists, the continent was an exotic land filled with the remains of ancient civilizations and jungles populated with feather-adorned natives.[60]

Like the Society's African collection, the museum's South American collection was small in comparison to its Pacific island and the Far East collections. Still, several important pieces were acquired from the continent and donated to the museum, including an impressive featherwork headdress for use in fertility and initiation rites, collected in the Amazon river valley by Salem merchant Henry P. Upton. The museum also possessed another object from Brazil, one that, while less visually impressive, unified the Society's collections from Africa and South America: it was the only piece of material culture on display in the museum that directly addressed the Atlantic slave trade.[61] In 1830, William Cleveland donated a West African *mbira* (a thumb piano or finger xylophone), recorded in the museum's catalogue as "a musical instrument used by the slaves at Rio Janeiro, probably brought by them from the West coast of Africa."[62] While few, if any, local vessels directly traded for African slaves in the colonial and antebellum periods, Salem mariners profited from portions of the triangle trade; and the specter of this terrible exchange was bound to other objects in the museum.

The majority of the South American collection was made up of Incan and Chimú anthropomorphic and zoomorphic ceramics.[63] While an active antiquities market did exist at this time, almost all of the pottery donated to the East India Marine Society was listed in the museum catalogue as having been taken or dug out "from the ancient Mounds in Peru."[64] An unknown sailor on board the Salem brig *Herald* in 1825–26 remarked in his diary about the "great many . . . Indian mounds or burying places, which are found in many parts of Peru & frequently contain many curiosities—some of them are very extensive."[65] This cavalier looting of pre-Columbian sites was condoned by the Spanish government. British traveler Gilbert Farquahar Mathison commented that "English gentleman . . . received permission from the Spanish Government" to open mortuary vaults, or *huacas*, and "made a valuable collection of Indian relics."[66] Lacking archaeological context or further interpretation in the museum catalogue, visitors would have had no means of understanding what these curious objects—such as a Chimú black pottery vessel in the shape of a llama's head—were actually intended for.

Closer to home, and outside of American overseas trade routes, the East India Marine Society collected and displayed objects related to First Nations in the United States. While many pieces in the collection were bound to American mythologies about a disappearing Native American presence in the country, indigenous cultures were in fact dynamic during this period—reacting, reinventing, and reforming themselves in response to an increased European-American presence.[67] In the early nineteenth century, there were few major collections of native North American objects in the United States. Peale's museum did contain some material culture from the Pacific Northwest and other regions.[68] In 1816, William Clark (1778–1838), then governor of the Missouri Territory after his expedition with Meriwether Lewis (1774–1809), opened his own museum in St. Louis. This museum, the first west of Cincinnati, was attached to Clark's house and was used as a council chamber for visiting Native American delegations.[69] The painter George Catlin also formed a large collection of native North American objects, acquired during his travels in the west during the 1830s, and displayed them alongside his portraits of Native Americans in the traveling installation he called the Indian Gallery.[70]

At the time the East India Marine Society was formed, indigenous communities in New England had been marginalized to small pockets within and alongside towns and cities.[71] Into the 1830s, Native American tribes camped around Salem or lived in liminal zones near the port, such as marshes. The museum had a major display of an object important to these active New England communities: the oldest recorded full-sized Passamaquoddy birchbark canoe, originally from the Penobscot River region in Maine (see figure 3, no. 2).

Still, few objects in the Society's collection accurately reflected these indigenous cultures. Instead, northeastern Native American populations were represented as ancient or extinct. Local residents uncovered prehistoric and historic artifacts in their fields or found them during road and house construction. These objects, such as a Woodland Period "Hatchet found on Col. Pickman's farm in South Salem," were donated to the East India Marine Society and then displayed alongside classical antiquities.[72] To emphasize the narrative of a disappearing culture, the Society commissioned two paintings that enhanced this distorted, inaccurate interpretation of native New Englanders. One, a fireboard painted by Cornè of a Native American encampment, depicts indigenous people as an embodiment of the wilderness, an object to be tamed (see figure 5, no. 11).[73] Twenty years later, Samuel Bartoll painted *Landing of the Pilgrims* for the newly opened East India Marine Hall (see figure 18). His fireboard presents an anachronistic depiction of Pilgrims dressed in nineteenth-century sailor's uniforms and includes Native Americans who were not present during this historical event. The overall message of these works is that Europeans encountered a desolate landscape that was ripe for the taking.

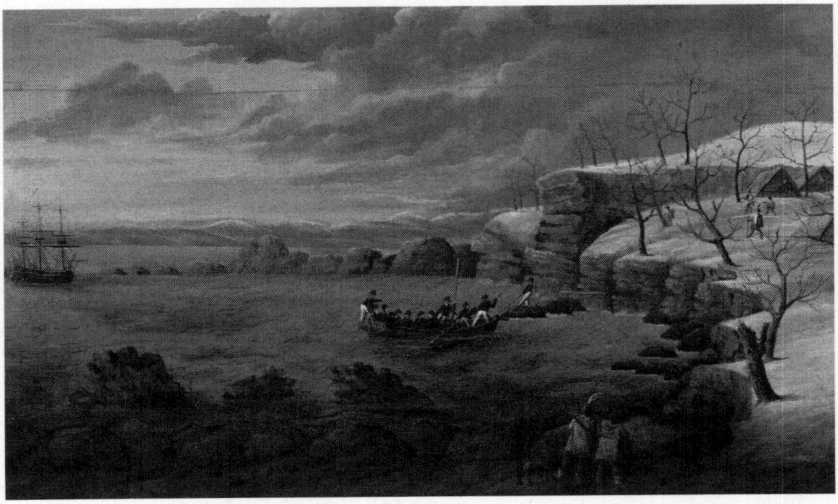

FIGURE 18. Samuel Bartoll, *Landing of the Pilgrims*, 1825. Oil on panel, 33¾ x 53 in. Peabody Essex Museum Collection, M293. © Peabody Essex Museum, Salem, MA. Photography by Mark Sexton.

The museum also displayed a number of objects from Atlantic and midwestern tribes. Many were collected during U.S. military campaigns in the first half of the nineteenth century and were donated by Army officers or officials who were related or connected to Salem families. The Great Lakes region and other areas of the Midwest had been sites of major conflicts between the U.S. government and Native Americans in the 1810s and 1820s. After the Treaty of Paris in 1783, the British had continued to maintain a presence and exert influence on indigenous communities, one source of tension that led to the War of 1812. Before and during that war, the American military often battled tribes that sided with the British; in 1811, William Henry Harrison defeated Tecumseh and the Shawnee at the mouth of the Tippecanoe River in one of many such conflicts. Afterward, the U.S. military continued campaigns to gain control of Native American land on the western frontier.

Native Americans in the Midwest, like those in the Pacific Northwest, had already been exposed to Europeans.[74] By the mid-eighteenth century, they were creating souvenir objects for trade, such as miniature canoes and dolls. Later, they began producing fancy boxes, trays, card cases, catlinite (red claystone) pipes, and other goods for sale to locals and visitors. East India Marine Society members, however, viewed these objects as exotic and assumed that they were traditional crafts.

David Bates Douglass (1790–1849), a native of New Jersey and assistant professor of natural philosophy at West Point Military Academy, collected and donated objects to the East India Marine Society while part of the 1820 Cass expedition organized by Lewis Cass (1782–1866), governor of Michigan Territory, and approved by Secretary of War John C. Calhoun (1782–1850) and President James Monroe (1758–1831). The expedition had scientific and geographic goals: to survey the western portion of Michigan Territory from the southern shore of Lake Superior to its connections between the Mississippi River. In addition, Cass hoped to locate the sources of important minerals in the Lake Superior region and obtain specimens of "virgin copper" that had been "procured by the Indians, or by half-breeds" and bring it to the Atlantic coast "for naval purposes."[75]

These goals, however, were secondary to larger political and military ambitions and part of Cass's terrible legacy of removing Native American people from their land. Cass was instructed to conduct "[a] personal examination of the different Indian tribes who occupy the country" and assess "their feelings towards the United States . . . their numerical strength . . . and of the various objects connected with them." The expedition was also organized to "procure the extinction of Indian title to the land in the vicinity of the Straits of St. Mary's Prairie du Chien, Green Bay," to move members of the Six Nations west from New York, and to subjugate Ojibwa people who were still loyal to the British.[76]

The objects that Douglass donated to the East India Marine Society (through his association with members William Story and Stephen White) were physical encapsulations of the expedition's scientific, ethnographic, political, and military goals. They included mineralogical specimens and Native American objects. Some Douglass intentionally collected, such as "very fine specimens of the sulph of strontian." Articles of clothing and pipes may have been reciprocal gifts from Native Americans employed as guides or as part of negotiations for land or allegiance. Douglass described in his journal a meeting with Broken Tooth (circa 1763–1828), chief of the Sandy Lake Anishinaabe, among whom Cass distributed gifts. He recorded that the Anishinaabe men were "quite astounded at the liberality of his gifts and express great attachment to the American government" and wrote that they agreed to Cass's proposal to "go down with him to St. Peters and have a council with the Sioux for a peace between the tribes." Douglass noted, "The pipe used today was given to the Governor."[77]

Native Americans also gave objects to the Society's museum to combat prevailing stereotypes of their culture. One donor was Elias Boudinot (1802–39), a Cherokee man educated in a Connecticut missionary school who had married into an established New England family. He urged his people to acculturate to survive this period of Indian removal. In 1826 he gave an address at the First Presbyterian Church of Philadelphia in 1826, part of a tour designed to raise money for the establishment of a printing press for a national Cherokee newspaper, the *Phoenix*. In his address he spoke about "[t]he rise of these people in their movement towards civilization," an attempt to dispel myths and misconceptions that "do great injustice to many of this race of beings." Boudinot provided several examples of Cherokee "progress" during his talk. He informed the audience about the "invention of letters" and writing and the translation of the New Testament into Cherokee. He pointed to this biblical text as a symbolic object, one that "has swept away that barrier which has long existed, and opened a spacious channel for the instruction of . . . Cherokees . . . of all ages and classes," and noted that they could now "read the precepts of the Almighty in their own language."[78]

In 1832, while on a speaking tour of the northeast to raise more funds for the *Phoenix*, Boudinot lectured in Salem. He visited the East India Marine Society Museum and donated examples of Cherokee writing and a translation of the Book of Matthew. His gifts to the Society and his appeals to white Americans reflected the complexities of Native American survival during the antebellum period. While his donation was an act of Native American agency, the objects themselves fell into line with larger missionary movements at home and abroad. (Salem itself was the headquarters of the American Board of Commissioners for Foreign Missions and was involved in international missionary activity between 1817 and 1883.)[79] In the end, Boudinot's efforts at Cherokee assimilation led to his demise. He accepted the mid-1830s Jacksonian policy that forced his people to migrate from their homelands in the southeastern United States to the Indian territory in modern-day Oklahoma (known as the Trail of Tears) and was assassinated by some tribal members who fought against this relocation. Despite Boudinot's efforts to promote the Cherokee as a "civilized" race, someone wrote "Indian" in pencil next to his signature in the museum visitor guestbook.[80]

Integrated into this global mix of cultural objects was a small collection of classical and Near Eastern antiquities acquired through maritime networks. American archaeological efforts in the Mediterranean and the Near East were sparse in the antebellum period, so mariners and travelers had a great impact on the growth of museum collections. Individuals on board merchant and naval ships had the best access to antiquities during this time, for many objects were acquired at ports connected to the opium trade, such as Constantinople and Smyrna (modern-day Istanbul and Izmir, Turkey), which were also major centers in the sale of antiquities.[81] Dealers sold material such as coins, relics, and forgeries at these ports of call and at the ancient sites themselves.

In 1803, working through the agency of Society member Elias Hasket Derby, Jr., Captain Apthorp of the British naval ship H.M.S. *Druid* donated a mummified ibis from the "Catacomb of Sakkara," the first Egyptian antiquity to be displayed in an American museum.[82] Twenty years later, Thomas Tanner, the commander of the British ship the *Antelope*, sent more than thirty objects to the East India Marine Society, including wooden *shawabty* (burial figurines), parts of a mummy, and a piece of an alabaster sarcophagus found by the Italian explorer and antiquarian Giovanni Battista Belzoni (1778–1823). In a letter addressed to "Members of the Museum of Salem," Tanner noted he had "lately visited the celebrated remains of antiquity on the Nile, & having personally collected a few trifles from the scite [*sic*] of the Ancient 'Diospolis'" presented them "with such explanation as it is in my power to give of them."[83] In 1824, Captain William Montgomery Crane (1776–1846) of the U.S. Navy gave four objects to the Society, including a fragment of papyrus with a painted vignette of the "Weighing of the Heart" scene from the Egyptian Book of the Dead.

Society members, too, contributed to this antiquities collection. As with the descriptions of pre-Columbian objects in the museum's catalogue, the descriptions of many of these architectural fragments, coins, and figurines note that they were "broken off" larger monuments or taken from burial mounds or ancient sites—for instance, "A model of a dog's leg, found in Herculaneum" by member Abijah Northey (1774–1853). While this object and dozens more were presented to the museum with more contextual information than most looted antiquities had, their provenance was not nearly as important as their physical representation of the ancient world coming to America.

Along with antiquities were relics connected to historical figures, events, or sites.[84] Many had been physically chipped out of historic or archaeological sites, including three fragments of Plymouth Rock and two bricks from Columbus's birthplace at Genoa. There were also many mementoes connected to Napoleon Bonaparte (1769–1821). No matter what American mariners thought of the emperor, they collected objects associated with him, particularly those connected to his demise. Some of the relics in the Society's collection served to augment the maritime experience in the museum, such as five pieces of the rock on which Captain Cook was killed in Hawaiʻi. Others instilled a patriotic fervor: a "Tassel taken from the bed curtain on board the Frigate *Guerriere* at the time of her capture" by crew members of the U.S.S. *Constitution* and a "Part of a chain which was stretched across the Hudson at West Point to prevent the ascent of the British fleet during the Revolutionary war."[85]

The Society's collection of relics also included religious objects. Along with a "Roman Catholic Rosary" and "A very minute figure of the Virgin

Mary and infant Jesus carved in ivory," the Society possessed a carved terminal rosary bead, known as a *pater noster*, or "prayer nut" (see figure 19). This object, donated by Elias Hasket Derby, Jr., in 1806, was one of the smallest objects in the collection but by far one of the most popular among visitors.[86] A lengthy description of it appeared in the museum catalogue, and a pamphlet titled *Description of An Ancient Carved Box in the Museum of the East-India Marine Society in Salem*—published by the Boston artist John R. Penniman (1782–1841) in 1819—was available for visitors to consult in the museum. Gothic boxwood rosary beads and other small devotional objects were produced in areas of the Low Countries in the late fifteenth and early sixteenth centuries. Their minute, detailed carving made them attractive to wealthy patrons, who commissioned beads of the finest craftsmanship and materials. The East India Marine Society's example contains one hundred and ten figures representing Heaven, with the Coronation of the Virgin in the upper hemisphere and Judgment Day in the lower hemisphere.[87] When examining it through a magnifying glass built into the vitrine in which it was encased, visitors marveled at its craftsmanship. Regardless of their religious affiliation, they considered this object to be one of the most exquisite pieces in the museum.

To augment the international array of objects, the Society amassed a substantial amount of European and American art in addition to commissioned paintings by Cornè and Bartoll. Alongside portraits of maritime heroes such as Cook, the East Indies merchants Nusserwanjee and Eshing, and influential Salem merchants such as Joseph Peabody and Elias Hasket Derby (see figure 6, nos. 12 and 13) were European paintings of biblical scenes.[88] They were eighteenth- and nineteenth-century versions of Renaissance paintings such as *Susanna and the Elders* by Delano and the *Adoration of the Magi* by Van Wyck of Antwerp (see figure 6, nos. 2 and 5), collected by local families such as the Derbys, Peabodys, and Gardners during grand tours to Europe. In 1825, George Peabody donated a nineteenth-century version of Antonio Balestra's (1666–1740) *The Death of Abel* (circa 1701–4), painted by an unidentified Antwerp artist (see figure 5, no. 7).[89] While these works are not considered masterpieces by modern standards, in the antebellum period they were displayed in homes as symbols of their owners' enlightened experiences. In addition to these works were American versions of European paintings, such as *View of the Temple of Apollo and Athens*. Painted in 1812 by the young Salem artist Theodore

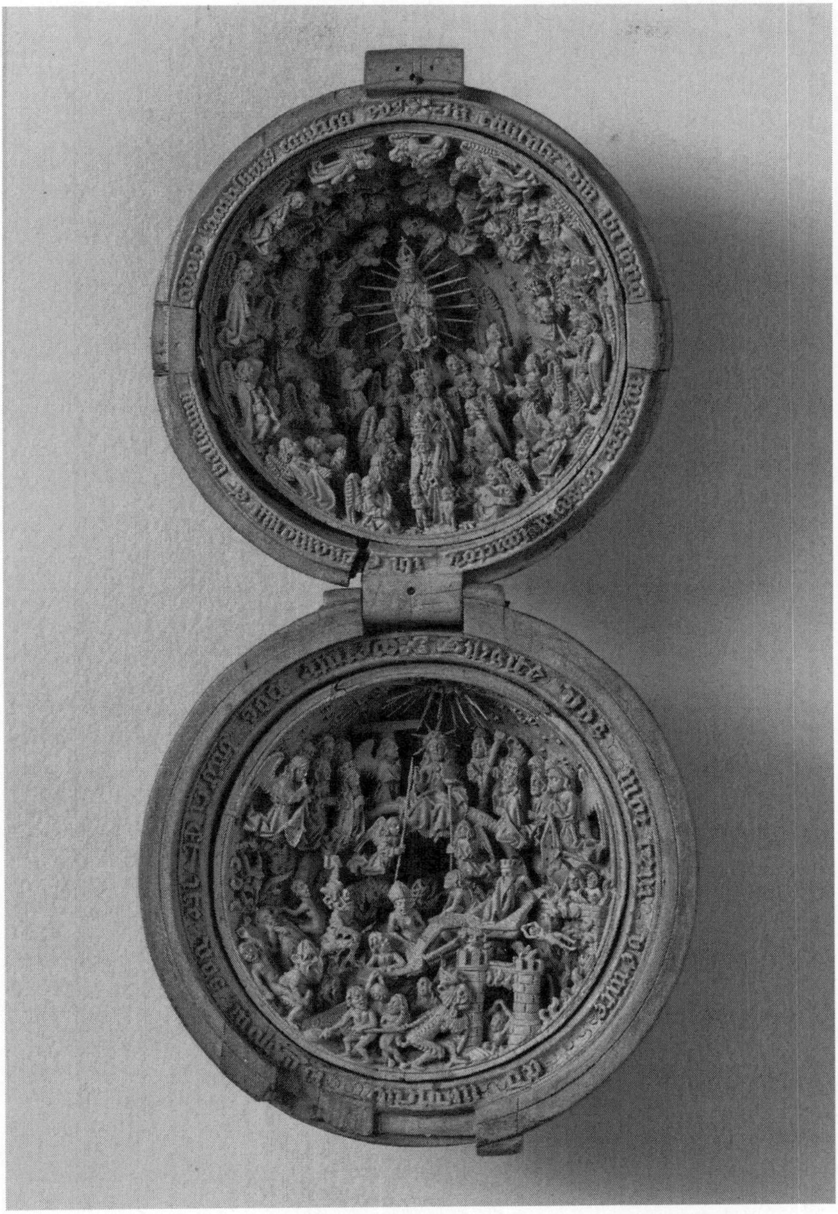

FIGURE 19. Adam Dircksz and the workshop of the northern Netherlands (county of Holland), prayer nut with *God in His Glory* and *The Last Judgement*, circa 1500–30. Boxwood, 4¼ x 2¼ in. (open). Peabody Essex Museum Collection, M557. © 2015 Peabody Essex Museum, Salem, MA. Photography by Walter Silver.

Fisher (1789–1819), after Claude Lorrain (1600–82), it augmented the classical antiquities on display in the museum (see figure 6, no. 15).[90]

To enhance the maritime flavor of its painting collection, the Society acquired a few marine scenes, starting in the 1820s. In the first half of the nineteenth century, American mariners commissioned Mediterranean artists in various ports of call to create ship portraits of their vessels for display in merchant counting houses or their homes. Member Nathan Cook (1783–1827) presented the Society with a painting of the ship *Erin* by the French artist Montardier (active 1812–48) of Le Havre, and an unknown individual gave the museum a portrait of the Salem ship *John* by Cornè.

These donations were followed by other scenes of maritime trade and naval encounters. Member William Henry Neal (1799–1851) gave a watercolor of American merchant ships involved in the coffee trade in the port of Mocha, and a year later member Henry Ropes (1791–1861) presented two paintings by his late older brother George Ropes, Jr. (1788–1819), a deaf and mute artist who was a pupil of Cornè. One of Ropes's paintings highlights early American naval heroism, depicting the capture of the Salem-built frigate *Essex* by the British ships H.M.S. *Phoebe* and H.M.S. *Cherub* in the Bay of Valparaiso. The *Essex*, built with public funds contributed by many local merchants and captains, fought valiantly for two and a half hours against heavily armed foes. The other painting depicts a British and French naval engagement during the Napoleonic Wars, a period of American neutral trade across the globe that contributed to Salem's maritime success.[91]

In addition to paintings, the East India Marine Society received maritime-themed prints that enhanced American patriotic sentiments in the museum. In 1824, the printmaker Benjamin Tanner (1775–1848) of Philadelphia donated six of his engravings. Three depict celebrated naval victories in the War of 1812: *Perry's Victory on Lake Erie,* after John James Barralet); *MacDonough's Victory on Lake Champlain,* from a painting by Hugh Reinagle (1790–1834); and *Capture of the "Macedonian" by the "United States,"* based on a painting by Thomas Birch (1779–1851). Another Tanner print, *America, Guided By Wisdom: An Allegorical representation of the United States, denoting their Independence and prosperity,* after Barralet, is extremely symbolic. According to Tanner's lengthy description on the bottom margin of the engraving, "Commerce is represented by the figure of Mercury . . . pointing out the advantages of encouraging and protecting

Navigation, signified by an armed vessel under sail." Described by some modern scholars as a "Neoclassical Allegory of American Exceptionalism," this print signals America's ascendancy in the world with the aid of naval strength.[92]

The East India Marine Society collected busts and statuary to round out its western art collection (see figure 6, nos. 4, 6, 14, and 16). Several members commissioned plaster busts of military heroes and patriots such as Washington, Lafayette, Hamilton, Jackson, and Adams.[93] In homage to European cabinets, the museum owned marble busts of the philosophers Rousseau and Voltaire, mathematicians such as Newton, classical writers and thinkers such as Homer and Cicero, and the Greek gods Apollo and Diana.[94]

Premier among the statuary in the collection (which included bronzed plaster casts of Hercules and the Erymanthian boar and Hercules and the Nemean lion, both donated by the Reverend John Prince in 1825) was a large cast of *Laocoön and His Sons* (referred to as the Laocoön Group) donated by William Osborn of New York in 1826 (see figure 20).[95] The cast of this impressive sculpture, one of the greatest in the classical world, was a major attraction among visitors to East India Marine Hall. Pliny the Elder (23–79), who attributed the Laocoön Group to three sculptors, described it as "of all paintings and sculptures the most worthy of admiration."[96] Praise continued through the centuries. After it was unearthed during excavations in Rome in 1506 and installed in a niche in the Belvedere courtyard of the Vatican, it was copied in plaster and bronze many times and placed in princely and noble cabinets. The American artist John Singleton Copley (1738–1815), writing to his wife from Florence in 1775, believed it was "not only the best work of art in the world now, but it was esteemed by the ancients the first in point of merit that the chisel ever produced."[97]

Until the end of the Gilded Age, America remained fascinated with plaster casts of classical sculptures. While they are most often associated with American museums collections from 1874 to 1905, they found their way into antebellum institutions such as Jefferson's small collection at Monticello; the Pennsylvania Academy of the Fine Arts, which began a cast collection for students in 1805; and the Boston Athenaeum, which acquired its first cast in 1822.[98] The East India Marine Society's Laocoön Group was integral to the collection for several reasons. As one of the greatest sculptures of the ancient world, it gave cachet to their small collection of

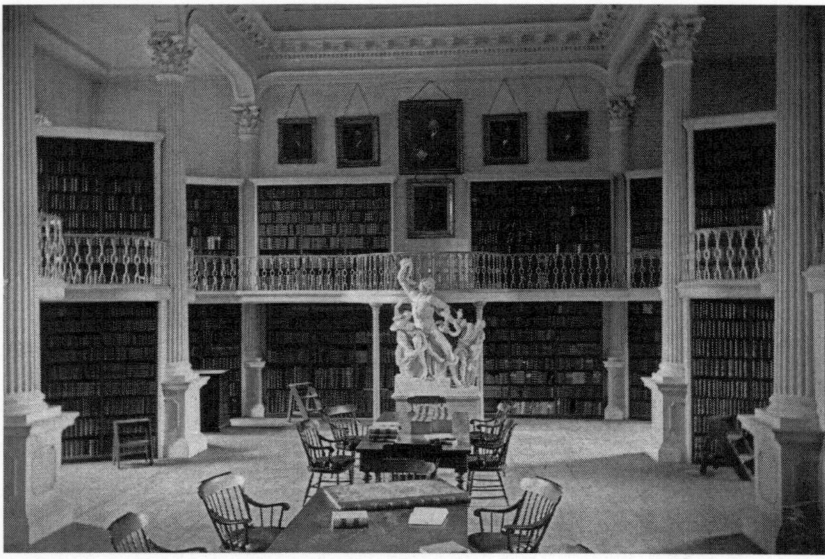

FIGURE 20. Plaster cast of the Laocoön Group installed in Plummer Hall of the Essex Institute in the last quarter of the nineteenth century. Peabody Essex Museum Collection, TR2016.27. © Peabody Essex Museum, Salem, MA. Phillips Library Collection.

western art. Likewise, its subject matter symbolized the dangers of the maritime experience in a particularly concrete manner. According to legend, Laocoön was a Trojan priest to Poseidon, and he and his sons were killed by sea serpents after angering one of the gods. The cast also served as a unifying force within the collection itself. The Society's museum was arranged in a manner akin to taking a voyage around the world, both above and below water. This object straddled both of these marine environments.

A decade after the Laocoön Group entered the East India Marine Society's collection, Salem's coastal shipping began to wane. In 1838, the Eastern Railroad was extended from Boston to Salem to transport granite, a sign that rail was starting to replace ships in the coastal trade. A year later, the Naumkeag Steam Cotton Company was constructed on the site of Briggs's shipyard, where ships now imported raw cotton and distributed textiles.[99] By midcentury, as the urban economic industries of leather and textile manufacturing were on the rise, the warehouses on Salem's wharves were being used to hold goods such as stone, coal, wood, and fish from the commercial fishing industry.[100]

Salem had never before had a maritime section, a sailortown, like other American port cities did because the entire town was tied to the sea. This changed in the first decades of the nineteenth century, as the port's merchant shipowners and captains built stately homes in new areas of Salem removed from the wharves or moved to Boston and beyond. Salem saw an influx of French Canadians who came to work in the Naumkeag Steam Cotton Mill in the 1840s, and boardinghouses were constructed in the area of the mill to accommodate them. Irish immigrants were attracted to the Salem waterfront after 1850. Once dominated by East Indies sailing ships, by the mid-nineteenth century the waterfront had transformed from a commercial trade center to a landscape dominated by bulk-good storage and industrial processing.[101]

The number of objects donated to the museum from the 1830s onward reflected the changing nature of American oversees trade and the decline of Salem's mercantile golden age. After 1837, only 567 objects were donated to the museum during the next thirty years. In comparison, the Essex Institute collected more than 2,000 "ethnographic" objects from 1845 to 1867.[102] During this time, some donors to the Society, such as John Henry Eagleston, also gave material to the Essex Institute—a telling sign that Salem's two collecting institutions were moving in opposite directions.

The few objects presented to the East India Marine Society in this period also symbolized changing dynamics in America toward continental expansion and the country's increased overseas presence. In Hawai'i, indigenous inhabitants embraced the Christianity of American Protestant missionaries in the early part of the century and as a result destroyed many vestiges of their prior religious practices. In 1846, John T. Prince of Boston donated one of the few remaining vestiges of pre-Christian Hawai'i, a sculpture of the god Kūka'ilimoku (see figure 21). In a letter accompanying this donation, Prince stated that the figure had been sent to him by a friend who lived in the "Sandwich islands," who had "procured after [it] considerable solicitation from one of the native chiefs, now a convert to Christianity, who intended to make an Auto de fe of him." Prince, fully aware of the rarity of "his godship," deemed it "worthy of preservation" and an "abiding place" in the museum, in "whose halls the curiosities of distant seas are so admirably arranged."[103] This masterpiece of Polynesian sculpture was created for Kamehameha I, who unified the Hawaiian islands in the early 1800s. It became a prominent figure in the East India

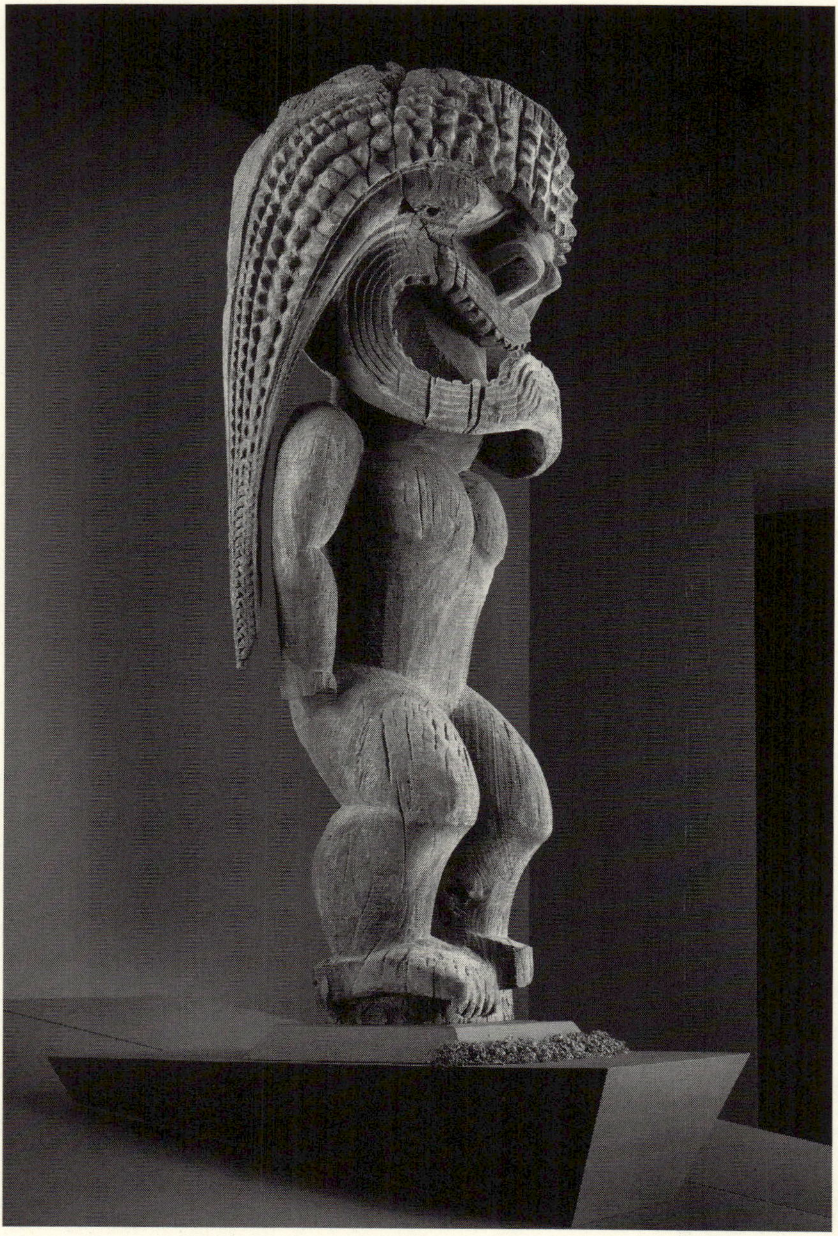

FIGURE 21. Figure of Kūka'ilimoku made by a Hawaiian artist, early nineteenth century. Breadfruit wood, 78½ x 28 x 20 in. Peabody Essex Museum Collection, E12071. © 2010 Peabody Essex Museum, Salem, MA. Photography by Dennis Helmar.

Marine Hall during the last twenty years of the Society's ownership of the museum.[104]

An influx of westerners into the Pacific Northwest in the nineteenth century had a detrimental impact on indigenous populations. William Cushing, the son of a successful Newburyport merchant in the fur trade, described a region wracked by disease, writing in 1844 that "the Indians have decreased very rapidly." He remarked that "ere many years have passed not a red man will be found in all the lengthe and breadth of America—from Hudson's Bay to the Gulf of Mexico—from the shores of the Atlantic to those of the broad Pacific."[105]

Continual western contact influenced artistic traditions. With the waning sea otter pelt trade in the 1820s and 1830s, local craftsmen created new tourist art in hopes of filling an economic void. Haida artists made pipes from argillite—a black, or sometimes red, shale indigenous to the Queen Charlotte islands—for sale to westerners in the region. Between 1830 and 1832, four different individuals donated examples to the East India Marine Society. While many were infused with indigenous artistic motifs and mythological scenes, others were geared directly to mariners. One, donated by John Coffin Jones (1796–1861) the first U.S. consular agent to the kingdom of Hawai'i, is in the form of an Anglo-American ship seen through the eyes of a local artisan. It contains exaggerated motifs, such as a rather large scroll underneath the bow of the ship intended to represent the vessel's decorative billethead.[106]

Until the late 1830s, the Society's collection of objects from China was the most significant of its kind in America. According to the British publication *The Gentleman's Magazine*, "the Museum at Salem, Massachusetts, . . . which has been accumulating through a long series of years by the intelligent and generous enterprize of the hardy sons of the ocean," had one of the three greatest Chinese art collections in the world along with "the collection at the Hague" and "that in the rooms of the East India Company in London."[107] In 1838, the American businessman Nathan Dunn (1782–1844) opened his Chinese Museum, or "Ten Thousand Chinese Things," in Philadelphia. Dunn was involved in the China trade as a merchant and had assembled a collection that was acknowledged by many as surpassing all others in the United States, including the East India Marine Society's.[108] Dunn's museum was a financial failure, though, and in 1849 P. T. Barnum purchased its remnants for his American Museum. In addition to this collection, the short-lived Boston Chinese Museum (1845–47) displayed Chinese objects to support the first Sino-American trade agreement at a time when the influx of opium into China—assisted by some local merchants and philanthropists—was spurring conflict in the Far East.[109]

While Dunn's enterprise and the Boston Chinese Museum both closed shop soon after they opened (as did many American museums in the antebellum period), the East India Marine Society Museum marched on. The few objects from China that entered the collection during this period mirrored the increasing conflict between China and the west. In 1855, Dr. Charles E. Parker of Pepperell, Massachusetts, donated "A Chinese Pin-Jall [cannon] taken at the Battle of Shanghai April 4, 1854 by Robt. C. Murphy Esq. U.S. Consul at Shanghai."[110] The most telling objects, though, were three portraits painted by the Chinese export artist Kwan Kiu Cheong (1801–60), better known as Lam Qua. Donated by William C. Hunter of Canton in 1838, they depict patients of the doctor and missionary Peter Parker of Framingham, Massachusetts, who treated people with large tumors or other major deformities at the Canton hospital. One portrait, of a forty-one-year-old shoemaker named Woo Pan afflicted with a football-sized cartilaginous tumor on the left side of his neck, may be viewed today as emblematic of the souring relationship between China and the west. During this period, Americans were coming to view Chinese people as an alien immigrant threat to the United States rather than as members of an exotic culture.[111]

A few donations to the East India Marine Society in the 1850s reflected the continuation of the federal policy of Indian removal. A print titled *Queenston and Lewiston Suspension Bridge! The Largest in the World!!!* was presented by Maungwudaus (circa 1807–after 1851), also known as George Henry, an Anishinaabe Methodist missionary and performer. He wrote on the print, "I have seen many wonderful works in Europe, but this Bridge beats all.—What would my grandfather think if he should rise up out of his grave and see this Bridge of the Yankees?!! March 21 1851." The development of the Niagara River region for interwater shipping impacted local indigenous populations, who used to supply fish and game to white settlers. When the print was made, there were little to no Anishinaabe in this area as they had moved to the headwaters of the Mississippi.[112] With no Native American presence on the print apart from Maungwudaus's handwriting, this object speaks to American commercial and geographic westward expansion and the people affected by Manifest Destiny.

One of the last objects donated to the East India Marine Society was perhaps one of the most telling—number 5255, "Frontier scene, A beautiful piece of sculpture representing the mother, and daughters." In 1863 Louisa Lander (1826–1923), a Salem-born sculptor, student of Thomas Gibson Crawford (1814–57), and granddaughter of Elias Hasket Derby, presented the Society with the plaster cast used for this work, which she had titled *The Captive Pioneer Mother and Daughters*.[113] The Society's president, Allen Putnam (1794–1868), remarked that it was "one of the most beautiful and attractive works of art that is in the Museum, and it being the work of a native Lady of the City, makes it doubly valuable on that account."[114]

The *Salem Observer* echoed Putnam's remarks, noting, "This interesting work manifests rare talant [*sic*] . . . indicative of the artist's genius and worthy of a pupil of Crawford." The *Observer* also stated that Lander's "artist aspirations were fostered and stimulated by her youthful visits to the Hall containing its unique collections" and believed the cast was "a superb acquisition to the Society and all the more interesting as being the work of a native of Salem and connected by family ties with several of the early and influential members."[115] This sculpture, though, held a silent parable for the country and the Society, one warning of the dangers of American westward expansion and foretelling the end of the Salem's golden age of maritime trade.

When William Story donated the ship model of the *Friendship*, he probably did not realize that this object signified the multifaceted nature of the East India Marine Society and its membership. It encapsulated the entire maritime experience in the antebellum United States, which was bound together in the Society's collection. The *Friendship* model was a reminder that ships had been the conduit for acquiring these objects of private and public contemplation. As Salem's fortunes changed over the course of the nineteenth century and the maritime port industrialized, fewer vessels like the *Friendship* were plying global waters. The ship model became a relic of a vanishing age, reflective of a virtual "united" Union and a "cohesive" American identity that that was coming apart in the decades leading to the Civil War.

The unusual objects that had once filled the *Friendship*'s cargo hold were now exhibited alongside her model to recount America's and the Society's past. The stories these objects told mirrored the tales published by Herman Melville (1819–91) and other sailor-authors of the period, which Daniel

Vickers believed "gripped the imagination . . . because their subject matter constituted such an extraordinary foil to modern life—so different from anything one encountered on the main streets of eastern cities, let alone in the cornfields of the Midwest."[116] The objects brought back and presented to the East India Marine Society functioned in a similar fashion, contributing to a sense of American identity among the more global citizens and visitors who came to Salem in the nineteenth century.

Chapter Four

EXHIBITION AND DISPLAY

To Form a Museum of Natural and Artificial Curiosities
—East India Marine Society Museum catalogue, 1821 and 1831

At the second formal meeting of the East India Marine Society, held on November 6, 1799, Benjamin Crowninshield, Jonathan Mason, Jr. (1757–1808), and Benjamin Carpenter were appointed "to list and arrange the articles in the cabinet (and to note by whom deposited)."[1] The men soon created a "Catalogue of the Museum of the Salem East India Marine Society," and one of their steady pen strokes recorded object number 1, a "Kemo from Tappanooly, Capt. Jonathan Carnes" (a giant clam from Sumatra). During the next twenty-two years, the descriptions of 982 objects were hand-entered into thirty lined sheets by either the donor or the receiving member, creating a written record of the work done to fulfill the Society's collecting goals as established in 1801. Like the *Friendship* model, the entries made by multiple members symbolized the communal nature of the endeavor.

Throughout the antebellum period, the East India Marine Society expanded, evolved, and regressed. The collection grew at an amazing rate in the Society's first thirty-one years of existence, but acquisitions decreased during the next three decades. After East India Marine Hall was constructed, the museum became more static in its arrangement, apart from the inclusion of new accessions. A careful examination of the collection within the context of the Society's disparate catalogues, its organizational meetings, and drawings of the hall gives us a unique opportunity to assess how an antebellum American museum functioned, note the antecedents of certain contemporary museum practices and procedures, and evaluate the cost and pains necessary to run the institution.

While Crowninshield, Carpenter, and Mason were creating the collection catalogue, the Society was searching for "a suitable room" to meet in. Eventually it rented quarters above a marine office, on the third floor of a brick building at the corner of Essex and Washington streets. Once the museum's quarters were established and the formal accessioning of donations had begun, the Society installed a partition in its new space "to deposit Books Charts etc . . . [and] secure the curiosities."[2]

Almost immediately, museum business became an important feature of bimonthly Society meetings. Operating the museum did not fall to one person alone; multiple members were tasked with improving and maintaining the collection. At the March 5, 1800, meeting, Carpenter, Clifford Crowninshield, and Josiah Orne were "authorized to get Perus voyages and charts bound & lettered," and a year later they were "requested to provide a Chinese face in the figure dressed." Beginning in 1800, certain object donors were acknowledged at every gathering, as when the Society offered thanks to "Mr. John Derby for the curiosities presented by him."[3]

In less than two years, the Society had built up a small museum worthy of notice. The *Mercantile Advertiser* of New York reported, "The Museum of the Society already contains many curiosities collected from the eastern quarter of the world."[4] By this time, though, its quarters were already proving inadequate for exhibiting the collection, so in 1804 the Society rented a larger space in a new building on Essex Street.[5] Twelve members worked to prepare the new gallery, examining "the Hall of the Society" and "removing & sorting the Curiosities at the New Hall." After William Bentley visited "the newly arranged Museum of the East India Society in the New Room" in June, he wrote in his diary:

> They have spared no pains to supply & to decorate it. On one Chimney is painted the landing of Plymouth & on another the launching of the Essex with devices. There is a delineation of the Cape of Good Hope, & of Wampum in China. They have the Eastern dresses & arms. Many American curiosities. A good collection of shells & some valuable things in natural History. Upon the whole their progress has been great & their success equal to any attempt in our country. They have many hundred Articles happily displayed. They have a painting of Capt. Cook done at the expence of the Society by Mr. Corne.[6]

Though his earlier account in 1801 had been less cordial, Bentley now seemed pleased with the organization and display of the growing global collection filled with eastern and "American curiosities."

Once established in the new space, the East India Marine Society focused on the internal operations of the museum. Most business revolved around day-to-day maintenance, but the Society also corresponded with other collecting institutions during this period. In 1806, Professor John Abbott of Bowdoin College wrote to the Society, "soliciting assistance for their museum."[7] Three years later, Daniel Bowen requested the loan of the Society's hall and museum, which was not granted. Bowen, a friend of Bentley's, had lost collections from his various commercial museums due to fires in 1803 and 1807, and perhaps his for-profit endeavors did not sit well with Society members.

The Society also started to grow its collection through means other than donations. In 1802, it purchased an assemblage of birds and butterflies from William Molloy for $64 and five years later bought "a collection of curiosities brought from New Holland by Capt. William Richardson."[8] It also obtained objects through exchange. On March 4, 1812, its president, Samuel Gardner Derby (1767–1843), and the committee of observation accepted a proposal from Obadiah Rich (1777–1850), the founder of the Boston Athenaeum, "for the exchange of shells belonging to the Society, if . . . it will be advantageous."[9]

By 1820, the collection had expanded to more than 2,500 objects and was difficult to maintain. The cataloguing system, too, had broken down by this point. One numerical digit was used for multiple objects, so the last recorded object in 1821—"A Box Contg Sundry Specimens of Corals and Fuci"—was actually the thirty-eighth object with the number 781.[10] The internal museum catalogue had become a disorganized mess, accounting for fewer than half of the objects the Society had collected. The museum's displays were also in disarray, a heterogeneous hodgepodge of objects. Nathaniel Bowditch noted, "The elegant arrangement which had been made soon after it was placed in the present Hall" had become "considerably broken in upon by the great accumulation of articles . . . stowed away wherever a spot could be found to place them in, so that things of a similar nature, instead of being collected together, were scattered about all over the Museum."[11]

Because Bowditch possessed a notable level of organization and attention to detail, he was voted in as president of the Society. During his tenure in the position, he put museum matters front and center. Donors to the collection were consistently acknowledged and that acknowledgment was always the first recorded item of business at meetings, preceding all other affairs. By the early 1820s, donation certificates were being sent to object donors. (In the nineteenth century these precursors to modern-day museum deeds of gift were commonly sent by learned societies to acknowledge contributions.)

To restore the "elegant arrangement" of the museum, Bowditch hired a local medical doctor, Seth Bass (1780–1867), as its first superintendent in 1820. Born in Quincy, Massachusetts, next door to John and Abigail Adams, Bass had received his medical degree from Dartmouth in 1815 and had practiced medicine in Salem for about twenty years. He was an avid collector of books and natural history specimens and purportedly owned about 3,000 volumes and an extensive collection of minerals, shells, and other curiosities.[12] Bass was the first of six successive superintendents with a medical and scientific background.

The East India Marine Society was established during a time of transformation in the field of natural history. Between 1780 and 1830, the study of the natural world had begun moving away from being strictly a theologian's pursuit in Europe and started to develop more specialized avenues of research. In addition, the field was becoming more professional. Amateur natural historians supported by learned societies, and clubs were now rivaled by expert researchers who were financed by new state-funded and -controlled institutions such as the Natural History Department of the British Museum in London, the geological and zoological museums of the University of Berlin, and the Musée National d'Histoire Naturelle in Paris.[13] In early nineteenth-century America, however, the lack of government-funded institutions kept the study of natural history in the hands of the amateur class, specifically those with medical training.

Natural taxonomies, primarily the artificial classification system of the Swedish naturalist Carl Linnaeus (1707–78), were viewed as one method of forging a national identity in the new United States.[14] Founding fathers Benjamin Rush (1746–1813), Thomas Jefferson, and others viewed natural taxonomies as a means of constructing an "American populace."[15] They viewed natural history as a possible rubric for unifying the nation.

Charles Willson Peale used Linnaeus's artificial classification system in a similar manner. It was the organizing principal for the natural specimens in his museum, which were installed below two rows of his portraits of Revolutionary War heroes, who were "presiding over the rational order of things, of which they were the superior extension."[16] Peale believed that one effect of this display would be the unification of people with differing political beliefs, who would be "drawn together for the purpose of studying the beauties of nature, while conversing on those agreeable subjects." His intended outcome was one in which visitors "may find a concordance of sentiments, and most probably from a slight acquaintance would think better of each other, than while totally estranged."[17]

Seth Bass was more versed in taxonomy and preservation than were most of the East India Marine Society members. Thus, by hiring him, the Society was able to project a greater degree of scientific clout in comparison to the strictly commercial museums that were opening around the country. He augmented the directions for collecting and preserving natural history specimens on the Society's blank journal forms, adding more than a full page of detailed directions. He also reorganized the entire collection of the museum, grouping natural history specimens based primarily on a Linnaean system, in which easily observable features of organisms are used to distinguish similarity or difference.[18] In addition, he was responsible for organizing and writing the museum's first printed catalogue. Within this publication, Bass created a special section titled "Catalogue of Shells in the Museum of the East-India Marine Society," where he used "The Linnean Genera" and occasionally "those of La Marck . . . and those of Perry."[19] Bass's knowledge of the invertebrate classification of the French naturalist Jean-Baptiste Lamarck (1744–1829), famous for his evolutionary theory of the inheritance of acquired characteristics, and the English naturalist George Perry (born 1771) speaks to his educated background in the field of natural history.

From the institution's inception, Society members worked to fulfill the objective of collecting natural artifacts. Jonathan Carnes donated the first natural history specimen, a large elephant's tooth. Other members followed suit, and by 1821 natural history objects made up more than half of the collection. In the museum, a visitor could see cases full of exotic birds and strange fishes, rocks and minerals, plants, assorted insects, *Chama gigas* (giant clams) and "enough corals to build a respectable atoll."[20] To reinforce the maritime aspects of their collection and interpretation strategy, large natural history specimens related to the sea took prominent positions in the museum. Two lower jaws of a sperm whale were installed along the western wall of East India Marine Hall, and Neptune's cups were placed in front of the northern windows (see figure 6, no. 7; figure 4, nos. 4 and 7).

Close inspection of the East India Marine Society's collection reveals that the museum exhibited another form of natural history: natural resources used to advance mercantile pursuits. Its display of economic natural history included fragrant sandalwood from Hawai'i and India, sea cucumbers from Fiji, sea otter skins from the Pacific Northwest, and silver ore reduced for specie, all of them used in obtaining tea and goods from China. Other displays featured undecorated sperm whales' teeth, used for barter with indigenous traders in Fiji, and samples of pepper from Sumatra and Siam. Set among other objects in the museum, these specimens revealed the global networks involved in acquiring trade goods as well as many elements of the collection.

Some museum visitors recognized these connections between economics and natural history. The noted British geologist Sir Charles Lyell (1797–1875), who came to the museum in 1845, understood that natural resources were key to Salem trade with China:

> [T]he early sea-captains of this port . . . had usually no capital, but started with a few beads and trinkets, and in exchange for these trifles often obtained the skins of sea-otters in the Oregon territory, each worth no less than 100 dollars. They also obtained sandal-wood in the Sandwich Islands, and bartered these and other articles in China for tea. On such slender means, and so lately as after the separation of the colonies from England, at a time when there was not a single American ship of war in the Indian or Chinese seas to protect their commerce, did many merchants of Boston and Salem lay the foundations of the princely fortunes they now enjoy.[21]

More often, though, visitors did not grasp the associations between natural specimens and trade unless they were overt. For instance, object 4570, listed in the museum catalogue as "Testudo imbricata, tortoise of commerce," literally made the correlation between this Atlantic and Indo-Pacific species and its use as a decorative inlay.

Bass's new position at the East India Marine Society Museum, one of the first curatorial appointments in the nation, also marked the first time that a non-Society member was given responsibility for stewarding the collection: "to enter the articles presented to the Society, in the catalogue, and to make such alterations in the arrangement of the Museum . . . as may be judged expedient."[22] The Society's officers, like modern-day museum directors and executive staff, still needed to sign off on all displays. Within a year of his hiring (at an annual salary of $100), the Society published the catalogue of the museum's collection. This hundred-page volume, titled *The East-India Marine Society of Salem,* lists 2,269 objects with donor names and includes the Society's act of incorporation, bylaws, lists of members and officers, a detailed breakdown of its funds, and an accurate list of the sixty-eight journals of voyages donated by members.[23] Bass was credited for the "new and more scientific" arrangement of the collection and acknowledged for his "very important services to the Society and to the public."[24] Part institutional history, part public relations piece, this publication—one of the earliest American museum catalogues—allowed the Society to both encapsulate its mission and collecting efforts and promote its endeavors to a wider audience. Copies were sent to other learned societies in the United States and abroad, and to former presidents Jefferson and Monroe. The Society also viewed the catalogue as a collecting guide, "to enable members when abroad to know what articles may be wanted to complete the collection." This volume is the first published encapsulation of the East India Marine Society's tripartite mission—benevolence, improving global navigation, and establishing a museum—and it contains examples of accomplishments made in all of these fields. The catalogue also documented the Society's promising depiction of its endeavors and bright future, as it "hoped, from the late accession of a great number of young and active members, that more will be done to increase our nautical knowledge, and to render the Museum a still greater object of attention to the man of science."[25]

Because the original numbering system had broken down, Bass renumbered all of the objects in the collection. He explained, "Some of the articles presented to the Society, several years since, were entered on the journals in a very imperfect manner; the donors, the names of the articles, and where they came from, being frequently omitted."[26] Along with creating a new paper record, Bass physically labeled objects in the collection with large and small numbers in paint or ink (see figure 10).[27] This new numbering system allowed him to apply Linnaeus's artificial classification system to the organization of man-made objects.

Bass recognized that the largest portion of the museum's collection was from the Pacific Islands. The first 156 objects listed in the catalogue are weapons predominantly from this region, followed by a few miscellaneous objects, twelve canoe models, twenty-four pipes (opium, hookahs, and so on), musical instruments, and some western armor. Bass likely followed a model portrayed in the plates of George William Anderson's volume on Cook's voyages, grouping objects by function rather than culture to achieve an organization similar to the one later used by anthropological museums at the end of the nineteenth century.

Next Bass numbered the first natural history specimens listed in the catalogue (horns of various species, the saw of a sawfish), the first figures of Indian and Chinese merchants and deities, and busts of poets and political figures. After this point, the catalogue organization jumps around, with natural history specimens followed by ethnographic materials. Bass listed a specimen of cava root, number 255, which he followed with a human intestine, donations from Japan (numbers 260–77), miscellaneous glass objects, a coconut-shell sugar pot, and fourteen teeth from various species, including an elephant and whales. His Linnaean organizational system returned with number 333, a pair of moccasins, the first native North American object listed in the new catalogue, which he grouped with other shoes from Asia and Africa. After the shoes he listed western paintings, ship portraits, and portraits of mariners. The first book in the catalogue is number 1419, *Chinese Art of Curing Diseases,* with more appearing as numbers 1527–62. The publication ends with "Catalogue of Shells," "Catalogue of Ancient and Modern Coins and Medals," "Catalogue of Paper Bills," and three objects that were late additions to the volume.

While sometimes erratic in its organization, the catalogue served as a useful document of Society members' worldly adventures at sea. Once the collection was moved into East India Marine Hall, displays were organized so that visitors could re-create a voyage around the globe. With this catalogue in hand and a clear numbering system in place on both object and in the printed text, they could easily identify what they were looking at (to the extent of the information supplied).

Three years after the publication of the museum catalogue, the Society tackled important museological issues. Their founding articles allowed for objects to be deposited in the museum "for the temporary use of the Society" and then returned to the owner. In 1824 it enacted further protocols for acquisitions: purchasing objects and "exchanging articles of curiosity." The Society also expanded the superintendent's authority, empowering him "to purchase any articles of curiosity for the use of the society to render their collection more complete" and create "an account in writing of all purchases made by him" to present at the first meeting of each new year. In addition, he was authorized to exchange any duplicate specimen presented by members or purchased by the Society "for other articles of which the collection may be deficient and which may be deemed not less valuable to the Society."[28] Like modern-day museum acquisition and deaccession policies, which require the approval of a director, a chief curator, and/or a collections committee, the East India Marine Society's bylaws stipulated that the superintendent must obtain written authorization from Society officers before adding and removing objects. Both measures allowed him to grow and refine the collection.[29]

Due to the continuing success of the museum, the East India Marine Society began looking into procuring another hall. President Stephen White, chair of a committee tasked with examining the Society's current quarters, reported, "[I]t would be inexpedient to alter or enlarge the Hall at present occupied by the society."[30] Instead, the committee advocated for creating a new building on a lot of land near the museum's current location. To pay for the cost of construction, the Society would rent out the bottom floor of the new building, which it believed would yield at least 5 percent annual interest, and create a new entity known as the East India Marine Hall Corporation.[31] This corporation would be a publicly traded body, but the Society would hold the majority of the shares ($100 each), and members would serve as officers.[32]

The first proposals for the construction of East India Marine Hall were made in May 1824, and news of the Society's plan to erect a new building appeared in publications across the country, including faraway newspapers such as the *Charleston Courier*. In July, the East India Marine Hall Corporation purchased a piece of land on the south side of Essex Street, opposite the junction of St. Peter Street, from John Andrew, a Salem merchant, for $4,000.[33] They engaged the Boston architect Thomas Waldron Sumner (1768–1849), the son of a housewright and a member of the Massachusetts Charitable Mechanic Association and the Society of Associated Housewrights (of which he was a founding member).[34] Sumner had designed the Massachusetts Charitable Mechanic Association building and the South

Congregational Church in Boston (1827) and had completed the designs and construction of Divinity Hall at Harvard University (after Simon Willard's original concepts) and the Congregational Church in Salem's Barton Square (1824–25). The *Salem Observer* believed that the town would be indebted to Sumner's "good taste and judgment . . . for some time to come" and "consider itself indebted for its two most ornamental public buildings."[35]

East India Marine Hall was reminiscent of the North and South Market Street blocks flanking Boston's Faneuil Hall Market, with a granite façade containing the words "East India Marine Hall" above seven arched windows and red brick side walls. Between 1825 and 1867 the first floor was rented out to other businesses, such as reading rooms and the Salem Post Office, and the second story contained a 100-by-45-foot hall used for the Society's museum, meetings, and dinners. The words "Asiatic Bank" and "Oriental Insurance Company" were chiseled above two entrances that flanked the door to East India Marine Hall. Not only did these names denote the first tenants on the ground floor, but they also demonstrated that the foundations of maritime commerce were literally supporting the Society (see figure 22, bottom).

Upon the hall's opening, the *Essex Register* wrote that it was "as chaste and beautiful a specimen of architecture as our country can exhibit," filled with "the rare and curious productions of nature and art from the four quarters of the globe . . . a cabinet unrivalled in this, and excelled by few in any country."[36] A period image illustrates how the hall's position and appearance wove the museum into the fabric of Salem's main thoroughfare, Essex Street (figure 22, top). It rose above all other buildings in its vicinity and undoubtedly attracted the attention of locals and visitors.

East India Marine Hall formally opened on October 14, 1825, an event attended by President John Quincy Adams, Supreme Court Justice Joseph Story, Boston's mayor Josiah Quincy (1772–1864), and numerous other American politicians and dignitaries.[37] The *Essex Register* reported that President Adams's visit to Salem "was one of filial duty to his venerable parent, the Society and the town . . . one of marked attention, for which he has our cordial acknowledgements."[38] A procession consisting of East India Marine Society members, invited guests, the Boston Brigade Band, and three constables left Hamilton Hall on Chestnut Street at two o'clock in the afternoon and proceeded along Cambridge, Essex, Newbury, Brown

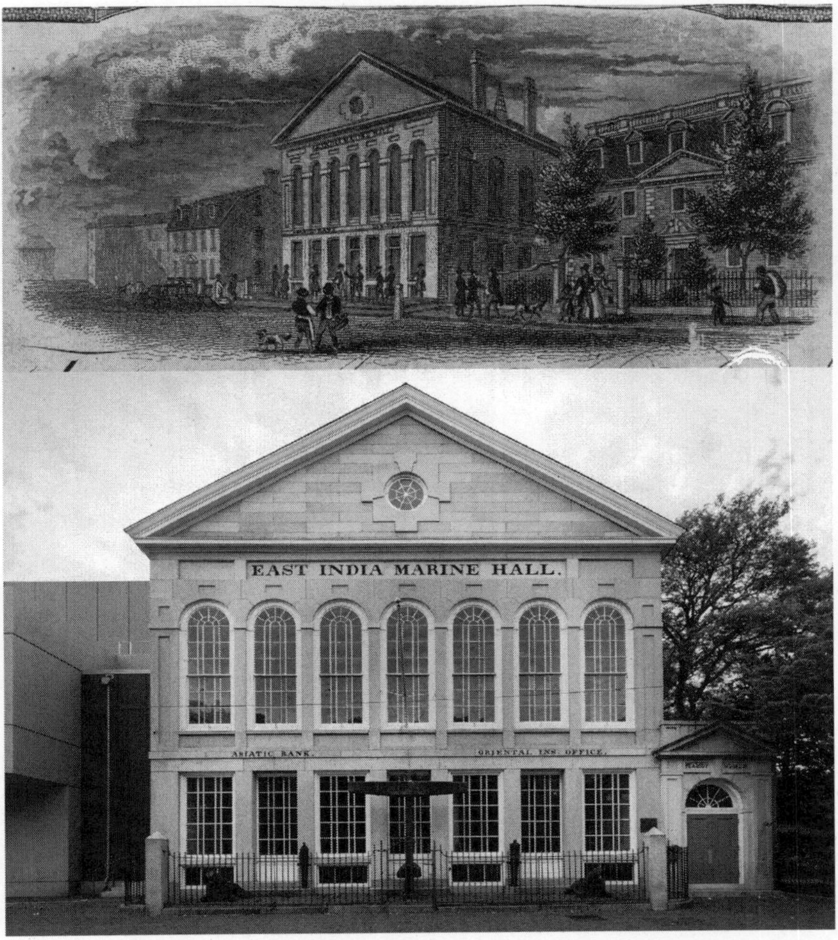

FIGURE 22. Top: Detail of East India Marine Hall, on a ten-dollar bill of the Asiatic Bank, circa 1840. Printed paper, 3 x 6¾ in. Peabody Essex Museum Collection, M20096. © 2016 Peabody Essex Museum, Salem, MA. Photography by Kathy Tarantola. This image is among the earliest known depictions of the building. Bottom: East India Marine Hall, circa 2016. © 2016 Peabody Essex Museum, Salem, MA. Photography by Allison White.

and St. Peter's streets before arriving at the new hall.[39] The *Essex Register* reported, "The occasion drew together a vast concourse of citizens as spectators, who lined the streets through which the procession moved."[40] All Society members wore tin anchor badges inscribed with "E.I.M.S." across the anchor stock and entangled with brass cord. The only physical emblems of membership the Society ever created, they were made especially for the occasion and were used in future meetings and processions. Once inside the new building, members and their guests—123 people in all—were treated to a sumptuous dinner complete with green turtle soup.[41] The *Salem Observer* glowingly recounted, "[A] splendid dinner was served up by John Remond, which for variety, elegance, and *taste*, was allowed by very competent judges, to surpass everything of the kind witnessed in this country."[42]

This banquet was recognized as an important local and national event, and accounts were circulated throughout the nation—in the *Christian Inquirer*; the *Columbian Centinel* of Athens, Georgia; the *Raleigh Register* of West Virginia; and other newspapers. The *National Intelligencer* of Washington, D.C., noted that the Hall was done in a "handsome and complimentary manner . . . the fruit of the enterprise and liberality of the Mariners of Salem, with which the Museum is stored."[43] Several news stories reprinted many of the fifty-one toasts delivered that night, "interspersed with appropriate music by the band" and mirroring those delivered during prior anniversary dinners.[44] In addition to honoring distinguished guests, past members, and Salem merchants, a number of toasts offered paeans to American patriotism.[45] One celebrated "Civil and Religious Toleration—produced and supported by commercial intercourse"; another honored "American principles—Like the Northern Lights, their radiance shoots across the political sky—Despotism beholds it trembling 'with a fearful looking for of a judgment to come.'" After the annual toast to Vasco da Gama was one to "The Merchants of the United States—May they inherit the spirit of Cosmo de Medicis [*sic*], and learning and arts bear testimony to their munificence."[46]

The day after the opening of East India Marine Hall, the *Salem Observer* published a laudatory piece on the Society, its tone resembling the praise penned by the anonymous author "X" in the *Salem Gazette* twenty years earlier. The *Observer* noted the value of belonging to the organization because of its strict nautical provisions and "the respectable standing, which it has already attained, and the advantages, which it holds out." This was contrasted with "the very general and almost indiscriminate admission of members into many of our societies for historical, literary, & philosophical purposes," which "has served to render the honor cheap and little valued; has lessened the sense of responsibility of the minds of the members to contribute to the objects of such institutions; and in the end has commonly produced a total indifference to their great purposes, and effectually defeated their usefulness." Part of the Society's national status, in the opinion of the paper, was linked to its museum, which had "already become extensive and valuable; and perhaps [is] not exceeded, we believe not equaled, by any similar establishment in the country." The paper also lauded "[t]he charitable purposes of the institution . . . to unite in the relief of those, who seem to have a peculiar claim on the proverbial generosity of their fellow sailors."[47]

Such effusions did not sit well with everyone. The *Richmond Enquirer* rebuked the Salem newspapers' coverage of the event, deriding "[t]he importance which too many of the Eastern papers attach to titles . . . 'Vitularies [*sic*] of Dignitaries of the Empire.'" The *Enquirer* found this "disgusting to every republican," an "absurd custom . . . growing upon our public Journalists," and believed this "man-worship in various modes, . . . too much the order of the day," should be diminished. Still, the *Enquirer* did not extend its criticism to the reason behind the gathering. The paper thought the Society "deserves of itself one moment's respectful notice" as "it is composed of persons who have *actually* navigated the seas beyond the Cape of Good Hope or Cape Horn."[48]

Seth Bass's tenure as superintendent of the museum ended before the opening of East India Marine Hall. In January 1825, the Reverend Elias Cornelius (1792–1832), an American missionary and a teacher of Elias Boudinot, claimed that Bass had "mutilated" one of the more than twenty minerals he had presented to the museum.[49] In addition, a member accused Bass of interfering with the election of the Society's officers at the prior annual meeting. Subsequently, a committee was appointed to look into these allegations. To further humiliate Bass, and perhaps as a sign of emasculation, they took the key to the museum away from him and placed it in the care of Abijah Northey, only permitting "an *Original* member" to posses it "until the opinion of the committee of OBS [observation] be known."[50] Bass was eventually exonerated, but the committee noted "a misapprehension of his powers" in exchanging duplicate specimens without consulting the committee "as required by the Vote of the Society." At this point Bass had tired of the "peculiarities" of the East India Marine Society and resigned his office as superintendent to become librarian of the Boston Athenaeum, a post he would hold until 1846.[51]

Bass's successor was Malthus A. Ward (1794–1863), born in Haverhill, New Hampshire, and one of the first doctors of the pioneer community of Hindostan Falls, Indiana, from 1819 to 1823. He attended the medical school at Bowdoin College in Maine, where he met Nathaniel Hawthorne. After graduating, he moved to Salem and set up his own medical practice; lectured on botany, horticulture, and chemistry; and was a founding member of the Massachusetts Horticultural Society.[52]

Ward, like Bass, adhered to a Linnaean system of classification and noted in an address to the Massachusetts Horticultural Society, "The mere Linnaean nomenclature is a gigantic effort, and itself a wonderful instrument of order and perspicuity." He also acknowledged the criticism more professional naturalists had for amateurs, "the severe sarcasms which are often, and, no doubt, in many instances, justly thrown upon 'closet naturalists' . . . the peculiar air of suspicion with which practical men and 'out-of-door students of nature,' regard all communications emanating from such a source." Ward used Linnaeus's taxonomy as a means to rebut these criticisms: "'I care not how learned my adversaries are, if they be only so from books!'" He also viewed natural history, "in its broadest acceptation," as embracing "a knowledge and description of all the objects in the material universe." This more inclusionary definition included astronomy and meteorology, subjects usual excluded from the field. Still, Ward, like Charles Willson Peale, believed that a higher power controlled the forces of nature, noting that "knowledge of the laws which regulate the phenomena of Natural History, strictly speaking . . . are employed by the great Governor of the Universe with the same determinate precision, as those which are opened to our view by the general sciences."[53]

Malthus Ward was tasked immediately with installing the Society's collection in East India Marine Hall. Following a Linnaean system for categorizing natural and artificial curiosities, Ward likely consulted books in the collection related to natural history, ethnography (such as George Anderson's), and art and antiquities.[54] He continued to update the gallery displays, incorporating new accessions that were entering the collection at a growing rate. Caroline Howard King commented in her memoirs that she and her companions were "rarely disturbed in our happy afternoons there, except by some old sea captain, who dropped in . . . to see if his last contribution from the East had been placed to advantage."[55]

Ward's displays in East India Marine Hall did not go unnoticed. The *Salem Observer* reported that the museum was "spacious and elegant; and the recent arrangement of their collections does honor to the taste and science of Dr. Ward and other gentlemen by whom it has been made."[56] Natural history specimens were integrated into the room with the rest of the collection and organized by type in their own cabinets. In 1830, an unidentified visitor was "much gratified, while on a late visit to Salem, to witness the many alterations and improvements which have been made [to the Hall] within a few years," which the person believed were extensive. The visitor also noted that "many curiosities in nature and of art, are continually increasing its well selected assortment; and they are all classified in such good taste and with so much judgment, as to produce the most happy effect." This patron declared "unfeignedly" that "*East-India Marine Hall* . . . contain[s] within its galaxy of beauties—the quintessence of all the Museum and Theatres, that adorn the cities of the U. States."[57]

The collection grew enormously during the 1820s, leading to new initiatives. On May 3, 1826, the Society insured East India Marine Hall for $5,000 and increased the insurance on "the Cabinet" to $10,000.[58] Members also voted to produce a new catalogue. Ward crafted this revised version in a style that was almost identical to the 1821 volume, beginning to number new objects at the point where Bass had left off (at 2,269). However, he did make some changes. He removed "Catalogue of Shells," "Catalogue of Ancient and Modern Coins and Medals," and "Catalogue of Paper Bills" from the revised version, reassigning the numbers in those sections as well as those used for natural history specimens that had decayed or been discarded. He inserted articles that had been added to the Society's bylaws after 1821, such as those relating to purchasing and exchanging objects and insuring the collection, and a list of new journals donated by members since the last volume had appeared.

By 1830 the collection had more than doubled, but in the fall of 1831 Ward resigned his post after being offered the chair of natural history at the University of Georgia.[59] The Society subsequently hired Dr. George Osborne (1798–1882) as the third museum superintendent, the first member to assume the position. Osborne, like his father and grandfather, who were ship captains, had gone to sea—in his case, as supercargo on two voyages to Sumatra and one to Europe. After returning home in 1826, he turned his focus to medicine and opened a practice in South Danvers (modern-day Peabody).[60]

Shortly after hiring Osborne, the East India Marine Society enacted further measures to support the superintendent's work in running the museum. Up to this point, anyone wishing to visit the museum needed to find a Society member at the Hall and obtain an admission ticket. As there were a "great and increasing number of visitors to the museum" (particularly during the summer), this method had become "exceedingly burthensome to that part of the society, whose business is in the immediate neighbourhood of the Hall."[61] To rectify the situation, the Society created a new position: assistant superintendent. This individual, ideally a member of the Society, would work during the high-traffic season (May 1 to November 1) "from 10 AM to 1 PM & from 3 to 5 PM to receive and wait on visitors, who may wish to see the museum" and aid the superintendent when requested. Member Joseph Preston (1780–1840) was elected to fill this role in 1832. Two years later, however, the position was terminated in favor of a custodian chosen by the president from the membership "to attend at the Museum such time as they may judge best . . . who shall admit visitors free of expence [*sic*] but under such regulations as the society or its officers, shall from time to time establish."[62]

Osborne stepped down as superintendent in January 1835, and the Reverend Charles Grafton Page, M.D. (1812–69), a naturalist and a founding member of the Essex County Natural History Society, replaced him at a salary of $75 per year (a reduction of $25 from Seth Bass's salary).[63] By the summer of 1837, 371 more objects had been added to the museum, and the Society voted to produce a catalogue supplement. Its new superintendent, Henry Wheatland (1812–93), who replaced Page after his short tenure in the post, crafted the *Supplement to the Catalogue of the Articles in the Museum, Journals &c. of the East India Marine Society*. Published in December 1837 and covering the years 1831–37, this short volume lists only new objects (by that time 431), new ship journals (14), and new members and officers.[64]

Wheatland, who became the Society's longest-serving superintendent (1837–48), was the foremost naturalist to hold the position. The son of a member, Richard Wheatland (1762–1800), a successful ship captain and merchant, he had graduated from Harvard University in 1832 and received his medical degree from Harvard in 1837. According to the *Salem Register*, "he did not take kindly to the College curriculum, but preferred to follow the bent of his own inclination toward science, natural history, and kindred studies."[65] Wheatland spent his entire life in Salem and was very active in the city's cultural and intellectual growth. An avid naturalist, he was a founding member of the Essex County Natural History Society. He served as secretary from 1835 until it merged with the Essex Historical Society (of which he was also a member) to form the Essex Institute in 1848. Wheatland was president of the institute from 1868 until his death and devoted much of his life to ensuring that it would become an enlightened cultural entity in the city.[66]

During Wheatland's tenure as superintendent, the museum reached its apex. In 1838, he undertook a thorough examination and modification of East India Marine Hall, creating a detailed report of the gallery's new arrangement and explaining to members that "Time, the great destroyer, had been making extensive ravages; the moth & corroding rust who, in their inventive gambols, do much serious injury to man, had been permitted to sport with boundless freedom." Thus, he wrote, "the Committee of Observation deemed it expedient that something should be done, and that quickly, to prevent further destruction. Accordingly in May I attempted to make a thorough cleansing of this Augean stable & devoted several weeks to the undertaking, aided at times by one or more assistants." Wheatland took all of the objects, both natural and artificial, out of their cases for cleaning and rearranged some displays "in order to bring together such articles as bore a resemblance to each other or were used for the same purposes in the economy of life by the different nations, such as the cooking utensils, shoes, hats, warlike instruments etc. etc."[67] Apparently, Bass, Ward, and Osborne had not fully applied Linnaeus's artificial system, and Wheatland was correcting these deficiencies as best he could.

He also reported that visitors had damaged many of the figures of Chinese and Indian merchants. As a result, he decided to encase a newly commissioned figure of a Canton merchant, recently carved by Joseph True (1785–1873), Salem's leading carver after Samuel McIntire's death. This figure displayed a full outfit—a blue silk coat heavily embroidered with flowers and many dragons, black crepe-pleated band sleeves, and brass buttons—that had been donated by China trade merchant Abiel Abbot Low (1811–93).[68] Wheatland installed this figure in a case "to prevent any injury or defacement that may arise from the exposure to the air, dust" but mostly to protect it from "excessive handling by visitors; A habit to which the Yankies [*sic*] are very much addicted and one which is said by some peculiar to this genius"[69] (see figure 4, no. 6).

The East India Marine Society followed many of Wheatland's recommendations and enacted further procedures to protect against "frequent depredations being committed by the visitors to the museum on articles." The president and the committee of observation required all visitors to leave umbrellas and canes at the museum entrance, and ten years later members voted unanimously to bar children under age fourteen from the hall unless they were accompanied by a parent or guardian "to take proper care of them." They also implemented measures to increase museum visitation. Free admission tickets signed by members were offered "to afford every practicable facility to strangers to gain access to the museum" and "to reli[e]ve the members from the tax of accompanying visitors personally to the doors of the museum and there pass them over to the doorkeeper as was required under the old regulations."[70]

Wheatland's arrangement of objects lasted for almost thirty years without considerable alteration, and many people came to Salem "for the purpose of visiting its celebrated museum, which contains a fine collection of curiosities from all parts of the world."[71] The custodian and Society members who were passing their time in the gallery worked to enhance the visitors' global voyage around East India Marine Hall. These men were usually willing to interpret objects for interested patrons and, in some cases, to offer guided tours.

One visitor, after climbing the stairs to the hall, recalled that he immediately felt the watery world before him. He was "transported in a moment to far-off tropic lands, where palms are waving in air, serpents and strange and terrible beasts lurking in jungles; or coral reefs were rising on the surface of shining seas,—for one is, in fancy, afloat on oceans of the Orient."[72] When examining the group of figures in the middle of the gallery, "so lifelike that they seem almost ready to speak to us in their unknown tongue," he engaged in conversation with the custodian, an "ancient mariner . . . first a sailor, and then a sea-captain for more than fifty years." This was member Joseph Hammond (1806–90), a fixture in the hall in the second half of the nineteenth century. At the time of his death, a local newspaper memorialized him as "one of those unique figures for which Salem has ever been famous . . . who would combine all of the interesting characteristics and be possessed of the charming gift of telling a sailor's yarn in the peculiarly talking style. . . . His audience came from every quarter of the globe and each went away with a pleasant memory of the old Salem sea captain."[73]

The visitor asked Hammond if he had been to India and if the figures on display were accurate "natural" representations. Answering in words that were "provincial and original, and not arranged according to rules of grammar or rhetoric," Hammond exclaimed, "'Natural! I guess you'd think so! . . . Bless you! I've talked with that fellow many a time,' pointing to a snake-charmer. 'And them, too, that is there in front with the beads, I've seen many a time saying their prayers; and that is one of their priests. They call him a Brahmin.'" When the visitor asked Hammond where he had ventured during his time at sea and if it was hard to now be shore-bound, he replied, "Well, I'd like to see any place I haven't been in. . . . Thirteen years ago I made a voyage to Cape Horn. We was drifted into the icebergs; nothing but ice all round us. . . . Two hundred forty-two days I wasn't heard from in Salem; and then I made up my mind, if we ever got home, I'd never set foot on ship again."[74]

Satisfied to think "that the captain had found so fit a place in which to rest, living over his former voyages," the visitor left the Hall and reflected on his unique experience in the museum: "Leaving the ancient mariner and all his treasures of foreign lands and many climes, I took my way through streets of stately and slumbrous houses, monuments of the old commercial prosperity, to where the sea itself rolls, as it rolled when these precious freights came over its waters, and was soon revelling in that 'odor of brine,' so grateful to the inlanders."[75]

Objects commonly associated with mariners such as Hammond, such as navigational instruments and ship models, were sprinkled throughout the museum to enhance the maritime flavor of the gallery.[76] Because sailor's nautical instruments were expensive items, crucial to a successful voyage, and viewed as objects of everyday knowledge, not curiosities, only those that were considered passé or experimental were donated to the museum. The Society received two Davis quadrants, or backstaffs, for the collection—one donated between 1815 and 1820, the other in 1844.[77] Invented by the English explorer John Davis (circa 1550–1605) in 1594, the Davis quadrant was used in the seventeenth and early eighteenth centuries to determine latitude at sea by measuring the sun's position in the sky relative to the horizon, with the measurer's back to the sun. This instrument was replaced by the octant, which allows a mariner to observe a celestial body and the horizon simultaneously while also facing forward, and then by the sextant, which is still used today. By the nineteenth century, the Davis quadrant was antiquated. Thus, the Society's examples were valuable historical illustrations of developments in navigational instruments and were likely admired for their craftsmanship as they were made with ebony, boxwood, and other expensive hardwoods that could withstand a marine environment.

The Society also displayed objects related to improvements in marine technology, such as a patent life preserver; a model of a machine made and used by Benjamin Carpenter on board the schooner *Benjamin* "to distil fresh water from that of the ocean"; and a model of a dredge, or pontoon, used to counter the silting of a harbor (like Salem's), made and donated by Elias Hasket Derby, Jr. The museum also displayed a novel device: a mechanical log watch designed by the English maker William Lovelace, the first navigational instrument donated to the museum.[78] This device would have been used along with a patent log like Gould's and was devised to replace the half-minute glass sand timer by measuring fourteen- and twenty-eight-second increments. Unlike most watches of the time, this log watch was square and its glass sides exposed its inner clocklike workings. It was never widely used, but on display at the East India Marine Society Museum, its unusual construction probably attracted speculation from both sailors and landlubbers.

Another unusual object in the gallery was created to exhibit mariners' resourceful thinking when encountering extreme circumstances at sea. In 1805, William Mugford donated a model of the ship *Ulysses,* which he had commanded on a voyage in 1804. The model depicts the ship without sails or masts in order to direct a viewer's eye to an unusual feature: heavy rope hanging off the sides of the model supports a cannon below a makeshift rudder. Mugford devised this after a severe gale destroyed the original rudder on the voyage, and the modification allowed him to safely bring the ship into port at Marseille, France. For his invention he received the Magellanic Premium from the American Philosophical Society, the oldest American prize awarded for scientific achievement, and an article titled "Mugford's Temporary Rudder" was published in *Archives of Useful Knowledge* in 1812.[79] Together with the Society's printed collection, this object and others helped exemplify the cutting-edge nature of the institution.

The museum displayed a small collection of ship models. Some had been acquired in overseas ports, such as models of Malay ships (see figure 4, nos. 1 and 2), while others invoked American patriotism and heroism. In addition to the model of the *Friendship*, a physical symbol of Salem's commerce, the museum contained a six-foot-long model of the U.S.S. *Constitution* made by the ship's crew around the time of its famed victory over the H.M.S. *Guerriere* during the War of 1812. The crew had presented the model to the *Constitution*'s commander, Isaac Hull (1773–1843), and he quickly donated it to the Society in 1813. Members often used the *Constitution* model in their parades and at other events. Oral accounts note that in the fall of 1813 it was brought to Hamilton Hall on Chestnut Street for a banquet in honor of the original's then-commander Commodore William Bainbridge (1774–1833).[80] A salute in Bainbridge's honor was fired from miniature guns (likely the working cannon taken from the model of the *Friendship*) and damaged the tiny replica. Without a model maker close at hand to repair it, the Society turned to British prisoners of war who were being held in a prison ship in Salem. They repaired the *Constitution*, and then presented the Society with a bill for their services![81] Years later, the *Boston Daily Globe* remarked, "[T]he British prisoners . . . got a little pocket money while forcibly reminded of the very cause of their imprisonment."[82]

By 1846, however, conditions in the museum were beginning to change. Wheatland was disgruntled by the state of the collections and frustrated by a perceived lack of support from Society members. He felt "almost ashamed to be considered the superintendent," given the museum's present condition, and threatened to resign "unless some effort is made to better its condition." In response, Society president Charles Moses Endicott, on behalf of the other members, informed Wheatland that they appreciated his "motives . . . to do something to infuse new life & interest into the Members of the Society" but took offense at "the manner" in which he proposed and dictated improvements. While they understood that his "zeal for science" had led him "a step in advance" of the members, they took umbrage at his use of language that was "anything but gratifying to the pride & feelings of the Society."[83]

Endicott alluded to the museum's finances as one reason for the Society's lack of support for Wheatland's progressive work with the collections: "The Museum has probably far outstripped the most sanguine expectations of its founders," and the expense of maintaining it had become a burden. He informed Wheatland that the museum needed to be run by "the strictest principles of economy," with "due regard being always had to the needful preservation & increase of its curiosities, so far forward as the condition of its funds will justify." If that meant putting finances above retaining Wheatland's "valuable services," they would choose the former, no matter how unwilling they might be to lose him. He emphasized this point by informing Wheatland that "the officers not possessing the enviable faculty of 'making bricks without straw,' cannot flatter themselves that by any 'efforts' in *their* power, a better state of things than now exists can be brought about by them."[84] Wheatland's frustrations were emblematic of a change in Salem's natural history landscape, and Endicott's statements reveal that the Society's role in this field was declining. Members were unable and unwilling to promote the new, more professional brand of natural history that Wheatland advocated. While finances played a part in the Society's decision to maintain the status quo, Endicott's words also characterized the Society's lack of interest in backing the very causes that had once been its mainstay.

The objects on display mirrored this change in attitude. While the installations constructed by Bass and Ward had attracted the attention of well-known naturalists of the day, such as the renowned American botanist Asa Gray (1810–88), they had also revealed the superintendents' inexperience in the field.[85] When George Hodges donated a penguin from the Falkland Islands in 1820, the earliest to be displayed in a North American museum, the taxidermist (who had obviously had never seen a penguin) stretched its neck like a giraffe's (see figure 23).[86] Not all of the donated animals were handled so inexpertly. The experienced taxidermist Jacques Kets (1785–1865), a Flemish naturalist and the first director of the Royal Zoological Society of Antwerp, donated a pair of well-mounted crested Java fowls in 1826. But the variations in quality among the specimens are emblematic of the amateur level of natural history practiced in many antebellum American institutions—a notable contrast to European ones, which had trained and educated specialists.

In 1840, the American conchologist and malacologist Augustus Gould (1805–66) praised "the collection in the Museum of the 'East India Marine Society,' at Salem," which is "of considerable extent and much notoriety," but believed "it was made as a matter of curiosity, rather than for scientific purposes."[87] His comments reveal a growing professionalism in the

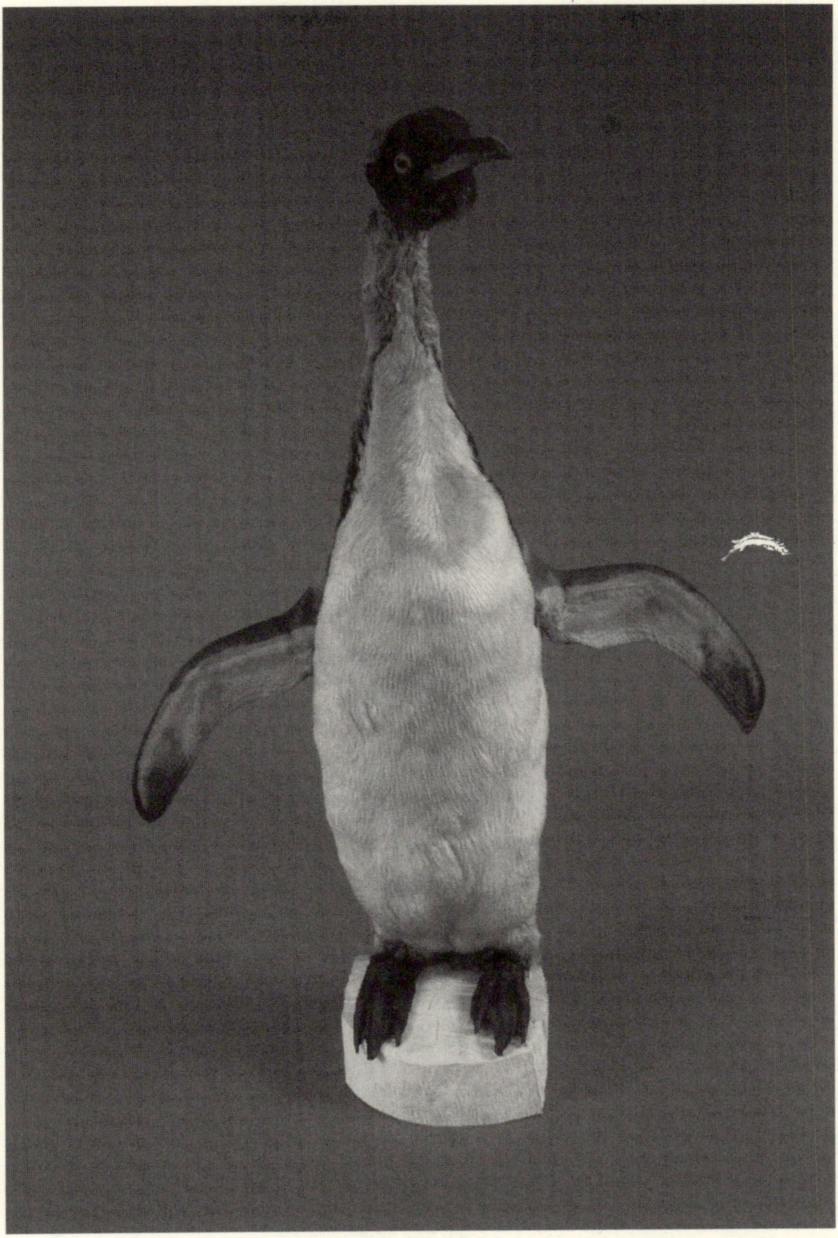

FIGURE 23. King penguin (*Aptenodytes patagonicus*) from the Falkland Islands, circa 1820. 32 x 20 x 7 in. Peabody Essex Museum Collection, EIMS1219.1. © Peabody Essex Museum, Salem, MA.

landscape of American science, a shift that occurred during Bass's and Ward's tenures as superintendent. There was now, as Gould made clear, a new type of discerning American scientist. In addition, his comments point to the museum's waning role as Salem's premier institution for conducting scientific research.

Charles Lyell echoed Gould's sentiments. When he visited the museum in 1845, he was pleased to have the opportunity to study "specimens of natural history, too large to be conveniently accommodated in any private house," such as "the great jaw-bones and teeth of the Squalus serridens, from the South Seas." Yet while he considered the museum's collection to be "really curious and valuable," he was unimpressed by the scientific classification displays at both the Society's museum and the Essex County Natural History Society, which he also visited: "In both collections there are a variety of objects which may appear, on a hasty view, to form a heterogeneous and unmeaning jumble."[88]

The East India Marine Society's waning interest in current trends in natural history was not the only factor leading to Wheatland's departure. Endicott informed the superintendent that the Society planned to relieve him of his duties at their November 1, 1848 meeting, explaining that members and officers had concluded that it would be best for the museum to have a leader "who has no divided interest by which his time or attention will in any way be abstructed [*sic*] or alienated from the Society." Specifically, he pointed out that Wheatland had not submitted a report of additions to the museum during the past year and accused him of not attending any meetings. Basing their actions on Wheatland's performance as well as on members' grumblings, the officers of the Society had decided, going forward, "to choose no one for Superintendent who holds any office under the American Academy of Arts & Sciences."[89]

Wheatland would not allow the Society officers to fire him and immediately resigned his post. He reminded Endicott that, when he took the job in 1837, he had made it very clear that his "affections were absorbed in the success of the Essex County Natural History Society." He also blamed the Society for a lack of support in recent years, noting that "not a single officer has been into the Hall to advise me in any manner whatever & even the members themselves have appeared to take very little if any interest." Wheatland could not maintain a positive attitude about the museum "when such apparent indifference is manifested by those who are its natural guardians & ought to be its well wishers." In reality, however, he was covering up for the conflict of interest that had developed between his roles at the East India Marine Society Museum and the Essex County Natural History Society.[90]

Despite his growing discord with the East India Marine Society, Wheatland had done his part to take care of the museum displays. In one of his final reports he noted that he had overhauled the wet preparations and replenished the alcohol in specimen bottles, which were then "cemented over [the bottle mouths] & painted so that they will need very little if any attention for several years."[91] He warned the Society that other portions of the collection "will by another season require considerable time & labor to be spent in the rearrangement of." His successor was his friend George Dean Phippen (1815–95), also the first librarian of the Essex Institute.[92] Wheatland likely trained Phippen in the proper methods of preserving natural specimens, and he remained in this position until 1855.[93]

When Phippen left, the Society decided to terminate the post of superintendent, given the state of its funds. Two years later, however, member Thomas Saul (1787–1875) assumed the duties of superintendent. Saul was a quintessential old salt, surly in his demeanor but endearing to visitors.[94] He had a great affinity for the museum and, when he retired from the sea, spent a considerable amount of time there. According to a period account, he was "rather short in stature, wore a stiff black satin neck stock with a 'dickey' that projected nearly up to the middle of his cheeks, . . . last year's stove pipe hat, winter and summer, and a black frock coat."[95] His conservative appearance was countered by a distinguishing feature: his forbidding countenance. According to one visitor, "if the very heavens fell, I do not think that such an unlooked for occurrence would have disturbed the rigidity of that countenance, which looked as though it would consign all evil doers to suffer the torments of the damned." Caroline Howard King remembered Saul as a "gruff and surly old janitor," but as he had a high esteem for her father, he was good to her. King noted that every time she visited the museum, he "went through his never-failing ceremony of presenting me with a slip of sandal wood cut from a huge log that stood near the door, or a sweet-smelling Tonguing Bean."[96]

Saul's work as superintendent was unpaid, a reflection of his love for the museum and his devotion to the Society's benevolent aspirations. At their November 1865 meeting, however, members unanimously voted to offer him a gratuity of $100 "in consideration of [his] faithful services" at a time when the Society had very little money.[97] Although Saul was not a trained doctor or caretaker, he did his best to maintain the collection and displays during the final years of the Society's stewardship of the museum. In his first superintendent report in 1857, he noted, "[D]uring the Spring & Summer the Articles in the Cabinet, has been carefully examined, and all those, especially of a perishable nature, has been properly attended to,—there is however some of the Cases, that requires some further attention—but those, being articles *not* liable to inquiry [injury], may be attended to at some future period. The large number of visitors during the last summer months, prevented me in part from accomplishing *all* I should wish and intended to do." He annually examined and attended to objects "of a perishable nature" and would add alcohol and other chemicals to jarred specimens that "by constant evaporation is subject to decay." He also reorganized some displays. In November 1860, he reported that he had "made some different arrangements in the Cabinet during the past year, by presenting them in more conspicous [*sic*] places. . . . The Articles of the Cabinet is now in quite good preservation, and with care will continue so."[98]

Regardless of its condition in the 1860s, the museum continued to be a preeminent Salem attraction. An individual named "L.P.H" told the *Sailors' Magazine & Seamen's Friend* in 1866 that "the Museum is a substantial granite building, very well adapted to the purpose for which it was intended, as a depository of rare curiosities, mainly from the East Indies, about six thousand of which it now contains, very conveniently arranged for exhibition." L.P.H. spent an hour at the museum "very pleasantly" and pointed to "the kind attentions of Captain Paul [*sic*] . . . connected with the institution more than forty year," whom the visitor would "long remember." L.P.H. advised those who go to Salem "not to fail to visit this interesting and instructive collection."[99] These words were not hollow. From 1799 to 1867, people came in droves to visit the East India Marine Society Museum.

Chapter Five

VISITOR EXPERIENCES

> The Salem Museum . . . has long been a subject of wonder and pride to our citizens.
>
> —"The Salem Museum," *Essex Register,* October 9, 1826

Visitors entering East India Marine Hall were asked to sign the museum's guestbook before beginning their journey around the gallery. These books contain the names and residences of more than 75,000 people who came to the museum between 1827 and 1867.[1] During this span, approximately two-thirds of the years that the museum existed under the Society's ownership, roughly 1,900 visitors came annually, with the highest number coming in the 1830s and 1840s.[2]

Careful reading of these guestbooks opens a previously unknown world. The logs list prominent figures in American history, such as Oliver Wendell Holmes, Sr. (1809–94), Clara Barton (1821–1912), Daniel Webster (1782–1852), and Horace Greeley (1811–1872).[3] The author Harriet Beecher Stowe (1811–96) toured the hall, as did the Salem-born writer and clergyman Samuel Johnson (1822–82), who "found his way to the old East Indian Museum, which the sea-captains had filled with curiosities from Calcutta or Bombay,—such wonders to a boy's eye."[4] American painters such as Asher B. Durand (1796–1886), Rubens Peale (1784–1865), and his brother Rembrandt Peale passed though the museum, as did the sculptors John Frazee (1790–1852) and Horatio Greenough (1805–52) and the jeweler Charles Lewis Tiffany (1812–1902).[5]

Most of America's states and territories are represented in the guestbooks. Trade routes, via sea and over land, brought businessmen from across the country into Salem and New England. Many people from New Orleans, Charleston, and other distant communities visited the museum with family members who still lived in Salem. The guestbooks list the names of American and foreign diplomats and travelers from across the globe. Lady Jane Franklin (1791–1875), the second wife of the explorer John Franklin (1786–1847), who commanded the ill-fated British naval expedition searching for a northwest passage through the Arctic (1845–1847), came to the museum with her daughter during a trip to the United States. She wrote in her journal that Salem "seems to be chiefly visited for its E. Ind[a] Museum."[6] Within these volumes are a litany of names unfamiliar to most people, such as the Indian author Joguth Chunder Gangooly. These, along with signatures written in Chinese, Greek, Arabic, and other languages, speak to the global character of the museum.

The guestbooks record events in the Society's history that had national significance. In late June 1833, during a trip to New England, President Andrew Jackson and Vice-President Martin Van Buren (1782–1862) visited the museum, and both men signed the guestbook. Jackson's presence in Salem did not sit well with many residents, particularly those from Whig-leaning families. Caroline Howard King, then eleven years old, recalled, "My friend Lucy [Saltonstall] and I, instructed by our fathers, were Whigs to the backbone," and the thought of "this dreadful President" being allowed "to admire our wonderful carving of Heaven and Hell . . . [and] perhaps shudder at our terrible Laocoon" was unbearable. She felt that her "beloved Museum would be desecrated by his presence and hoped that the group of stately orientals opposite the door, would rise up in a body and forbid his entrance."[7]

A day or so after the president's visit, the girls went to the museum. When they "went to inscribe our valuable autographs in the visitor's book, an often repeated ceremony," they were disgusted "to see scrawled across the page in large straggling characters the hated name of Andrew Jackson and beneath it Martin Van Buren." The next afternoon, the two girls returned to the museum. When Captain Saul "was conveniently absorbed in his newspaper," they cut out "the offensive signatures . . . stole home like two guilty little conspirators, half gleeful and half frightened, burned the cut out names, and for years kept our own counsel."[8]

When word of the girls' political prank leaked in the fall of 1834, it caused a great stir in Salem and beyond. A partisan war of words began in national newspapers. The *Alexandria Gazette* called it a "Petty Malignity," and the *Commercial Advertiser* of New York threatened on September 3 that if the East India Marine Society did not publicly denounce the act, their members' names were to be published in "glaring capitals, and they were to be hissed and booed at in the streets."[9] That same day, at the Society's bimonthly meeting, William Story asked his fellow members to consider disavowing "all knowledge of the individual who erased the name of Andrew Jackson from the album of this Society" and to use "all the means in our power to ascertain the person, or persons, who committed such a dishonourable act against this society."[10]

The East India Marine Society stayed true to its 1802 bylaw forbidding partisan politics in its quarters. Members did not rise to the bait of the *Advertiser* and failed to pass the resolution.[11] The *Salem Gazette* backed the Society's stance. In the reporter's view these "gross, wanton, . . . unprovoked insults" were "more than common human patience can be expected to endure": "There is not a more respectable, liberal, enlightened body of men in New England, than those connected with that society."[12] To immortalize the incident, the Society wrote next to the gaping hole in the guestbook that it had "once contained the signature of Gen. Andrew Jackson" and had been "mutilated by some unknown person."

Like King, some of the people who visited East India Marine Hall wrote personal reminiscences, newspaper articles, or works of fiction pertaining to the museum. These accounts, many of which have long been forgotten, provide a window into the minds of these early museumgoers and illustrate that all segments of antebellum life—from the slave trader Isaac Franklin (1789–1846) of New Orleans to the abolitionist Rush R. Sloane (1828–1908) of Ohio—visited the museum.[13] In today's museums, staff analyze such visitor feedback when designing and assessing exhibitions and programs. For the historian, nineteenth-century patron accounts are enormously valuable ways to balance a museum's internal mission with public perception. In the Society's case, the reflections of visitors from the United States and across the globe clearly show that the museum was not simply a Salem institution but was woven into the fabric of American life.

Sometimes Society members mediated visitors' experiences at the museum, but patrons were also able to walk around East India Marine Hall on their own. A copy of the museum catalogue, crafted to impart information through the Society's lens, was always available for consultation.

Like Society members, many visitors gave their experiences at the museum an Orientalist slant. Several accounts are tinged with Anglo-Eurocentric views of certain global cultures; for instance, a number present Pacific Islands cultures as savage or barbaric. Very few visitors had knowledge of the multiple meanings imbued within certain objects, nor were they conscious of the symbolism these objects reflected. Still, this object-based epistemology gave patrons a more in-depth look at the world and at America's place in it. Visitors entered the Hall with preconceived notions of other cultures based on published travel narratives and print images; but when confronted with material evidence, some changed their opinions. Like their modern-day counterparts, many nineteenth-century museum visitors also focused on objects with which they had a personal connection or affinity.

In *Sketches of History, Life and Manners, in the United States* (1826), Anne Royall (1769–1854), among the first American female journalists, wrote one of the earliest depictions of the museum in its new home in East India Marine Hall.[14] She told her readers about the maritime origins of Salem's wealth and noted, "You find few gentlemen in Salem, who have not visited almost every part of the world, and who do not possess more general knowledge than those of any other town in the Union."[15] She then listed the founding principles of the Society, likely extracted from the museum catalogue, and proclaimed, "The collection is one of the richest in the United States . . . worth all the cabinets and museums put together in the United States . . . that I have seen."[16]

Royall presented an overview of the collection—"67 Journals . . . of voyages"; artificial curiosities "primarily from . . . Islanders of the Indian Ocean and the southern seas"; and natural curiosities "scientifically arranged . . . an intellectual feast to the naturalist"—before launching into those objects that caught her fancy. She was attracted to both common and unusual objects in the museum, denoting her eclectic tastes and the effect of a display that was organized according to a rudimentary ethnological and scientific classification system. Royall listed more than thirty objects in succession—"a candle made of the tallow of the tallow-tree of Japan. . . . An instrument to find the two chief corrections of a lunar observation, . . . branches of cocoa and cinnamon trees, . . . busts of Cicero and Shakespeare . . ."—and then commented that "a repetition of any one specimen in the museum is useless, the whole is equally interesting, particularly portraits of the principal Chinese merchants, and the most beautiful variety of coral and pearl."[17]

Royall saw one object above all that was worth describing in detail: the carved terminal rosary bead depicting the "day of judgment, and hell and purgatory," which also appears in most extant visitor accounts. She called it "the greatest curiosity. . . . A most extraordinary piece of ingenuity": "The figures are complete, and so small that you have to look through a magnifying glass to see them; and there appears, in every face, a most surprising degree of expression."[18] The museum's smallest object and the artistic talent of a master carver captivated Royall more than any other object from a distant land on display.

Not all visitors appreciated the encyclopedic arrangement of East India Marine Hall. The Boston-born writer Caroline Howard Gilman (1794–1888), who visited in 1832, thought the arrangement detracted from her interests. Gilman penned several popular works and in 1832 became the editor of the juvenile weekly newspaper, *Rosebud* (later renamed *Southern Rose*).[19] In her volume *The Poetry of Travelling in the United States*, she wrote that "Salem is justly proud of her Museum, and its peculiar value has arisen from the marine taste of the people . . . a race of men notorious for their warm hearts and open hands."[20] Gilman saw the museum as the benefactor of sailors' "generosity," which "is very perceptible in the elegant contributions . . . lavished on this pet of the community." In her view, "the scientific eye ranges with delight over such vast collections," yet she, a non-scientist, felt "a weariness of head and feet in the well-filled galleries." For her, "[o]ne bird flying in solitary freedom over the green trees, . . . one painting hanging without competitors, where I can take in the whole expression, one relic of antiquity bringing up the strong associations of the past, give me more delight than the most crowded halls."[21] Gilman's tastes aligned more with twenty-first-century museum installations than those of her own time.

In general, visitors greatly admired the East India Marine Society Museum. International visitors were particularly enthusiastic. After a visit in 1826, the Italian traveler Giacomo Constantino Beltrami (1779–1855), who claimed to have found the source of the Mississippi River, expressed his admiration in Latin verse:

> Siste Viator! Siste, mirare! Est Orbis in Urbe,
> Et praebet pulchrum cunctata miranda Salem.

Obstupui, hie Superum, hinc hominum prodigia vidi,
Pontus, Magna Parens, Ignis et Ipse favent.
Oh America! Oh, felix tellus, populusque beatus!
Quam nobis tollunt dant tibi fata vicem.

Stand still, Traveler! Stand still, to look! There is a World in the City,
And beautiful Salem offers all wondrous things [joined together].
I was astounded: here I saw prodigies of the Gods, from here [prodigies] of men,
The Sea, [our] Great Parent, and Fire itself are well disposed!
Oh America! Oh, happy land, and blessed people!
What the fates have taken away from us they give to you in turn.[22]

The *Essex Register*, which printed Beltrami's untranslated poem "from a manuscript placed in our hands by the author," viewed his words as proof of the museum's international standing, "superior to any European collection with a like design." His poetic "stamp"—"the testimony of a distinguished scientific traveler . . . who had seen and studied the most celebrated collections in other countries"—proved that Salem and its museum could claim to be, "without question, the first in the world."[23]

On October 1, 1827, Basil Hall (1788–1844), a British naval officer from Scotland and a fellow of the Royal Society, visited the East India Marine Society Museum and later recalled with nostalgia its maritime flavor: "As my eye fell on numberless carefully cherished objects, which I had often seen in familiar use on the other side of the globe, my imagination revelled far and wide into regions I may never live to see again!"[24] For Hall, a stroll around the museum was a link to wistful memories of his seafaring past.

In the 1830s, the English social theorist Harriet Martineau (1802–76) wrote about Salem and the East India Marine Society Museum in the second volume of her book, *Society in America.* She praised the city's ascendancy to the world stage as a global port with international connections and trading routes.[25] A Salem mariner, she wrote, would head to "some semi-barbarous place, where he procures some odd kind of cargo, which he exchanges with advantage for another, somewhere else . . . bringing home a freight of the highest value." In her view, the museum was a reflection of the city's economic life: "the commerce of Salem . . . may be seen in the famous Salem Museum."[26]

Writing of the strict nautical requirement for membership in the Society, Martineau called it "a very harmless kind of monopoly . . . an unalterable condition of the honour of being a member." That restriction, she noted, was not extended to the public: "Everybody is freely admitted to visit the institution; and any one may contribute, either curiosities or the means of procuring them." Martineau believed that the Society's collecting interests, more than the "handsome hall" built "for the reception of their curiosities," created an atmosphere in which it became "discreditable to return from a long voyage without some novel contribution to the Museum."[27]

Martineau was drawn to many objects in the Hall, particularly "some Oriental curiosities, which might never otherwise have blessed my sight." A group of "wonderful figures, made of an unknown mixed metal, dug up in Java, being caricatures of the old Dutch soldiers sent to guard the first colonies" also stood out. She remarked that a "reasonably grave person might stand laughing before these for half a day" and said that she had previously had no idea "there had been so much humour in the Java people." For Martineau, these eastern depictions of Europeans were more intriguing than any other object of an "Oriental" character.[28]

The British traveler James Boardman (1801–55) visited the museum at about the same time as Martineau, and his *America, and the Americans* (1833) recounts that trip as well as those he took to several other museums around the United States. He wrote of visiting "the principal Museum of New York" (Scudder's American Museum), which "is private property; but open to the public by payment at the doors," as well as Peale's museum and the Museum of Natural History in Philadelphia.[29] When he arrived in Salem, he noted the port's decline, thanks to "the successful rivalry of New York, and the other great commercial marts of America."[30] According to Boardman, Salem had thus lost "much of its mercantile importance; and, after having numbered its sixty ships, which almost annually sailed round the Cape of Good Hope, or Cape Horn, it now only reckons a tenth part of that number." Still, the city "has an air of neatness, and contains a handsome square, and many good buildings, but its chief attraction is its Museum, which had recently been arranged in a capacious hall, erected expressly for its reception." Like other visitors, he linked "[t]his extensive depository of the wonders of nature and art" to maritime trade and admired Salem mariners' ability to create "a valuable Museum" through donors who "are neither professed naturalists, artists, antiquarians, or lettered 'travelling fellows,' but plain nautical 'business men.'"[31] This characteristic, according to Boardman, was a uniquely American quality.

In East India Marine Hall, Boardman viewed the many objects from the East Indies and the Pacific. Unlike other visitors, however, he focused primarily on the Society's collections from the ancient world, which allowed patrons to travel to "the classic shores of the 'blue Mediterranean,' those inexhaustible mines of ancient art," and to "pore over the half-obliterated hieroglyphic, study the bold features of the Caesars in the corroded medal, or dwell upon the sublime contortions of the Laocoon."[32] Boardman noticed an object "[a]mong the heterogeneous trifles which chance has thrown in the way of the contributors," one that most visitors might have passed by: "a note in the hand-writing of the immortal Byron . . . which was written during the bard's residence in Genoa . . . addressed to a friend."[33] For this visitor, the contents of the letter were not nearly as important as its material connection to Lord Byron (1788–1824): "Every relic of the lamented author of 'Childe Harold,' even the most trifling, is so precious, that we could not peruse this half-angry, half-humorous, and hastily-scribbled note, without painful emotions, accompanied by regret at his untimely, although glorious end."[34]

James Silk Buckingham (1786–1855), a British journalist who published several narratives of his travels around the world, also highlighted the global nature of the East India Marine Society Museum. Like Edward Peron Hingston, Buckingham, who visited the United States in the 1830s, felt that most American museums were "almost always the property of some private individual, who gets together a mass of everything that is likely to be thought curious—good, bad, and indifferent—the worthless generally prevailing over the valuable. The collections are then huddled together, without order or arrangement . . . and there is generally a noisy band of musicians, and a juggler . . . to attract visitors . . . and mere amusement, and that of the lightest and most uninstructive kind, is the only object sought in visiting them."[35] He did not lump the Society's museum into this characterization of American institutions. Rather, he believed that, along with Nathan Dunn's Chinese Museum in Philadelphia, it could "furnish abundant information and amusement to visitors of all classes, from the venerable navigator and hydrographer to the holiday pupil, as there is as much to entertain as to inform."[36]

In the narrative of his travels, Buckingham wrote that he "made several visits to the Museum and was, on each occasion, abundantly gratified."[37] Like other visitors, he provided an overview of the museum installations, but he also commented on the positive attributes of Malthus Ward's (and his successors') organization of the hall: "The articles are well arranged, and kept in excellent order, and there is never so great a crowd of visitors as to prevent the careful and uninterrupted examination of any article at leisure." He noted a "singular mixture and variety of curiosities in the Salem Museum . . . and not a tithe of even the singular things are here mentioned." Moreover, physically the hall, with its "large size, and numerous and spacious windows" made "an imposing appearance."[38]

Buckingham provided a lengthy list of objects on display: "War-clubs, sceptres, battle-axes, paddles, spears . . . from almost all the tribes of the Pacific and Indian oceans, in every conceivable variety" and a "Helmet, coat of armour, sabre, and cannon-ball from the plain of Waterloo, with the skulls and bones of some of the warriors." He noted a "Box made from the keel of the ship Endeavour, in which Captain Cook circumnavigated the globe; and a part of the rock on which he was killed at Owhyhee" and "The Chinese Art of curing diseases . . . by a Chinese author, with a Latin translation by a Jesuit priest." Many of his descriptions of these objects appear to been have extracted directly from the museum's catalogue, but when writing about the carved rosary bead, he carefully detailed its features, describing it as "undoubtedly one of the most curious specimens of skill and patience united, that I have ever seen."[39]

Other Europeans mentioned visiting the museum during their time in the America. Adolphe Fourier de Bacourt (1801–65), the French ambassador to the United States in 1840–42, visited Salem in September 1840.[40] He had "a very gloomy view of American society and manners" and found "the men vulgar, the women grotesque, and American society ridiculous."[41] He did not extend this opinion to the East India Marine Society Museum, however. While staying in Boston, where he believed they "hate the French," De Bacourt went up to Salem, "a pretty little seaport town." He visited the "maritime museum . . . founded forty years ago by a club whose members must prove that they have doubled Cape Horn and the Cape of Good Hope," and who are "bound to bring some object of antiquity on their return from every voyage, and deposit it in the museum, which has been filled in this way."[42]

Dr. Francis Pulszky (1815–97), a Hungarian archaeologist and curator, came to the United States in the retinue of Lajos Kossuth (1802–94), the regent-president of the kingdom of Hungary during the revolution of 1848–49.[43] The *Salem Register* of May 10, 1852, described this group's visit to Lynn, Salem, and Boston and noted, "Count Pulzsky [*sic*] and several of the strangers were conducted to the East India Museum, which they examined with great interest."[44] In 1853, Pulszky and his wife Theresa wrote in their published account of their travels that the Society's museum showed "how the New England spirit of gathering information pervades every class."[45]

People of varying religious faiths visited the Society's museum, and some reflected on their experiences through scripture and verse.[46] Rolfe Ricker, in an essay on his travels for the *Juvenile Reformer, and Sabbath School Instructor*, saw the museum as on par with the Bible itself. He believed, "No one, whatever may be his taste or pursuit, can enter the magnificent hall in which it is arranged, without experiencing the highest pleasure, and deriving an amount of instruction which he could gain otherwise only by years of travel and toil." In Ricker's view, "No where can Christians go, except to the Bible, to get richer and more useful instruction."[47]

Ricker, like many other museum patrons, gave his readers an overview of the collection. He divided the pieces by field of interest, noting, for the natural historian, "There is hardly one of the natural sciences which is not here illustrated"; for the antiquarian, "statues, busts and pictures for the Artist, old coins, remains of unknown animals, pillars, urns, sculptures, the wrecks of former ages"; and for the curious, "figures as large as life from heathen lands, in their real costume and about their usual employments, specimens of their manufactures, instruments of war, of agriculture and of art; the idols which they worship and models of their pagodas and temples." He saw "a thousand other wonders, all opening to the moralist and the Christian, an exhaustless field for contemplation." Still, he suggested that visitors "must bring the Bible here, just as they would take a candle with them into a dark room, or they will lose one half the beauties of the objects which they see." Overall, Ricker believed that the museum "is full of instruction" and if any of his "young readers ever go to Salem," they could "spend a summer there quite profitably."[48]

While many accounts give the impression that Salem was an enlightened city, it, like the rest of antebellum America, was entangled with the "peculiar institution" of slavery. Salem is often seen as a center of the New

England abolition movement, but it had had a complex association with African Americans since its founding in 1626. In the early years of the republic, a large percentage of the town's free black population had settled in a few sections of the town—for instance, the Salem end of the turnpike to Boston (an area known as "Roast Meat Hill") and "Knocker's Hole" (home to about a hundred huts, near the wharves and named after the noise of shipbuilding).[49]

Salem's black inhabitants had to deal with daily restrictions, including areas of the city where they could not walk and sections of church where they could not sit.[50] In 1835, as public schools became available in the city, Salem's young African Americans were forced by local ordinance to attend segregated institutions. The impetus came from 175 Salem residents who had signed a petition asking that black children not be allowed into the local public schools, and the resulting decision ignited a decade-long fight to reintegrate the schools.[51] Through the hard work of an outraged black community—supported by the city's mayor, Stephen Clarendon Phillips (1801–57), a noted abolitionist, as well as John Remond—race distinction in Salem public schools was terminated in the 1840s.[52]

The East India Marine Society played its part in this division between abolition and segregation, adding to the complexities within the Society, its mission, and its collection. In 1827, John Brown Russwarm (1799–1851), an editor of *Freedom's Journal*, one of the first African American newspapers in the United States, chronicled his experiences at the museum in a letter published in the paper.[53] He praised the Society's collection, "the richest in the country," and declared, "There are but few museums equally valuable."[54] However, "I can say but very little concerning it, owing to the shortness of my visit, which had to be regulated by the time which the gentleman who had charge of the Museum had to spare; for you are to be informed, that it was an act of great condescension in allowing us persons of colour to peep at it, as no money is ever taken as the price of admission."[55] Six years later, Society member Joseph Ropes (1771–1850) put forth a resolution at the September meeting "[t]hat people of Colour shall be excluded from visiting the Museum of this Society, during the usual hours of admission, excepting as attendants on visitors," which passed at the next bimonthly meeting by a vote of twenty to seven.[56] While the names of the members who voted for and against the measure is unknown, it was not repealed until just after the end of the Civil War, on May 3, 1865.[57]

Until 1850 most Salem residents had no knowledge of the East India Marine Society's decision to bar people of color from the museum. In that year, however, the *Salem Register* ran a column written by "a very respectable source" wishing to counter a published statement in a previous edition that the Society's museum was "a Museum free to all."[58] The writer reported, "It may not be generally known that tickets of admission to the Museum are not granted to *colored persons.* It is a fact which I have learned from officers of the society, that one of their rules prohibits the admission of colored persons, except upon terms requiring on their part a sacrifice of self-respect. Foreigners, paupers, convicts, if white, can obtain tickets, while our native citizens, however respectable, if colored, are denied admittance." Still, the author noted, "The city of Salem is distinguished, above all others in the United States, for the equality of rights and privileges enjoyed by all classes of her citizens, without regard to color or condition. . . . No invidious distinction is here permitted in the public schools. Our churches have no 'negro pews.' Public opinion countenances no proscription in the Lyceum or the concert room." Yet there is an air of revisionism in these claims. Though the city had integrated many of its public institutions by this time, the author was ignoring Salem's prior segregated history. In conclusion, the author argued that the East India Marine Society, "a Charitable Institution, founded and maintained by men renowned for their generosity and honorable deeds—the Navigators and Merchant Sailors of Salem," should not be a refuge for a "senseless remnant of the injustice of past times." The editor of the *Salem Register* believed that this report would surprise the majority of its readers "as much as it did ourselves" and hoped that this public declaration, "when brought to the notice of a Society so liberally disposed as this is, will be promptly expunged, and the admission of colored, as of white, persons, be safely entrusted to the discretion of the members." While the editor shrugged off the Society's decision to bar people of color from entering the museum as "a relic of ancient prejudices, established many years ago," the article demonstrated that racial prejudice was alive throughout the country.[59]

This issue of race represents another duality inherent in the Society. While "people of color" were not allowed into East India Marine Hall between 1833 and 1865, the museum's guestbooks included the names of Native Americans such as Maungwudaus; Indians such as Rustomjee Hirjeebhoy Wadia of Bombay (1837–71), who visited in 1860; and others who were not barred entrance because of their race.[60] Unlike other contemporary institutions (for instance, Peale's museum, which displayed images of other cultures beneath portraits of white Americans), the East India Marine Society exhibited portraits of Nusserwanjee Wadia and Eshing alongside white maritime heroes such as Cook and displayed busts of American political and military heroes next to religious sculptures from the East Indies.

Nonetheless, several Society members revealed their acceptance of the cultural and racial stereotypes that infiltrated antebellum American society. Some of the toasts given during their annual dinners denote these racial attitudes—for instance, one delivered in 1807 that proclaimed, "*Our Museum*—May these emblems of the wants of the *savage*, teach us to value the blessings of the *civilized* state."[61] In 1849, member Ephraim Emmerton (1791–1877), a veteran of the India trade and later an investor in the Zanzibar trade, argued against the sale of pews to African Americans in the city's First Congregational Society Church.[62] These examples, along with the decision to exclude African Americans from visiting the museum, adds to the complexities imbued in the Society's parades, collection, and displays.

Many Salem residents recorded their experiences at the museum. Joseph Hodges Choate (1832–1917), a lawyer who succeeded John Hay (1838–1905) as ambassador to the United Kingdom during the McKinley administration, wrote about its influence on him as a boy. He made particular mention of the lack of great western art in Salem, stating that there were "some pictures and statuary . . . of no great account." Choate believed "there was no opportunity for the study of art except at the famous East India Marine Museum," which held "two wonderful casts that made a great impression on my mind, one of the Laocoon, and the other of the boy seated and picking a thorn out of his foot, which are still very famous among the artistic treasures of Europe." (Unbeknownst to Choate, "a distinguished artist of Calcutta" had created this version of *Boy with Thorn*.)[63]

Caroline Howard King wrote the most extensive local description of the East India Marine Society Museum. Her reminiscences and reflections on her multiple visits as a young girl in the 1830s also provide some of the best insights into children's experiences at the museum. In her memoir, she described the sense of exotic wonderment evident in Salem at this time, when "there was an Eastern flavor" and "the Spice Islands seemed to lie very near our coast." King recalled how at each visit the museum held "a mysterious attraction . . . for an imaginative child." Unlike visitors who only had a short period of time to tour the museum, perhaps during the one trip they would ever make to Salem, King spent entire days perusing the collection, sometimes "until the hour of closing came."[64]

Upon entering the "beautiful old hall," King was greeted by "the solemn group of Orientals who, draped in eastern stuffs and camel's hair shawls, stood opposite the entrance." They were supplemented by the "circle of sitting and standing figures, who were placed in the centre of the hall in those days," all of whom "became real friends of mine" (see figure 6). She recalled, "I never heard their exact history, but I came to know their dark faces well, and Mr. Blue Gown, and Mr. Camel's Hair Scarf and Mr. Queer Cap, each had his own pleasant individuality and must be greeted whenever I went to the Museum."[65] For King, it was not important whether eastern or western hands had crafted these figures or whom they represented. Instead, they became the childhood acquaintances of an imaginative girl. The hall and its trappings helped her create a place "full of enchantment . . . as near fairy-land as one ever can [experience] in this workaday world."[66] It was a land far away from the realities of mercantilism, the prosaic details surrounding the acquisition of objects, and the sphere of international commerce and exploration.

Martha Nichols, the granddaughter of Society member George Nichols, who "cherished a love for the institution throughout his life," also wrote about her time at the museum as a young girl. She recalled, "[T]here was an especial artistic charm about the place when I was a child." When her grandfather offered to take Martha and her oldest sister to the hall, they "always wanted to go" and "started off gaily, each one holding a hand," until they "reached the magic door which opened onto so many wonders." Once inside, Nichols "joined a group of sea captains (for there always seemed to be a group there)," and Martha and her sister "wandered almost breathlessly around the hall, glad to stay there for hours if . . . permitted."[67]

A former Salem resident identified as "E. H. F." recounted his or her childhood experiences when returning to the city after being away for many years. Unlike other observers, who bemoaned the former glory of the city as compared to its more dilapidated state by the 1860s, E. H. F. found it "rare . . . to come back after a long absence and find a city looking as 'natural' as Salem does . . . [f]ree from the vulgar fever of unrest, from the vulgar dream of ambition, from the vulgar thirst for gold," reposing with "dignified ease, glorying in her past, content with her present, and serenely trustful of her future." Even while characterizing this attitude as "the slow, silent process of fossilization," E. H. F. celebrated "[r]ich, quiet, stately, self-respectful, polite old Salem! May she live ten thousand years, and her shadow never be less,—nor greater."[68]

E. H. F's vision of Salem was epitomized in the East India Marine Society Museum, the city's "favorite child," whose "management is an admirable illustration of her character." He or she praised the museum for adhering to its founding principles during hard financial times, specifically resisting the temptation to charge admission: "And now that, from some temporary collapse in the funds, it is unable to pay a salary to a keeper, it utterly refuses . . . to accept any entrance money, refuses even to allow a keeper to take voluntary perquisites from visitors, choosing rather to be itself a door-keeper, than to do for hire what its father did for love." The museum's collection of objects was E. H. F.'s key to unlocking the past. "I wanted very much to see the wonders of my childhood . . . the Indiamen sitting and standing in sedate perpetuity—the throng of wooden people crowded into a sixpenny globe—the awful whale's jaw, and the bugs, and the beetles, and the lizards." To do so, the visitor "hunted up a director, who showed us the riches of his house, with as much suavity and patience, and detail, as a professional showman, but with the modesty, the quietness and the *knowledge* which belong only to a gentleman."[69]

In an article for the periodical *Old and New*, George L. Chaney offered another childhood recollection of East India Marine Hall. He noted, "Strangers [visiting] from afar have felt repaid by the variety and suggestiveness of its collection." For Chaney, "[t]o walk around this room was to circumnavigate the globe," and "only the retrospect of maturer years can estimate the influence of such a hall of wonders upon a growing youth." A ticket to the hall allowed him to "enter the chamber of all nations, travel around both capes, and come safely home again in one afternoon." Chaney's voyage began and ended "with a group of figures, which, once seen, could never be forgotten. . . . [They stood in] immense glass cases, dressed in the cool linen and silk of the tropics, with bronzed cheeks and shining black hair, and small, piercing black eyes." These life-sized figures of Indian merchants "met the boyish visitor's wondering gaze."[70]

Salem's native son Nathaniel Hawthorne had a unique relationship with the museum that contrasts with the euphoric musings of King, Nichols, and others. The East India Marine Society played a central role in forming Hawthorne's understanding of the world, particularly the East Indies. Salem's trade and the movement of ideas and material objects, along with Hawthorne's readings about the Orient, helped shape his conception of the region. In addition, the legacy of his father, Captain Nathaniel Hathorne (circa 1775–1808)—a Society member who died in Surinam—must have had a profound impact on him: not only the souvenirs, curios, and logbooks his father left behind but also the loss and hardship experienced by many families connected to the sea.[71]

Hawthorne's short story "A Virtuoso's Collection," originally published in the *Boston Miscellany of Literature and Fashion* (May 1842), was inspired by his visits to the East India Marine Society Museum.[72] The connections between the fictional and the real institution are evident from the outset.[73] Hawthorne's narrator chronicles a visit to a collection in a manner akin to the way visitors recounted their experiences in the Society's museum. "[H]aving a leisure hour at my disposal," the narrator is attracted by "a small and unobtrusive sign: 'To be seen here, a Virtuoso's Collection,'" and decides to leave "the sunny sidewalk of our principal thoroughfare" (a place similar to Essex Street) and enter the museum. He mounts "a sombre stair-case," pushes open a door at the top of the landing, and encounters a doorkeeper who charges him admission. The description of this attendant recalls contemporaneous descriptions of Society members such as Thomas Saul: "He wore an old-fashioned greatcoat, much faded, within which his meagre person was so completely enveloped that the rest of his attire was undistinguishable. But his visage was remarkably wind-flushed, sunburnt, and weather-worn."[74]

Hawthorne's narrator then begins his tour through the gallery with the owner of the museum, a mysterious virtuoso. He describes him as "a middle-aged person," perhaps a former "scholar or . . . man of action," but "all outward and obvious peculiarities had been worn away by an extensive and promiscuous intercourse with the world." Similarities abound between the virtuoso's museum and East India Marine Hall. At various points in the tale the narrator describes the interior as "extensive" and "spacious."[75] He remarks on an incongruous display of objects, "the tendency to whimsical combinations and ludicrous analogies, which seemed to influence many of the arrangements."[76] Displays include "the golden thigh of Pythagoras . . . on the same shelf with Peter Stuyvesant's wooden leg" and "the wooden statue, so well known as the Palladium of Troy, . . . with the wooden head of General Jackson, which was stolen, a few years since, from the bows of the Constitution." Some objects are directly connected to those in the Society's collection, such as "the shell of the egg which Columbus set upon its end," a reference to Corné's painting *Columbus Breaking the Egg*.

The narrator's overall impression of the virtuoso's collection—and, by extension, the Society's museum—is not flattering. He proclaims at one point that he has "little interest in . . . science"; and when he is shown numerous magical objects such as "Cornelius Agrippa's magic glass," he tells the virtuoso that these illusions "have grown wearisome" now that there are "so many greater wonders in the world, to those who keep their eyes open and their sight undimmed by custom, that all the delusions of the old sorcerers seem flat and stale."[77] After seeing countless apocryphal objects, such as a finger from the Colossus of Rhodes and the skull of King Philip, and "complet[ing] the circuit of the spacious hall," the narrator takes his leave. As he is departing, the virtuoso points out that "the inner door of the hall was constructed with the ivory leaves of the gateway through which Æneas and the Sibyl had been dismissed from Hades," denoting the dark, unnatural character of the virtuoso's collection—and perhaps for Hawthorne—the Society's museum.[78]

Regardless of Hawthorne's true feelings about the East India Marine Society, his time spent as corresponding secretary for the Salem Lyceum helped expose more people to the museum. He had varied connections to transcendentalism—a philosophical, literary, and political movement that developed in New England in the 1820s and 1830s—and drew transcendentalist writers to speak in the city. In November 1848, he wrote to Thoreau to arrange a lecture and likely did the same for Emerson, who gave more than fifty lectures at the lyceum between 1836 and 1871.[79] This influx of transcendentalist speakers in Salem inspired the city's own contributions to the movement, in the form of the Reverend Jones Very, Elizabeth Palmer Peabody (1804–94), Samuel Johnson, and others.[80]

Naturally, the transcendentalists found their way to the museum and left their signatures in the visitor guestbooks. Thoreau, who visited in September 1858, wrote in his journal that he "[s]aw at the East India Marine Hall a bay lynx killed in Danvers July 21 (I think in 1827); another killed in Lynnfield in March 1832" and was amazed to learn that this animal was "much larger than I expected."[81] Thoreau was especially taken with objects connected to New England's past, such as "a sword in its scabbard, found in the road near Concord April 19, 1775, and supposed to have belonged to a British officer"; a "pestle and mortar found in making Salem Turnpike"; and "what was called the blade of an Indian knife found on Governor Endicott's farm, broken, three or four inches long, of a lightcolored kind of slate, quite thin, with a back."[82]

Hawthorne and the transcendentalists were not the only literary figures to record their experiences at the museum.[83] The American poet Hannah Flagg Gould (1788–1865) wrote about her visit in 1847, capturing the sense of mystery and wonder she felt when walking through the displays. She brought her readers on a tour of the gallery, a "comprehensive repository of wonderful works of nature and of art . . . together in so close a compass from so widely distant parts of the world." She felt magic within the hall, "witchery enough to bind your feet to the floor of that charm-working cabinet by an irresistible spell," which for her was akin to time travel, "while you felt that you ought to be off, since time and the steam-cars wait for no man, and to send your thoughts radiating at once into every direction where the sun darts its beams."[84]

Like other visitors, Gould marveled at the museum's ability to transport patrons to distant lands. "As you surmounted the flight of steps that ushered you abruptly into the hall," she wrote, almost immediately "you felt . . . transported to the eastern hemisphere!" She described the "group of oriental statuary" that "first met your eye, . . . so exactly to the life were the figures represented in their various castes and conditions, from the proud, erect Hindostanee, with his rich Cashmere shawl and turban, to the half-naked, dusky Bengalese fakir, in his squalid, beggarly appearance and squat position." She was particularly taken with the statue *Boy with Thorn*, telling her readers that the child depicted is "seated on a block—his head bowed in close attention to his work . . . busily engaged in picking at a puncture in the sole": "You felt as if the thorn in his foot had riveted yours to the floor beside him." This synesthetic association transfixed Gould: "you could hardly have the heart to leave him till you saw the cruel thing extracted, and the face of the little sufferer turned up towards yours with the glad expression of relieved childhood."[85]

Eliza Leslie (1787–1858), a popular domestic theorist and the editor of *Miss Leslie's Magazine* and the annual *The Gift*, wrote extensively about the museum in an 1844 essay "Pencillings of Boston." She considered it the town's main attraction for tourists and wrote that "A veteran captain is always in attendance to give whatever explanation may be desired concerning the curiosities, all of which are numbered—and catalogues are kept in the room for the convenience of visitors while there." Leslie thought "[t]he contents of this liberal and public-spirited museum are admirably classed and arranged, and in excellent preservation."[86]

She was most intrigued by some of the mainstays of the collection: the Indian palanquin and the figures of eastern merchants. Her essay offers a window into her preconceptions of palanquins, most likely formed by turn-of-the-century travel narratives and Anglo-European prints, noting that she expected them to be light and "rather elegant vehicles." Instead, when confronted with a physical example, she altered her opinion and exclaimed that palanquins were "surpassingly clumsy, and indeed ugly . . . the most cumbrous, awkward, and tiresome mode of conveyance imaginable; and it must be almost equally fatiguing to the carriers and the carried." Leslie quipped, "I have long been sceptical as to the boasted luxuries of India."[87]

Writing of the figures of Chinese and Indian merchants, Leslie revealed that she believed they were the products of eastern artists: "Like the Chinese, the people of India are surprisingly skilful in making these effigies." She interpreted the variety of facial features and expressions as evidence that they "undoubtedly have been modelled from life—the only way to obtain a variety, for there is usually a most monotonous similarity in faces created according to the imagination of a human artist."[88] Leslie thought these depictions of merchants made for a western gaze were superior to the other "idols" in East India Marine Hall, which were from "different parts of the yet-uncivilized world." She is amazed that "such ugly and uncouth objects could, even by savages, be regarded as emblematic of the deities whom they believed it their duty to worship. Does the North American Indian adore any but the One Being, to whom he gives the true and sublime titles of the Great Spirit and the Master of Life?—and of him he presumes to carve no image."[89] In this instance, she was not able to part with her biased views of other cultures.

Leslie reserved her highest admiration for "a little work of ingenuity which must have been very gladly admitted into the collection . . . not furnished by any of the hardy brotherhood that 'go down to the sea in ships, and behold the wonders of the deep.'"[90] This was Lucy Hiller Cleveland's (1780–1866) *The Sick Chamber*, a 17½-inch-high vignette of a bedroom with five figures, made for a charitable fair in 1831 and then donated to the museum. Cleveland was married to Society member William Cleveland (also her second cousin) and accompanied him on voyages to the east in 1828 and 1829. She made many cloth figural pieces for similar charitable fairs in the antebellum period and also anonymously wrote children's books published in Boston between 1827 and 1842.[91] Through both media, she focused on abolition, temperance, and social benevolence.

The Sick Chamber was displayed on top of a low case on the eastern wall of the hall, just below Benjamin Tanner's prints (see figure 5, no. 4). Leslie commented that it was made by a "Lady of Salem . . . of unrivalled genius in that branch of the art of dollmaking whose productions are shamefully slandered by the degrading and unjust title of rag-babies."[92] Leslie had a personal connection to *The Sick Chamber* as she had made similar pieces of a "genteel sort" that had "no rags in their composition." In her lengthy description of this work, longer than her other musings about the museum, she declared that "the most admirable resemblance of the human form and face," done with "such consummate skill and exquisite neatness," was a "curious and astonishing testimony of the skill and patience" of the artist.[93]

Leslie recommended "a visit to the Salem Museum; and those who have been there already, will find much pleasure in going again."[94] She noted with surprise—as did many other visitors—that admission was free of charge. During their visit, one of Leslie's companions "said to the venerable curator—'As so many strangers come to Salem for the purpose of seeing your museum, I think you would find it very profitable to make a charge for admission.'" The attendant handled this question as his brethren had done so before, indignantly replying, "I'd rather dig clams!"[95]

The Society's museum made its way into other literary works. In Day Kellogg Lee's (1816–69) 1854 novel *Merrimack: Or, Life at the Loom*, about an orphaned thirteen-year-old girl who goes to work in a textile mill, one character, Mr. Keezle, is likened to the "little alabaster image with a squatted lump of a body, a flattened head, and shining face, which the sea captains brought from India and set up in the Salem museum."[96] *Lottie Wilde's Picnic*, published in 1867 by "Grandmother Hope" (possibly Henry Gally Knight), contains a whole chapter devoted to a school excursion to the East India Marine Society Museum.[97] In chapter 6, the teacher Mr. Homer announces to his class that they will be visiting "the East-India Marine Museum in Salem" during their vacation, and a "suppressed murmur of applause [is] heard through the school."[98] Chapter 7 then reads as a narrative version of the museum catalogue. After a brief description of the institution's origins—the usual boilerplate material taken from prior museum or newspaper publications—the class enters the hall and is "startled at the sight of a number of images, large as life, sitting round in a semicircle before them." Like King and other children who visited the museum, these boys and girls are captivated by what they see. A character named Will Freeman exclaims, "Look here, Harry . . . here is an instrument made of the bone of a whale, used by the natives of New Zealand as a war-weapon, and a paddle called patoo-patoo." As in the narratives of Ann Royall and others, all objects in the museum are briefly mentioned except for one, which receives closer treatment—the carved rosary bead donated by Elias Hasket Derby, Jr., "the greatest curiosity of all."[99]

Unlike most real and fictional accounts of the museum, *Lottie Wilde's Picnic* challenges gender stereotypes. The tour guide, Mr. Preston, attempts to steer the boys to look at objects deemed appropriate for males, and vice versa. The children, however, have other ideas:

> "Alice, see this frock, made of the intestines of the sea-lion!" said Lillie Rutter. "Yes, Lillie; and you come and look at this one, made out of the intestines of the whale," replied Alice.
>
> "Young ladies," said Mr. Preston, "you will like to examine this elegant shawl: it is made of red and yellow feathers, and worn by the ladies in Owhyhee. The boys, I suppose, will prefer to look at the specimens of marble from Herculaneum and Pompeii."
>
> "I had rather look at those than the handsomest shawl that ever was made," said Eva Ingersoll. "So had I," said many voices.

Rather than force the children to look at certain objects, the guide admits his error. "'Ah, then I was mistaken!' said Mr. Preston. 'I thought the young ladies were more fond of dress than any thing else.' But the young ladies were so intent upon the curiosities, that they had no time to resent such an unwarrantable assertion."[100] In the nineteenth century, as in today's world, children had a unique ability to challenge established norms and change adult attitudes and opinions.

At the end of the class's four-hour visit, "[s]everal gentlemen, members of the society, were present, and pronounced themselves so highly gratified with the exemplary conduct of the young ladies and gentlemen, that they extended them a cordial invitation to visit the Museum on their next vacation." When the protagonist, Lottie, arrives home, she gives her parents an account of her experiences at the museum. Again, the rosary bead takes center stage, the "[o]ne thing I shall never forget." Lottie does not comprehend how anyone can "study those countenances [on the bead] for any length of time, without resolving to give themselves to Christ as their Saviour." After she stood gazing at the "wondrous" object, she felt "more resolved than ever to take Jesus as my portion and friend forever."[101]

In all of these accounts, it is clear that visitors' experiences at East India Marine Hall were integral to the museum's wide fame. Some visitors gained an appreciation for other cultures or new perspectives on the world outside of their city, state, or country, while others reconfirmed preconceived notions of faraway lands and people. In the end, though, almost all acknowledged that East India Marine Society members had built a unique American museum.

These themes are encapsulated in E. D. Eliot's short story "The Lost Deed: A Legend of Old Salem," which touches upon the city's golden age of maritime trade and the founding of the Society's museum. At one point in the story, the character Dick Seaward takes his friend George to meet his father, a ship's captain, and "eat cocoa-nuts, and see the curiosities which the captain had brought home." Captain Seaward takes a liking to George, and, in the manner of Society members in East India Marine Hall, "spare[s] no pains to entertain him." The old salt "appeared like some hero of romance to his wondering guest" and "ransacked his memory, stored by voyages of five-and-twenty years, for marvelous adventures, unheard of perils by shipwreck, pirates, etc." The captain's narrative produces an effect on George's "excited imagination, [such] as Don Quixote might have experienced at hearing the adventures of Amadis de Gaul from his own mouth."[102]

Material culture augments the mariner's stories. Following his tale, the captain "displayed his curiosities" for George. They are "numerous and strange, . . . [an] elephant's tusks and ostrich's eggs, . . . a nautilus' shell, which might have carried a boat's crew; and . . . the entire skin of an enormous snake, which the captain intended to have stuffed and hung as a capital ornament round the best room." These objects serve "in some sort as illustrations of his discourse." To George, they are wonders of the unknown world and physical proof of the tales he has just heard, and "he look[s] upon the possessor of them with a feeling almost amounting to awe." These are not merely sailor's heirlooms, however. Rather, they are "among the first deposited in the Salem Museum upon its being founded; and they there formed a nucleus, around which has been gathered, from time to time the present noble collection."[103]

By the end of the Civil War, the museum's global fame was cemented in the minds of both Americans and individuals abroad. A writer for the *Edinburgh Review* claimed, "The name of the village of Salem is as familiar to Americans as that of any provincial town in England or France is to Englishmen and Frenchmen," not simply due to the witchcraft trials of 1692 but also because of its museum. In the years before the war, he wrote, "[t]he houses were hung with odd Chinese copies of English engravings, and furnished with a variety of pretty and useful articles from China, never seen elsewhere." He noted that the East India Marine Society had spread global awareness through the collection and display of objects: "Each speculative merchant who went forth . . . was determined to bring home some offering to the Museum . . . and, whether the adventurer came home rich or poor, he was sure to have gained much knowledge, and to have become very entertaining in discourse."[104]

The author wrote that Salem "was suffering its share of the adversity which has fallen upon the shipping trade, while . . . still mourning the loss of some of its noblest citizens in the late civil war," yet he could still sense "the same vigorous pursuit of intellectual interests and pleasures" in the city. This stemmed from its "cultivated and travelled community [members]," who were acquainted "with people of all known faiths, and [their] familiarity with all known ways of living and thinking, while adhering to the customs, and even the prejudices, of their fathers." In his view, "[t]he Salem Museum was the glory of the town, and even of the State."[105] His words recall those printed thirty-five years earlier in the *New-York Journal of Commerce*: "Has the reader ever visited the Salem East India Museum?—We have many a time: and we do not hesitate to say that to *us* it is the most interesting Museum which we ever entered."[106] This praise still rings true, and the institution started by a group of worldly mariners continues to thrive and inspire visitors today.

Conclusion

"THAT THUS THEIR EXPLOITS, ON THE OCEAN WAVE, FROM AGE TO AGE MIGHT STILL BE HANDED DOWN"

> I am glad to know that the old East India Marine Hall has been restored by the Peabody Museum so that its usefulness will be continued through the years. All who cherish the sagas of the old Salem sea captains and merchants will be thankful that this glorious memorial to the Golden Age of New England shipping is to be perpetuated.
>
> —President Franklin D. Roosevelt, letter to Augustus P. Loring, Jr., president of the trustees of the Peabody Museum of Salem, read at the rededication of East India Marine Hall, November 4, 1943

Between 1846 and 1848, Nathaniel Hawthorne worked as a clerk in the Salem Custom House overlooking Derby Wharf. In the preface to *The Scarlet Letter*, as part of his reflections on his employment in this federal office, he recounted watching the decline of Salem's maritime fortunes. The once bustling wharf "in the days of old King Derby" were now "burdened with decayed wooden warehouses," exhibiting "few or no symptoms of commercial life." With a tinge of bitterness, he wrote, "Salem was a port by itself; not scorned, as she is now, by her own merchants and shipowners, who permit her wharves to crumble in ruin."[1]

Other depictions of Salem during this period echoed Hawthorne's. The Reverend Octavius Brooks Frothingham (1822–95) commented that, when he was in Salem in 1847–55, the "splendor had departed. Derby Street was deserted, the great warehouses were tenements for laborers. . . . The sailors had disappeared; the commerce, owing mainly to the shallowness of the water in the harbor, had gone to Boston and New York." While he noted that "traces of the old glory still lingered" and that "[h]ere and there a great merchant was seen on the streets," he made it clear that Salem's reign as one of the nation's leading commercial ports was at an end.[2]

Like many other American towns, Salem was unable to fight the advances of the Industrial Revolution. The coastal trade waned as canals and railroads became the primary means to transport goods back and forth from cities into the interior. The wharves in Salem were now used to warehouse goods such as stone, coal, wood, and catches from the commercial fishing industry.[3] Salem merchant George Augustus Perkins (1813–95), writing from Fishtown, Cape Palmas, in West Africa, surmised, "Railroads & Factories must make more business for the town. . . . I should perhaps find it difficult to recognize Salem if set down in some places in it."[4]

In this climate, the East India Marine Society's ability to support benevolent activities also diminished. Members had expended funds to construct a museum and now needed to take care of a burgeoning collection. This included paying staff, caring for the objects, publishing catalogues, and cleaning the museum. When they compared their charitable disbursements in the 1830s to those of prior decades, they were disturbed. In 1831, $112 was distributed among fourteen beneficiaries; two years later, $142 was shared among seventeen. Society meeting minutes called this "trifling . . . a mere apology for Charity."[5] They understood, however, that conditions were changing. In 1834, the Society's capital funds totaled $9,135.57, but seventy-four shares ($7,012.21) were tied into the East India Marine Hall Corporation.[6] In addition, the Society paid an annual $200 to the corporation for rent.

To counter this alarming financial situation, some members put forth a proposal in 1834 to charge admission (twenty-five cents to adults, half price to children) to visitors not accompanied by a member. Those in favor noted, "The Museum, from a small cabinet of curiosities, has become one of the largest collections in the country, and has obtained a celebrity, that strangers from all parts of the world visit it; to gratify them it would require too great a sacrifice of time, and too heavy a tax on the members in returning to the old regulation [that visitors should be accompanied by a member]."[7] Tickets were printed, but the idea was tabled because the majority of members believed that admissions fees were antithetical to the public nature of the museum and the charitable principles of their organization.

Still, funds continued to decline, and by the end of the 1830s the Society was forced to enact some extreme measures. The president and the committee of observation were ordered to "collect the sums now due from such persons as in their opinion are able to pay the same"—that is, collect outstanding dues for membership, totaling between $600 and $700. This move, however, did not result in increased funds; rather, these members were ousted for nonpayment. In all, between 1839 and 1867, nine members were expelled; only four had ever been expelled from the Society in previous years.[8]

Dwindling funds directly correlated with declining membership. After the East India Marine Society was formed in 1799, 115 members joined the organization between 1800 and 1819, 110 between 1820 and 1830. After that point, membership plummeted. Between 1830 and 1840, thirty-five members were admitted, and after 1843 (the apex of total living members, at 136) membership took another sharp decline. In the 1840s, only seventeen members were voted into the Society, and only twelve joined between 1850 and 1860. With Salem's overseas trade near its end, few captains were venturing beyond the capes, and thus few could fulfill the unchanged qualifications required for membership.[9] In the last seven years that the Society operated its museum, only four mariners joined the rolls.

The pomp and circumstance associated with the early days faded as a result of diminishing funds, but the East India Marine Society attempted to maintain a public presence. On April 19, 1841, members took part in a local procession held in memory of the late president, William Henry Harrison.[10] Plans for an 1837 dinner were shelved, but in 1841, the Society decided to hold an anniversary celebration.[11] On this occasion, the *Salem Gazette* noted that it had "revived the old custom, established at its foundation, of an anniversary dinner, and partook of a dinner got up in Mr. Dow's best style."[12] The toasts, however, were more somber and more reflective than usual, with five memorials for past members and a final sober toast to "*Our Meeting this Evening*, As it is the first festive meeting here, to some of us, may it be the last to none of us."[13] Only twenty-three members attended the proceedings that November night.

The last public event the East India Marine Society took part in was on October 25, 1848: the celebration of the newly integrated Cochituate water supply into Boston. On this occasion, as in days of old, members were "escorted by the Salem L[ight] Infantry and Salem Band."[14] The procession also included "the old Palanquin, which has not been before seen in public for about forty years," which was carried "by six stout negro bearers, dressed in white oriental costume, with white turbans" and held "a fair young boy reclining in oriental style." The parade continued "to the northern entrance of the Tunnell [*sic*]," where members "took the [train] cars appropriated for their reception." In Boston, they "formed again at Lewis's Wharf . . . and the Procession marched into State Street, proceed[ed] by the Military, and Band and also accompany'd by the two Ships, on the Car, and by the Palanquin carried by the bearers."[15]

Three years later, during Salem's celebration of the seventy-fifth anniversary of national independence, the *Salem Observer* reported that the parade contained "a wagon carrying on a platform, the two models from the East India Museum: the 'Constitution' and the 'Friendship.' The ships were followed by a procession of some twenty boys in sailor costume. The East India trade of Salem was represented by the Palanquin from the Museum, in which half a dozen East Indians, in costume, were carrying a pretty little boy, also dressed in Oriental style."[16] What was missing from this procession, oddly, were the Society members, who declined to take part in the parade.

In September 1855, the Society's income was not sufficient to meet current expenses, given that a large part of its funds was invested in East India Marine Hall "which was not at present occupied" by businesses on the ground floor.[17] Members voted to call a special meeting to discuss the situation and decided to "dispense with the services of a door-keeper."[18] At the next meeting in November, the Society voted to forgo the "Duties of Superintendent" during the wintertime. The treasurer's reports for 1858 show that gross income fell by more than a third from 1851–53 to 1854–56 (from an average of $922.37 a year to an average of $590.23 a year), "which is accounted for by less rent from Building, less dividends, less assessments from members who are decreasing in numbers."[19] At the May 1858 meeting, member William D. Waters presented a motion for an admission fee, which was tabled for further consideration and spurred "several spirited debates" at the next "fully attended" meeting.[20] Eventually, the Society voted to indefinitely postpone the discussion.

A year later, the East India Marine Society made a last-ditch effort to support its museum's operations by petitioning the state's general court for aid. The legislative committee on education noted in its report on the Society's application that the "collection is unequalled in value in this or perhaps it might be said in any country" and has been "from the first open to the public without fee or charge of any kind, . . . visited by persons averaging 10,000 per year." Still, the petition was dismissed because it "came to the Committee after all the bills granting aid from the proceeds of the sale of land in the Back Bay had been finally reported." In addition, the Committee called out "the S. E. I. M. Soc." for its inability to comply "with the condition inexorably attached by them to all their bills granting aid to institutions, namely that of raising by subscription, an equal sum.'"[21]

By midcentury, the East India Marine Society's intellectual clout was also diminishing as Salem's maritime sector began supporting new Essex County industries. Society members had always been businessmen, but in the early days of the organization they had been cutting-edge mariners mapping uncharted waters and bringing back one-of-a-kind objects. Now their scientific curiosity was amateurish in comparison to the professionalization of the field occurring in the country and the world.

One dramatic event mirrored this downturn. In 1859, the Society made U.S. naval lieutenant Matthew Fontaine Maury (1806–73), a leading cartographer and oceanographer, their first and only elected honorary member.[22] They believed Maury was worthy of their recognition because he had "devoted a very considerable portion of his life to nautical research and ha[d] done more to promote the interest of the Mercantile Marine than any other living man." Bestowing this title on him fulfilled "one of the principle objects of this Society, . . . to advance Nautical Science, and Knowledge."[23] Maury willingly accepted the honor, believing that "the members of this Society are . . . experts in Navigation, and that in token of the value that they set upon the labours of this Office, they have conferred the most signal honor that ambition could crave."[24] News of his election was published in newspapers across the country, including the *Augusta Chronicle*, and he was also elected an honorary member of the Salem Marine Society shortly thereafter.[25]

In the fall of 1859, Ripley Ropes of Salem presented a "beautiful Photograph likeness" of Maury, which was hung in East India Marine Hall. Today, a discerning eye might marvel at its still-pristine condition, surprising given that the light-sensitive salted-paper photograph was apparently on display in a well-lit interior space. In fact, however, the object's impeccable condition reflects a nation in turmoil. Two years after the photograph was donated to the museum, the Civil War broke out, and Maury declared his allegiance to his native state of Virginia and thus to the Confederacy. At the Society's July 3, 1861, meeting, President Allen Putnam (1794–1868) characterized that decision as shameful, accusing Maury of "abandoning his duty and loyalty to his Country and Flag."[26] Those gathered in East India Marine Hall on that summer night unanimously voted to strike his name from the rolls and expel him from the Society, calling him "unworthy of holding a name or a place as a member of this Institution." In addition, Maury's portrait was "taken from the Hall, and placed in some obscure corner of the Building," for it was "unworthy of a place among the collections of the Cabinet of the Museum."[27] The words "Lieut/ M. P. Maury/ Traitor" were inscribed on the back of the frame, an indelible record of this decision.[28] Maury's association with the East India Marine Society had brought embarrassment to the Hall, and the incident signaled the end of the Society's national and international scientific influence.

In these years the museum's collections and displays continued to be properly maintained, but by 1860 Thomas Saul's reports were somber in respect to donations. He told his fellow members that since their last annual meeting only one object had been presented to the museum, "from Capt. Joseph Hammond . . . the Streinur [*sic*] or part of the mouth of the Grey whale from, California."[29] In 1861 his report mentioned only the donation of a portrait of member Henry Elkins, and in 1862 he alluded to the Essex Institute, not the East India Marine Society Museum, as Salem's principal institution for donations. "Since the Plummer Institute has been erected," he wrote, "I presume most of the donations formerly received by this Society have been presented to that Institution."[30] Saul listed only four donations to the Society that year, and in his final extant report, from 1863, only eight objects are mentioned.

When the Reverend Jones Very wrote "The East India Marine Museum" in 1865, he was memorializing a fading institution. Without outside funding, the Society voted that year to drop the insurance on the "curiosities of the Cabinet."[31] In addition, at their November meeting, they again brought up the idea of charging admission and this time also suggested looking into the "sale of curiosities" in order to "invest proceeds . . . [and] divide interest among indigent members and families." While charging admission was again voted down, the Society continued to explore ways to raise funds, as their organization was "dying out and many members need assistance, more than can be obtained from present funds."[32] The motion to look into the sale of the collection was tabled, and as an alternative, the Society voted on February 21, 1866, to bestow honorary membership on anyone donating $100 or more. Only one person, John Robinson (1846–1925), the son of a Society member, took advantage of this option.[33]

It appears that the idea of selling the collection leaked out of East India Marine Hall and into the ears of local reporters.[34] On November 30, 1865, the *Salem Register* published a scathing editorial concerning the rumor that P. T. Barnum was going to purchase the Society's collection. The paper reported, with humorous hyperbole and disgust, that this news had "caused considerable sensation in the community and especially among the families of deceased donors." Selling the collection would be "a libel on the very respectable gentlemen who hold the Museum in trust"; "the bones of the noble old mariners who won such renown for themselves, their seaport and their country" would "rattle in their coffins at the bare mention of such a sacrilege." The *Register* was confident that the community would rally to the cause if called upon rather than "suffer the memory of their maritime fathers to be dishonored by such an act . . . such a stigma," for "[t]he idea that this unique collection . . . is in the remotest danger of being associated with the Joice Heths, and Feejee Island Mermaids, and the heterogeneous humbugs of a metropolitan show room, is too monstrous to be tolerated for a moment."[35] The talk of Barnum's takeover was mere conjecture, but the promises of public relief for the East India Marine Society proved to be empty.

On the night of May 18, 1866, a fire broke out in a shed behind East India Marine Hall and spread to the adjacent Lynde block on Essex Street, which was completely destroyed. Luckily, the museum's objects were saved without harm, but the building suffered some water damage.[36] The incident may have been an omen, as a year later the Society's collection was saved yet again by timely aid. Henry Wheatland and the trustees of the Essex Institute, looking to acquire East India Marine Hall for their growing collection, caught the ear of philanthropist and Essex County native George Peabody (1795–1869). Born in South Danvers, he was distantly related to successful Salem merchant Joseph Peabody but grew up with lesser means. George Peabody had made his fortune in banking and finance and later used that money to support and establish many institutions, most of them in New England but a few in other parts of the United States.[37] Instead of expanding the Essex Institute, he made a $140,000 gift to form a new Salem museum—the Peabody Academy of Sciences, to be constructed in the mold of the new natural history and anthropology museums that were developing in postwar America.[38] East India Marine Hall was purchased from the Society, its collection was deposited in the new institution, and the Essex Institute gave its natural history and ethnographic collections to the Peabody Academy so that the institute could focus on Essex County history.

When the Peabody Academy of Science was formed in 1867, the trustees of the new institution assured the East India Marine Society that its collection would be "properly cared for and arranged, . . . giving to the same equal care and protection bestowed upon other collections . . . to be kept by them and their successors." The academy planned to redesign East India Marine Hall, however, and to place all of the Society's archaeological and ethnological objects and "such articles as have reference to the history of said Society" in cases on the east wall alongside similar objects from the Essex Institute "or other collections." Natural history objects from both organizations would be arranged with "the general collections in said Hall," and any duplicate material would be exchanged.[39] Finally, the academy assured the Society that its members would continue to have free access to East India Marine Hall, along with suitable rooms and accommodations, free of charge.

According to the *Cape Ann Light and Gloucester Telegraph*, the trustees of the Peabody Academy of Science had invited the public to see the hall one last time before renovations were made, noting that "Providence . . . put it into the heart of one of the most favored of our contemporaries to rescue from both time and Barnum all that was not perishable of this ancient and honored society."[40] The renovation and reconfiguration of East India Marine Hall took place in 1867–69 under the direction of new superintendent, Frederick Ward Putnam (1839–1914), an important figure in American anthropology; and the new Peabody Academy of Science opened in August 1869.[41] It, like its predecessor, was free to the public. Moreover, as visitors no longer needed to seek out a Society member for free tickets, there was a major increase in attendance.

The Peabody Academy of Science emphasized natural history in the museum. In a new Darwinian world, the display of specimens was having

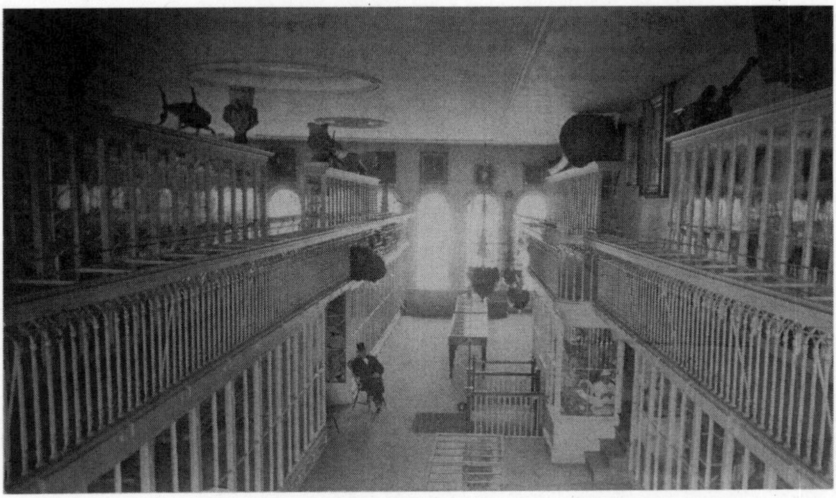

FIGURE 24. *East India Marine Hall Looking North,* circa 1876. Peabody Essex Museum Collection, TR2016.26. © 2008 Peabody Essex Museum, Salem, MA. Phillips Library Collection. Captain Joseph Hammond is seated in the center of the photograph.

less influence on cutting-edge scientific discoveries, which were now arising from field and laboratory research, yet natural history museums continued to thrive.[42] Many of the academy's officers and staff were former students of the Swiss-American biologist Louis Agassiz (1807–73) of Harvard University—such as Putnam and Edward Sylvester Morse—and were likely influenced by Agassiz's work at the Harvard Museum of Comparative Zoology.[43] These staff members completely altered East India Marine Hall. The architecturally spacious gallery filled with eclectic objects was turned into an encyclopedic zoological installation with floor-to-ceiling cases and a second-floor balcony encircling the room (see figure 24). The hall ceased to appear "as if each sea-captain had lounged in and hustled down his contributions in any convenient vacant space."[44] While academy staff appreciated the roots of the organization and the Society's important ethnological collections, they classified other objects not connected to the early days of the Society as "historical specimens."[45] This group included the plaster casts, relics, and other western artworks and artifacts. Starting in 1875, this material, along with the Society's library, was deposited in the Essex Institute at Plummer Hall, located five hundred feet away on Essex Street, to make room for new accessions.[46]

Although the Peabody Academy of Science was moving the institution into a new direction, the public still viewed it as the East India Marine Society Museum. Alice M. Guernsey (1850–1924), a writer and editor for children's and family publications, wrote a detailed description of her visit to the museum for the magazine *Household* in October 1871.[47] Her essay resembles those from the antebellum period, acknowledging the watery world of the exhibits and emphasizing the Society's collections of natural and artificial curiosities such as "the famous statue of the Laocoon" and the "Neptune's cup sponges, fit, indeed, for the revels of the mighty monarch of the sea."[48]

Without a museum to care for and operate, the Society continued to hold regular meetings and distribute funds to beneficiaries. Occasionally members were given objects that they transferred to the Peabody Academy, but their glory days were long gone. Some of them, such as Nathaniel Brown (1827–79), recognized that the Society needed to adjust to this new era.[49] In 1869, he was asked to investigate whether the stipulations for membership should be altered from navigating "near" the capes to "up to or beyond" them. He reported that every year Salem was becoming "less of a commercial place," with fewer mariners who "navigate distant seas than in years gone by."[50] He pointed out that "the days too for Supercargoes . . . has gone by." New modes of overseas exchange had replaced old trading routes; a merchant might now send ships and cargo "consigned abroad to his American friends, who were never within many thousand miles of the great capes, but who have reached their foreign abode by a quiet and easy overland journey." Brown speculated that "the *whole* current of trade, in these days of Pacific Rail Roads & cutting of Isthmuses, may be changed. . . . [C]onsequently there is becoming each year less material of which to keep up the Society."[51] He warned his brethren that these factors would keep membership stagnant if the bylaws remain unaltered. Yet his plea, like that of Laocoön, when he warned the Trojans not to take the wooden horse into their city, fell on deaf ears. Ultimately, the Society and maritime trade were trapped by American industrialization, just as Laocoön and his children were ensnared by the serpents.

By 1880, the officers of the Peabody Academy of Science had come to realize that their institutional mission was not aligned with the strengths of the collection, and they reversed course, returning to their organizational roots—the East India Marine Society Museum.[52] The academy's director, Edward Sylvester Morse, known for his work in zoology and later his research on Japanese prehistory, pointed out the futility and incongruity of the museum's natural science focus.[53] He argued that the museum "should relinquish all effort towards building up a large general collection, as it could not hope to compete with the great museums of the Boston Society of Natural History, and the Museum of Comparative Zoology at Cambridge." Instead, he suggested, the academy should "endeavor to perfect those departments which already give it pre-eminence above all other museums in the country . . . [such as the] widely known . . . unrivalled Ethnological collections, the result of the intelligent interest of Salem Sea Captains, who during the height of Salem Commerce, founded the East India Marine Society."[54] In other words, at a time when the country was establishing temples to fine art that rivaled their European counterparts (such as the Metropolitan Museum of Art) and vast government-supported institutions (such as the Smithsonian), Morse and the academy's officers and trustees decided to promote their own museum's unique, century-old global character.

After Morse left to work in Japan, John Robinson became acting director of the museum. In the mid-1880s, he worked to preserve and record the memories of the East India Marine Society, with the help of living members and Henry Wheatland, who was compiling his own genealogical record of members in a scrapbook. In 1884, Robinson sent out printed sheets to all descendants of Society members and asked recipients to contribute whatever biographical information they could, for "[t]his unique institution is now passing into history and it is hoped, before it is too late, to obtain the materials for a sketch of its work and those who conducted it."[55] These sheets reassured the Society and its members that the Peabody Academy of Science was "endeavouring to preserve with care all the memorials of the East India Marine Society," as it had promised to do in 1867.[56] Likewise, Robinson asked the families to donate portraits of Society members to augment the growing collection at the academy. With the help of Wheatland and others, he commissioned drawings of the interior of East India Marine Hall from all four directions to visually capture the museum as it existed before 1867 (see figures 3 through 6).[57]

Robinson published an article on the East India Marine Society in the *Salem Gazette*, an attempt to preserve the not-so-distant history of the Society, which was rapidly disappearing in the local and national consciousness. He wanted readers to understand that "[a]side from the munificent charities of the Salem East India Marine Society" and "the fame of the East India Marine museum," there was a scientific history "which at this late day is by many persons forgotten, and to the younger generation is unknown." He acknowledged the Society's national presence, noting that for years members had been "in constant communication with the United States government," and reminded readers that "the endorsement of the society was ever considered a guarantee of the highest character." Although Society members did not have the advantage of "any knowledge of the methods familiar to the modern scientist," they still "devised for themselves methods and plans, based upon the orderly ways of transacting business at that day, which the modern scientist has not improved upon." For this reason, according to Robinson, Salem should be proud of the East India Marine Society "and claim for it a high rank among the scientific institutions of the day for the large amount of original work contributed to general knowledge by its members."[58]

At the same time, Robinson oversaw the reorganization of the museum's ethnological collection, classifying objects by culture rather than function in the mold of other anthropological institutions in the United States. He realized the museum needed additional space to adequately display the academy's growing collection; and with approval of the trustees in 1885, the construction of a new gallery commenced off the southeast corner of East India Marine Hall. Four years later, this new wing, named East Hall, opened, along with a three-hundred-seat lecture hall on the ground floor known as Academy Hall.

With its displays of global art and artifacts, East Hall became a satellite version of the older installations of East India Marine Hall. Portraits of shipmasters were hung on the north and south walls of the gallery above a case containing "Relics of the East India Marine Society." In the middle of the room stood a most unusual "sculpture": *The Ship Trophy,* a stack of numerous Society ship models arranged above their palanquin. This votive homage to Salem's maritime past, which included many East India Marine Society objects, also signaled a new direction for the Peabody Academy of Science—one focused on cementing the legacy of its founding body, not only in the minds of Salem residents but among all museum visitors.

Beginning in 1885, several newspapers, including the *Boston Advertiser*, were reporting that the academy wanted to build a new wing to hold the "mythological collection" or "mythological department" of the museum.[59]

The *Boston Evening Transcript* of July 2, 1887, referred to a glass case in the museum in which the Society's relics were preserved and highlighted "the mighty china punch-bowls, richly decorated in gilt and colored figures . . . which once decked the curved table set out for the annual banquets of the jolly salts. What strong New Amsterdamian heads, what potent stomachs, what nerves, those fellows must have had!"[60] The same year, the *Times of London* published a series of essays titled "A Visit to the States."[61] When the traveling correspondent visited Salem and wrote about the museum, he did not call it the Peabody Academy of Science, which by this point had been in existence for twenty years. Instead, it was "the East India Marine-Hall . . . the great lion of the place."[62]

Just before the turn of the century, Robinson expanded his preservation work to highlight the East India Marine Society's link to Salem's maritime past. At the height of the port's overseas trade in the early nineteenth century, navigational instruments, builders' half-hull models, and ship portraits were considered either tools of the industry or mementos for display in merchant offices. By the end of the century, this had changed, and the museum started to collect these objects and others connected to American and global maritime history. When East Hall was opened, Robinson devoted a space underneath the gallery at the north end of the room to exhibit some of these objects, many of which had been stored in the attic of East India Marine Hall. It became the first maritime installation in an American museum.[63] As maritime objects continued to pour into the museum from the Pacific Islands and Japan (the latter through the work of Morse and Boston-based philanthropist Charles Goddard Weld [1857–1911]), a new space was sought for the growing collection.[64]

The rooms on the ground floor of East India Marine Hall, once used for businesses such as the Asiatic Bank, were converted into a new gallery. Dedicated to the ingenuity of John Robinson and supported by Weld and others, the Marine Room opened in 1905. In 1920, an extensive catalogue was published to document this new space, which reflected the museum's stature as the nation's premier institution for maritime art and history.[65] Among the many displays were "Relics of the Society" and other objects once on view or used in East India Marine Hall, such as the Venetian crystal chandeliers donated by Benjamin Carpenter in 1804.

In an address marking the opening of the Marine Room, Robinson, internally known as the "keeper of the E.I.M.S. relics," stated, "The exhibit in the Marine Room is intended to illustrate the history of the East India Marine Society, the development of its Museum and, in a broader sense, to be a memorial of the foreign commerce of Salem. Practically the three objects cover the same period and the Museum alone continues to perpetuate the story of the others."[66] The opening of the room signaled a continuing shift in the museum's mission. In 1915, the Peabody Academy of Science was renamed the Peabody Museum of Salem, as the institution refocused on its maritime roots and the voyages that were the conduit for collecting objects from across the globe.

The East India Marine Society was still extant, and its members recognized that further changes were necessary. After East India Marine Hall was sold and the Society ceased operating the museum, it did away with assessments and fines and admitted forty-five new members to the organization.[67] The Society's funds rose to more $23,000, and between 1873 and 1883 approximately $1,400 was distributed annually to beneficiaries. Further funds came in from bequests. In 1883, the Society received $5,000 from the will of member John Bertram (1796–1882) and a $200 bequest three years later from member Charles Roundy (1794–1886). Still, given that Salem voyages "beyond the capes" were all but defunct, membership declined as the nineteenth century came to a close. In 1866, the Society had 114 living members, but by 1897, there were only 27 remaining.[68]

Members knew that the end of the East India Marine Society was unavoidable. On January 1, 1908, a committee was created to ensure that any remaining beneficiaries would be paid when the final members passed away.[69] As a result, they reincorporated in 1910 as the Trustees of the Salem East India Marine Society. In the publication of their new bylaws, the Society trustees officially recognized that the Peabody Academy of Science would continue to keep their memory alive, as promised in 1867. "No trifling amount of money has been expended for benevolent purposes, and the world-renowned East India Museum, now in the care of the Peabody Academy of Science, will long testify to the patience and fidelity of the members of the Society."[70] They also stipulated that, once membership dwindled to seven individuals, Peabody trustees would be eligible to join this corporation. By 1944 all of the original Society members had died, and in 1959 the East India Marine Society merged into the fabric of the museum as the Trustees of the Peabody Museum of Salem. In 1981 the

Society's memory was also kept alive as a level of charitable giving to the museum, the East India Marine Associates, which still exists at the PEM.

By the early twentieth century, novels and short stories were memorializing the glory days of the East India Marine Society but in a new way—as a literary device to denote a part of America that was disappearing. Katharine Holland Brown (died 1931) used Salem's past and the Society as the backdrop of 1830s family strife in her story "Brewster Blood," published in *Scribner's Magazine*.[71] Nineteenth-century Salem and the Society were the backdrop for Joseph Hergesheimer's (1880–1954) novel *Java Head* (1919), which centers on a Salem captain who brings back a Cantonese woman as his wife and includes multiple perspectives on the issue of miscegenation.[72] The East India Marine Society also made an appearance in Rudyard Kipling's (1865–1936) novel *Captains Courageous* (1897). As some old salts in the novel converse about ship models, one states, "Wa-al, Enoch Fuller he made a model o' the old *Ohio,* and she's to Salem museum now. Mighty pretty model, too."[73]

Early twentieth-century travel writers, historians, and journalists also wrote about the Society and Salem's golden age of maritime trade. In *The Romantic Shore* (1915), focusing on the North Shore of Massachusetts, Agnes Edwards Rothery (1888–1954) pointed to the objects donated by Jonathan Carnes (such as the two-stemmed pipe from Sumatra) as "undoubtedly responsible for the present institution [Peabody Museum]." She felt that "in glancing back to them we cleave a swift path through one of the most varied and glowing bits of history in America."[74] Ralph Delahaye Paine's (1871–1925) article "Old Salem Ships and Sailors" in the *Outing Magazine* (January 1908) reached beyond Rothery's provincial study, arguing that "the story of the struggles and heroisms of the Western pioneers has been told over and over again" but "the work of the seafaring breed of Americans toward the building of a great nation has been somewhat suffered to remain in the background." Paine viewed the Society's collection of logbooks and ethnological objects—"which can so vividly recall a vanished era and make it live again"—as the key to recovering this past, "[f]or those heroic seafarers not only made history but they wrote it while they lived it."[75]

Twentieth-century artists were also inspired by the East India Marine Society's collection. Like their nineteenth-century counterparts, they came first and foremost as visitors. The modernist painter Marsden Hartley (1877–1943), a New England native who often painted seascapes, frequently visited the museum, calling it his "second most beloved . . . in our country."[76] Hartley claimed to know "every ship model—every painting of ships—every coil of rope—every [illegible] box in that invaluable display," and felt a "sense of personal ownership" in showing the museum to others. His visits to the museum likely inspired several of his later works.[77] In the summers of 1943 and 1944, the abstract expressionist painter Barnett Newman (1905–70) and his wife Annalee visited the Peabody Museum of Salem while vacationing in East Gloucester.[78] The East India Marine Society's collection particularly struck Newman. In a letter to his friends Adolph and Esther Gottlieb, Newman encouraged them to visit the museum, specifically writing about objects donated to the Society in "the NW Coast case," such as some "fine slate pipes and a good Chilkat blanket." Newman believed that "the Salem Museum may not have as extensive a collection as the Smithsonian but is considered to have choicer things."[79]

In the 1940s, after expanding and restoring other portions of the museum, the Peabody Museum of Salem turned its attention again to East India Marine Hall. Recognizing that the East India Marine Society had created the defining character of their museum, staff members believed that the hall's 1867 zoologically themed organization was incongruous with the museum's current emphasis on maritime history and international exchange via the sea.[80] The cases and galleries constructed in 1867 were demolished; the ceiling cove, which had been destroyed when the gallery was refitted by the Peabody Academy of Science, was remolded; and the stairway was reconstructed. Benjamin Carpenter's crystal chandeliers were rehung, some original cases were reinstalled, as were the figures of East Indian merchants, and new objects such as ships' figureheads were added to the maritime ensemble. The hall was rededicated on November 4, 1943, and from this point on it was used in a manner akin to its roots—as a museum gallery, a venue for public programs, and a function hall.

Outside of Salem, though, the Society's impact on the field of museology went unnoticed or was misconstrued. In 1943, Robert Maynard Hutchins (1899–1977), then president of the University of Chicago, delivered an address marking the fiftieth anniversary of the Field Museum in Chicago. Speaking of the state of museums as educational institutions, he argued that "the purpose of the second museum established in this country, that of the East India Marine Society at Salem, illustrates the problem that all museums are still trying to solve." Hutchins classified it as "simply a co-operative curio cabinet," and while this type of museum is "interesting and amusing, and sometimes produce[s] . . . sensational results," he alleged it is "usually ephemeral and often false—my sea-captain grandfather told me most atrocious lies—and such material, whether it is words or objects, should hardly be central in education." Hutchins concluded, "Whatever educational value it once had has now almost wholly disappeared, and its presentation is no longer the special function of a museum," as newspapers, magazines, movies, and department stores have taken on the role of "gratifying the public appetite for the odd, the quaint and the amazing."[81]

Yet contrary to Hutchins's claims that the East India Marine Society Museum was simply a collection of oddities to entertain the masses, the Peabody Museum of Salem continued to expand the Society's collection and build upon the work of Robinson, Morse, and others throughout the twentieth century. In addition to Robinson's maritime post, curatorial departments were formed around the strengths of the collection, including Oceanic art, Chinese art, Japanese art, Native American Art, and South Asian and Indian art. The 1984 merger of the Peabody Museum of Salem and the China Trade Museum in Milton, Massachusetts, and the subsequent merger of the Peabody Museum and the Essex Institute in 1992, brought additional departments and collections into the fold, many of which resonated with Salem's and America's mercantile past. Today, the museum interprets the transnational collection started by the Society in a modern global context using an art and culture paradigm.

In the twenty-first century, the PEM's holdings of the East India Marine Society, and East India Marine Hall itself, inspire a new generation of museumgoers and artists. The museum established a contemporary art program in 2008, and the first initiative under this new course, *FreePort*, sought to explore the ways in which "trade, exchange and translation drive cultural change" through the work of living artists.[82] When two of the first three artists chosen to collaborate in the project visited the museum for the first time, they immediately gravitated to East India Marine Hall.

In 2010, Charles Sandison (born 1969), a Scottish-born artist residing in Finland, created an immersive experience in the hall. Sandison is known for his animated digital text projections in and on dramatic architectural settings such as the Grand Palais in Paris. In the projection he created in

Salem, *Figurehead*, he animated handwritten words scanned directly from Society members' journals and logbooks. This display was intended, he said, to "make visible the trade routes, the politics, the competition, the emotions that led to the founding of the museum and the origins of PEM's remarkable collection." He also commented, "Instead of sea water, the words from the captains' log books will represent liquid. Thus the words of the mariners themselves become the ocean of light in which the viewer swims." Sandison reflected, "When I stood for hours in that hall I saw all of this. We all see this. It is always there. My aim is not to add something to the hall but to reveal what is already there."[83]

A year later, Turner Prize–winning artist Susan Philipsz (born 1965) created *If I With You Would Go* in East India Marine Hall. Philipsz, also Scottish-born but living in Berlin, creates sound installations of "her disembodied voice—in settings where you least expect to have such an intimate experience."[84] Eight speakers placed around the hall played her singing eight different versions of the Scottish ballad "The Daemon Lover." Like the conscious and silent narratives created by the Society, her piece "responds to both the tangible maritime history, as well as what is not displayed—the stories of longing and loss, the paradox of the sea as provider of opportunity and taker of life." For both of these transnational artists, the historical origins of the museum resonated with their contemporary creative milieu.[85]

In late 1899, a luncheon was held at the Peabody Academy of Science to celebrate the centennial of the East India Marine Society, "lunching, chatting and spinning yarns of the ancient mariners who started the museum."[86] During the afternoon participants were able to view the first objects donated to the Society, which "were given a place of honor before the company."[87] John Robinson gave a short talk on this collection, particularly noting the double-ended pipe donated by Carnes. The *Salem News* reported that it "had not been smoked for a century," and "Prof. Morse filled it with tobacco and each of the smokers present took a whiff at it." Another of Carnes's donations, the cup made out of rhinoceros horn, "which had not been used for an equal time was filled with 'West Peabody Cider' and the president of the trustees, G. A. Peabody, drank to the health of the institution in a veritable drinking horn."[88]

Modern-day museum staff would be horrified at the idea of using the collections in such a manner. On this occasion, however, it was a fitting means to celebrate an important moment in the museum's history, adding to the lore and symbolism of these founding objects. With the East India Marine Society nearing its end and Salem's overseas trade all but defunct, the pipe and the cup bound the guests to the past. For twenty-first-century visitors to the PEM, these objects illuminate the interconnected global world that existed in the nineteenth century, and the place of Americans—culturally, intellectually, and politically—within it.

NOTES

Introduction: "A Cabinet, that every mariner may possess the history of the world"

1. Caroline Howard King, *When I Lived in Salem, 1822–1866* (Brattleboro, VT: Stephen Daye Press, 1937), 29–30.
2. Upon his arrival, Cornè had a profound impact on the marine painters of the newly formed United States, and painted gouache scenes of local ships, historical and allegorical images in oils, and portraits based on engravings. He also taught his craft to other aspiring artists. See Daniel Finamore, "'To Paint a Storm': Perception and Meaning in Marine Painting," in *Romance of the Sea: An Exhibition of Marine Painting from Members' Collections* (Boston: St. Botolph Club, 2002), 2.
3. Local artist Samuel Bartoll painted these words on the banner. See bills and receipts, box 9, folders 1 and 5, East India Marine Society Records, MH 88, Phillips Library, Peabody Essex Museum, Salem, MA. Prior to the construction of East India Marine Hall, the Society rented quarters in two other buildings on Essex Street.
4. "Museum at Salem," *Juvenile Rambler, or, Family and School Journal*, November 13, 1833, 182. This was apparently not the first article the *Rambler* published on the museum, as the author noted, "You once gave us an account of the Museum at Salem."
5. "East-India Marine Hall, Salem," reprinted in the *Sailor's Magazine, and Naval Journal,* December 1, 1830, 109.
6. Herman Melville, *Moby-Dick; or, The Whale* (New York: Harper, 1851), 11–13.
7. John Cowe, staff writer for the *Salem Evening News*, noted that some people think John Quincy Adams became the prime mover in establishing the Smithsonian Institution when he was in Congress due to his multiple visits to the East India Marine Society Museum. Cowe also humorously imagined the Society as "crusty old merchants meeting in their club room-museum Hrumph, hrumphing and hrumping their way about from one deep leather chair to the next, grumbling about the weather and the decline of trade revenues" ("Museum Helpful in Wartime," *Salem Evening News*, August 20, 1969).
8. "Art. VI.—THE SALEM EAST INDIA MARINE SOCIETY," *Merchants' Magazine and Commercial Review* 9, no. 3 (September 1843): 268.
9. Steven Conn, *Do Museums Still Need Objects?* (Philadelphia: University of Pennsylvania Press, 2011), 127.
10. This vast archive of twenty-nine boxes and thirteen volumes—consisting of correspondence, financial documents, guest books, scrapbooks, catalogues, and ships' journals from the founding of the Society in 1799 to 1972—is preserved at the PEM's Phillips

Library (East India Marine Society Records, MH 88). Almost a third of the objects the Society acquired in the nineteenth century survive. As a curator at the PEM, I came into the project speaking the language of the East India Marine Society collection. The Society accessioned objects in a variety of ways (outlined in chap. 4), producing disparate internal and external catalogues that were very familiar to me. A systematic merging of information has been done for the entire collection for the first time.

11. Quote from "Salem East India Marine Society," *Essex Register*, October 13, 1825. This book is the most comprehensive study of the Society and its museum to date. It is the first volume on the subject since Walter Muir Whitehill's *The East India Marine Society and the Peabody Museum of Salem: A Sesquicentennial History* (Salem: Peabody Museum, 1949), published to commemorate the 150th anniversary of the museum, and builds on the following works by Peabody Essex Museum staff produced since the mid-twentieth century: Mary Malloy, "Sailors' Souvenirs at the East India Marine Hall: 'Gathered, With Cost and Pains, From Every Clime,'" *Log of Mystic Seaport* 37, no. 3 (1985): 93–103; Daniel Finamore, "Displaying the Sea and Defining America," *Journal of Maritime Research* 4, no. 1 (2002): 40–51; Susan Bean, *Yankee India: American Commercial and Cultural Encounters with India in the Age of Sail, 1784–1860* (Salem: Peabody Essex Museum/Mapin Publishing Company, 2001); and John R. Grimes, "Curiosity, Cabinets, and Knowledge: A Perspective on the Native American Collection of the Peabody Essex Museum," in *Uncommon Legacies: Native American Art from the Peabody Essex Museum*, ed. John R. Grimes, Christian Feest, and Mary Lou Curran (New York: American Federation of Arts/University of Washington Press, 2002), 1–11. Other essays on the museum that inform this book are James M. Lindgren, "'That Every Mariner May Possess the History of the World': A Cabinet for the East India Marine Society of Salem," *New England Quarterly* 68 (June 1995): 179–205; and Patricia Johnston, "Global Knowledge in the Early Republic: The East India Marine Society's 'Curiosities' Museum," in *East-West Interchanges in American Art: "A Long and Tumultuous Relationship"* (Washington, D.C.: Smithsonian Institution Scholarly Press, 2012), 69–79.
12. National Parks Service, *The Salem Project: Study of Alternatives* (Denver: U.S. Department of the Interior, 1990), 127.
13. Ibid.
14. Daniel Vickers, *Farmers and Fishermen: Two Centuries of Work in Essex County, Massachusetts, 1630–1850* (Chapel Hill: University of North Carolina Press, 1994), 283.
15. Sidney Perley, "Commercial History of Salem," *Essex Antiquarian* 1, no. 1 (1897): 4.
16. Daniel Vickers, with Vince Walsh, *Young Men and the Sea: Yankee Seafarers in the Age of Sail* (New Haven, CT: Yale University Press, 2005), 250, 177.
17. Ibid., 249.
18. East India Marine Society, *The East-India Marine Society of Salem* (Salem: Palfray, 1821), 4.
19. George Schwartz, "'Collecting and Arranging . . . A History of The Globe': A Reconsideration of the Salem East India Marine Society and Antebellum American Museology," Ph.D. diss., Boston University, 2015.
20. "The Salem East India Marine Society," *Salem Gazette*, November 9, 1841.
21. Peabody Essex Museum general archives, Phillips Library.
22. This study is informed by the methodologies of the anthropologists Clifford Geertz, Arjun Appadurai, and Igor Kopytoff.

Chapter One: Origins

1. George Granville Putnam, *Salem Vessels and Their Voyages: A History of the Pepper Trade with the Island of Sumatra* (Salem, MA: Essex Institute, 1922), 1:7–11; John Frayler,

"Pepper and Providence," in *Pickled Fish and Salted Provisions: Historical Musings from Salem Maritime NHS* 7 (July 2005): 2–3.

2. Arlo Bates, "Introduction," in *Old Salem*, by Eleanor Putnam [pseud. of Harriet Leonora Vose Bates], ed. Arlo Bates (Boston: Houghton Mifflin, 1886), 14.
3. Daniel Finamore, "Displaying the Sea and Defining America," *Journal of Maritime Research* 4, no. 1 (2002): 40.
4. National Parks Service, *The Salem Project: Study of Alternatives* (Denver: U.S. Department of the Interior, 1990), 135. Salem's merchant ships also included smaller brigs that carried less crew and tonnage than the East Indiamen did. Almost 5,000 of the more than 75,000 sailors who sailed on Salem ships between 1799 and 1879 were listed as having a colored, black, or brown complexion, and some were born overseas. See "Salem Crew Lists, 1799–1879," http://research.mysticseaport.org.
5. Herbert P. Adams, "Origin of Salem Plantation," in "Village Communities of Cape Anne and Salem, from the Historical Collections of the Essex Institute," *Johns Hopkins University Studies in Historical and Political Science* 9–10 (July–August 1883): 26.
6. National Parks Service, *The Salem Project*, 132.
7. Margaret Pardee Bates, ed., "Some Letters of Mary Boardman Crowninshield," *Essex Institute Historical Collections* 83 (1947), http://landmark.salemstate.edu.
8. Phyllis Whitman Hunter, *Purchasing Identity in the Atlantic World: Massachusetts Merchants, 1670–1780* (Ithaca, NY: Cornell University Press, 2001), 173.
9. Dan Finamore, "Object 001," connected.pem.org. A painted ring containing the number "194" is obscured by the tobacco stains on the bowl. This number was put on the pipe in 1821 when the collection was renumbered. To date, no Indonesian scholar has ever seen such a curious-looking smoking device.
10. Robert Booth, "Salem as Enterprise Zone, 1783–1786," in *Salem: Place, Myth, and Memory*, ed. Dane Morrison and Nancy Lusignan Schultz (Boston: Northeastern University Press, 2004), 63, 76. The American Enlightenment was a period of intellectual, social, and political awakening in the mid-eighteenth and early nineteenth centuries, inspired primarily by philosophers and scientists in England and France.
11. On the origins and evolution of cabinets of curiosity, see Arthur MacGregor, *Curiosity and Enlightenment: Collectors and Collections from the Sixteenth to the Nineteenth Century* (New Haven, CT: Yale University Press, 2007); Oliver Impey and Arthur MacGregor, *The Origins of Museums: The Cabinet of Curiosities in Sixteenth- and Seventeenth-Century Europe* (London: British Museum, 2000); Paula Findlen, *Possessing Nature: Museums, Collecting, and Scientific Culture in Early Modern Italy* (Berkeley: University of California Press, 1994); and Krzysztof Pomian, *Collectors and Curiosities: Paris and Venice, 1500–1800* (Cambridge, MA: Blackwell, 1990). These cabinets had evolved from European *studioli* (private studies) formed during the Italian Renaissance.
12. Carol Duncan and Alan Wallach, "The Universal Survey Museum," *Art History* 3, no. 4 (1980): 451.
13. On the founding of the Louvre, see Andrew McClellan, *Inventing the Louvre: Art, Politics, and the Origins of the Modern Museum in Eighteenth-Century Paris* (Berkeley: University of California Press, 1994).
14. Anne Goldgar, "The British Museum and the 'Virtual Representation' of Culture," *Albion* 32, no. 2 (2000): 195–231.
15. Joel J. Orosz, *Curators and Culture: The Museum Movement in America, 1740–1870* (Tuscaloosa: University of Alabama Press, 1990), 11–25, 14.
16. Joyce Henri Robinson, "An American Cabinet of Curiosities: Thomas Jefferson's 'Indian Hall at Monticello,'" *Winterthur Portfolio* 30, no. 1 (1995): 45.
17. Mary Malloy, "Sailors' Souvenirs at the East India Marine Hall: 'Gathered, With Cost and Pains, From Every Clime,'" *Log of Mystic Seaport* 37, no. 3 (1985): 94–95.

18. Mary Malloy, *Souvenirs of the Fur Trade: Northwest Coast Indian Art and Artifacts Collected by American Mariners, 1788–1844* (Cambridge, MA: Harvard University, Peabody Museum of Archaeology and Ethnology, 2000), 31–32.
19. See Hina Hirayama, *"With Éclat": The Boston Athenaeum and the Origin of the Museum of Fine Arts, Boston* (Boston: Boston Athenaeum, 2013).
20. For the most comprehensive examination of Peale's American Museum, see Charles Coleman Sellers, *Mr. Peale's Museum: Charles Willson Peale and the First Popular Museum of Natural Science and Art* (New York: Norton, 1980).
21. Finamore, "Displaying the Sea and Defining America," 42.
22. On Barnum, see Neil Harris, *Humbug: The Art of P. T. Barnum* (Chicago: University of Chicago Press, 1973); and James W. Cook, *The Arts of Deception: Playing with Fraud in the Age of Barnum* (Cambridge, MA: Harvard University Press, 2001).
23. Edward Peron Hingston, *The Genial Showman. Being Reminiscences of the Life of Artemus Ward, a New Edition* (London: Chatto and Windus, 1881), 18.
24. Lawrence Levine, *Highbrow/Lowbrow: The Emergence of Cultural Hierarchy in America* (Cambridge, MA: Harvard University Press, 1988).
25. Daniel Bowen, "Columbian Museum, at the head of the Mall, Boston" (Boston: Daniel Bowen, 1798). Also see Peter Benes, "'A few monstrous Snakes': Daniel Bowen and the Columbian Museum, 1789–1816," in *The Dublin Seminar for New England Folklife Annual*, ed. Peter Benes (Boston: Boston University, 2004), 22–39.
26. "The Great Bygone Museum Tour," https://blog.mcny.org; "New American Museum," *Columbian,* March 23, 1810, 3; "American Museum," *Columbian,* November 3, 1810. Scudder's Museum was founded in 1791 as the American Museum of Tammany Hall.
27. Quoted in *Georgian*, August 14, 1830.
28. Dennis Andrew Carr, "Optical Machines, Prints and Gentility in Early America," M.A. thesis, University of Delaware, 1999, viii.
29. Charles W. Upham, "Memoir of Rev. John Prince, L.L.D.," in *Collections of the Massachusetts Historical Society* (Boston: Eastburn, 1836), 5:278–79.
30. William Bentley, *The Diary of William Bentley, D.D.*, vol. 2, *1793–1802* (Salem, MA: Essex Institute, 1907), 322. Bentley created a library that was one of the largest in America at the time of his death, with upward of 4,000 volumes.
31. Thomas Knoles, "William Bentley's Cabinet," unpublished inventory, American Antiquarian Society. A few of the earliest objects Bentley obtained in the 1780s and 1790s are listed in brief entries entitled "Collection. Nat. Hist." and "Curiosities." Bentley lived in rented rooms in the house of Benjamin Crowninshield, which survives today as the Crowninshield-Bentley House of the Peabody Essex Museum.
32. Photostats of Bentley papers at American Antiquarian Society, box 1, folder 24, William Bentley Papers, MH 36, Phillips Library, Peabody Essex Museum, Salem, MA (hereafter PLPEM). Bentley bequeathed the majority of his collection to the American Antiquarian Society, established in Worcester, Massachusetts, in 1812. Despite this large donation, Isaiah Thomas (1749–1831), founder of the society, bemoaned the fact that Bentley's cabinet was "not so extensive" as he had hoped and incorrectly believed he "had given a great part of it to the Salem Museum [East India Marine Society Museum] some time before his death" (Isaiah Thomas, letter to Timothy Alden, May 8, 1820, quoted in Thomas Knoles, "'An Equal Taste for Antiquities': Reverend William Bentley and the American Antiquarian Society," in *The Dublin Seminar for New England Folklife Annual Proceedings* [2004], 20). Bentley's will clearly states that he gave his "Cabinet with all it contains to the American Antiquarian Society, & all my paintings and engravings," and no Salem institution is mentioned in this document (copy of the will of William Bentley, May 8, 1819, box 1, folder 17, William Bentley Papers, MH 36). While Bentley used his relationship with Society members to grow his collection, he only occasionally returned the favor. He

donated only nine objects to the Society: two Chinese porcelain figurines and floral or faunal specimens.

33. Bentley, *The Diary of William Bentley*, 2:316. Gibaut was not one of the East India Marine Society's influential members. He did not serve in any executive capacities in the organization or on any committees. In addition, Gibaut did not donate any objects to the Society's collection, even though he had given material to Bentley for his personal cabinet.

34. Ibid., 2:321. Since Bentley penned these words, nineteenth-century and modern scholars have interpreted them as evidence that he played an instrumental role in the founding of the East India Marine Society and the construction of its bylaws or have credited him as the founder of the Society. Compounding this misinterpretation is a mythology surrounding Bentley's role in the formation of the Society, which began shortly after his death. His name does not appear anywhere in the Society's drafts of its articles and bylaws or in its minutes. For a more in-depth analysis see George Schwartz, "'Collecting and Arranging . . . A History of The Globe': A Reconsideration of the Salem East India Marine Society and Antebellum American Museology," Ph.D. diss., Boston University, 2015, 47–57.

35. Nathaniel Silsbee, Jr., letter to Benjamin H. Silsbee, December 19, 1867, scrapbooks, box 28 (OS), vol. E, East India Marine Society Records, MH 88, PLPEM. Silsbee served as both a U.S. representative and a U.S. senator.

36. "The 'East India Marine Society,'" *Salem Observer*, February 20, 1892. Peabody Academy of Science scrapbook 4, 1890–1903, PLPEM. The bylaws of the first American marine society, the Boston Marine Society (founded as the Fellowship Club in 1742), were the template for all subsequent marine societies in the country. During the centennial celebration of the Boston Marine Society, a toast from the East India Marine Society's president Charles M. Endicott—who could not attend the commemorative event—was read aloud: "*The Boston Marine Society*—The great progenitor of all similar societies throughout the Union—may the prosperity of its members be as universal as their enterprise and liberality are unbounded" (*Gleanings from the Records of the Boston Marine Society, Through Its First Century, 1742–1842. Compiled by Nath'l Spooner* [Boston: Boston Marine Society, 1879], 172).

37. *Charter of the Marine Society of the Town of Newport in the State of Rhode-Island* (Newport, RI: Mercury Office, 1806), 11. The Providence Marine Society and the Portland Marine Society also allowed for this exception.

38. John Fenno (1751–98), the founder of the pro-Federalist newspaper *Gazette of the United States*, proposed an American marine society similar to these European models. His *Plan for Establishing a General Marine Society Throughout the United States, and Systems of Regulations Therein* (1798) envisioned an organization that would give sailors "protection and secure their safety"; "provide and bind out, receive and recommend proper boys as apprentices to vessels of the United States"; and "provide for the health, protection, and regularity of the seamen of the United States." His concept never reached fruition due to its complex funding system (Gautham Rao, "The Creation of the American State: Customhouses, Law, and Commerce in the Age of Revolution," Ph.D. diss., University of Chicago, 2008, 235–38).

39. *Rules and Bye-Laws of the Baltimore Charitable Marine Society* (Baltimore: Pechin, 1798), 7.

40. Historical currency conversion is based on information at http://futureboy.homeip.net. Votes were cast in a mahogany voting box purchased from William Gavet in 1802.

41. East India Marine Society, *By-Laws and Regulations of the Salem East-India Marine Society* (Salem, MA: Cushing, 1800), 7.

42. Stephen Wheatland, "Appendix H: The Salem East India Marine Society: A Report of Its Funds and How They Were Acquired," in *The East India Marine Society and*

the Peabody Museum of Salem: A Sesquicentennial History, by Walter Muir Whitehill (Salem, MA: Peabody Museum, 1949), 190.

43. Vol. A., minutes/records, 1799–1824, East India Marine Society Records, MH 88.
44. Vol. B., minutes/records, 1824–1852, East India Marine Society Records, MH 88.
45. Salem Marine Society, *Laws of the Salem Marine Society, with the Several Acts of General Court Relating to the Society, &c., and a List of Members* (Salem, MA: Observer Steam Book and Job Printing, 1873), 5.
46. In 1918, membership was opened to the grandsons of members and then extended to great-grandsons in the 1930s and great-granddaughters in the 1990s. The first female member, Joan Vaughan Ingraham, became the first female master (president) of the Salem Marine Society in 2015. Today, the Salem Marine Society has a robust membership and is an active charitable organization promoting and maintaining Salem's maritime legacy. On the history of the Salem Marine Society, see *A History of the Marine Society at Salem, Established 1766, Incorporated 1772. Together with the Laws of the Society, the Acts of Incorporation, Portraits of Members, 1766–2016, and a List of Members, 1766–2016* (Salem, MA: Marine Society at Salem, 2016).
47. List of subscribers agreeing to formation of East India Marine Society, August 31, 1799, founding documents and meeting minutes, box 1, folder 1, East India Marine Society Records, MH 88. Many local residents did not realize that the two organizations were distinct entities. An article in the January 19, 1846, *Salem Register* suggested that most people were unaware of the Salem Marine Society and its charitable endeavors as they were performed "so quietly and unobtrusively. . . . For generous impulses, the sailor's genuine modesty restrains them from giving publicity to their good deeds." Locals were more familiar with the East India Marine Society, "which formed and owns the noble Museum that has acquired so wide a renown." Despite this confusion, the Salem Marine Society held no animus toward its fellow organization, and the two societies worked together in 1807, 1815, and 1816 to improve buoys and piers in Salem Harbor (among other occasions of collaboration in the nineteenth and twentieth centuries). In 1814, they were designated by the Commonwealth of Massachusetts as the principal organizations to consult when hiring Salem's pilot (the local mariner who helps incoming ships sail through local waters). See *The Public and General Laws of the Commonwealth of Massachusetts, from February 28, 1807, to February 16, 1816* (Boston, 1816), 4:395–96.
48. Whitehill, *The East India Marine Society and the Peabody Museum of Salem*, 4. On Lambert, see Edwin B. Hewes, "Jonathan Lambert, of Salem, King of Tristan D. Acunha," *Essex Institute Historical Collections* 71, no. 1 (1935): 1–6.
49. Whitehill, *The East India Marine Society and the Peabody Museum of Salem*, 3. President Monroe visited the Society during his stay in Salem.
50. At times, the Salem Marine Society did poke fun at the more public face of the East India Marine Society. During the Salem Marine Society's centennial celebration, then master Nathaniel Brown, a member of both societies, remarked that the Salem Marine Society was not known for "ostentatious displays and parades" like its "younger brother" ("Centennial of the Salem Marine Society," *Salem Register*, June 12, 1871).
51. East India Marine Society, *By-Laws and Regulations of the Salem East-India Marine Society*, 12.
52. The palanquin was donated by captains Edward West, Moses Townsend, Benjamin Lander, Josiah Orne, and William Mugford (series I, B, correspondence, reports, information relating to EIMS objects, box 3, folder 1, East India Marine Society, MH 88).
53. *Salem Register*, January 6, 1803.
54. *New-York Herald*, November 26, 1806.

55. Christine L. Garlough, *Desi Divas: Political Activism in South Asian American Cultural Performances* (Jackson: University Press of Mississippi, 2013), 56. Garlough's analysis is part of her ethnographic study of contemporary South Asian American women who use cultural performances as a means of public discourse.
56. See Anirudra Thapa, "The Indic Orient, Nation, and Transnationalism: Exploring the Imperial Outposts of Nineteenth-Century U.S. Literary Culture, 1840–1900," Ph.D. diss., Texas Christian University, 2008, 30.
57. *Salem Gazette*, November 8, 1805.
58. *Salem Gazette*, November 6, 1807.
59. Bentley, *The Diary of William Bentley*, 2:361.
60. Alternatively, Bentley's comments might stem from bitterness surrounding the mechanics of the China trade, where Canton officials sequestered western merchants to a complex on the Pearl River known as the Foreign Factories, or to the fact that his turn to dine with the Society did not come until 1804. The Society voted in 1799 that "one of the clargemen [*sic*] of the town be invited by the President to dine with the Society when ever they dine together (and that they are to be invited agreable [*sic*] to age)." See Finamore, "Displaying the Sea and Defining America," 44; and Whitehill, *The East India Marine Society and the Peabody Museum of Salem*, 17.
61. "White's Voyage to the China Sea," *Essex Register*, June 30, 1823. This was originally published in the *New England Galaxy*.
62. Silas Pinckney Holbrook, *Sketches, By a Traveler* (Boston: Carter and Hendee, 1830). This was originally published in the *New England Galaxy* and *Boston Courier*.
63. They were paid $6.25 for their services (bills and receipts, box 9, folder 2, East India Marine Society Records, MH 88).
64. In 1855, the Society's president, Charles M. Endicott, remarked that "the citizens of Salem were annually gratified with the novel and interesting spectacle of its procession through their streets," but by midcentury, "the spectacle" was incongruous to a period he characterized as a "utilitarian age" and had become "among the dull things of memory" (Charles M. Endicott, "East India Marine Society, Salem," *Monthly Nautical Magazine and Quarterly Review* 2, no. 1 [1855]: 63).
65. John Robinson, *Visitor's Guide to Salem* (Salem, MA: Essex Institute, 1895), 88.
66. See George Schwartz, "'The Chief Spirit . . . Our Venerable Fellow Citizen': The Life of John Remond in Antebellum Salem, Massachusetts," in *The Dublin Seminar for New England Folklife Annual Proceedings*, ed. Peter Benes (Boston: Boston University, 2012), 118–29. Remond also catered the dinner marking the two hundredth anniversary of the first settlement of Salem and a public dinner on Thursday, September 3, 1829, in honor of Judge Joseph Story.
67. Sharron Wilkins Conrad, "Nineteenth-Century Philadelphia Caterer Thomas J. Dorsey," *American Visions* 15, no. 4 (2000): 36.
68. Early in 1835, Society members voted "that all wines, liquors, etc usually provided for the use of the Society at their meetings be from this time discontinued." This attempt to curb excessive drinking at bimonthly meetings did not last long. In May, the prohibitionary vote was rescinded and the dinners were "placed on the same footing as before" (Whitehill, *The East India Marine Society and the Peabody Museum of Salem*, 29).
69. Augustus P. Loring, Jr., "Mr. Joseph Peabody of Salem, Massachusetts, and His Punch," *American Neptune* 2, no. 1 (1942): 42. Loring was a trustee of the Peabody Museum of Salem and a descendent of Joseph Peabody. The punch is more closely associated with the Salem Marine Society.
70. Starting in the late eighteenth century, potters in European and Asian ports produced specialized ceramics for American sailors, an emerging and distinctive clientele. Some of these bowls, pitchers, plates, and mugs contained symbols and scenes confirming

national pride in the newly formed United States. The distinctive cream-colored vessels from Liverpool, an important center for trade in the Atlantic world, documented a mariner's engagement in this trade network. A ship portrait would be emblazoned on one side of a pitcher or bowl and the other side adorned with transfer prints with patriotic, romantic, or Masonic motifs.

71. The other two transfers are a scene of the 1799 engagement between the U.S.S. *Constellation* and the French frigate *L'Insurgente* (the first American naval victory over a foreign nation) and *Washington Securing Liberty to America,* depicting George Washington and Liberty looking toward a map of the United States from the Atlantic coast to the Mississippi River.
72. The toasts come from the following sources: *Salem Register*, November 12, 1804, also transcribed by William Bentley in his diary entry on November 10; *Salem Register*, November 6, 1806; *Essex Register*, November 9, 1807; toasts 1808–15, East India Marine Society Records, MH 88; and Whitehill, *The East India Marine Society and the Peabody Museum of Salem*, 26. For a complete list of the toasts given at all Society dinners, see Schwartz, "Collecting and Arranging," 542–55. Bentley's diary suggests that toasts were chosen in advance of the dinner, noting that before the 1802 dinner "A Committee for the Toasts were chosen, and the Toasts selected" (2:408).
73. The *Salem Register* reported, "When this toast was drank, a salute of 16 guns was fired from a full rigged ship in the museum." The model used was likely one of the *Friendship* (see chap. 2). The *Register* quotation was republished in the *Columbian Centinel*, November 8, 1806.
74. Other objects related to Washington in the museum's collection were a small bust donated in 1820 and Chief Justice John Marshall's (1755–1835) five-volume biography *Life of Washington*, published in 1804.
75. Several toasts from this dinner were published in the *Bombay Courier*, May 16, 1807: "The Toasts given at a late meeting of a New England Marine Society, while they show the rise of a great body of their people, are fostidiously [*sic*] technical, that the reader will probably be ammused [*sic*] in glancing at the specimens which we select from an account of the proceedings of the Meeting."
76. This toast to Cook also had a literal connection to other objects in the collection: five pieces of the rock in Kealakekua Bay, Hawai'i, where he was killed in 1779.
77. Corné worked from the frontispiece print to George William Anderson's 1784 volume *A New, Authentic, and Complete Collection of Voyages Round the World Undertaken and Performed by Royal Authority*, donated by Jacob Crowninshield to the Society in 1801.
78. Bentley was not overly impressed with Corné's painting, noting that it spoke to "the infancy of the Arts" (William Bentley, *The Diary of William Bentley, D.D.*, vol. 3, *1803–1810* [Salem, MA: Essex Institute, 1911], 481).
79. "An Act to Incorporate Benjamin Hodges and Others into a Society by the Name of the Salem East India Marine Society," in East India Marine Society, *Bye-Laws and Regulations of the Salem East-India Marine Society*, (Salem, MA: Pool and Palfray, 1808), 3.
80. Dirk Jan Struik, *Yankee Science in the Making* (Boston: Little, Brown, 1948), 108.
81. East India Marine Society, *The East-India Marine Society of Salem* (Salem, MA: Palfray, 1821), 3.
82. A. Hunter Dupree, *Science in the Federal Government: A History of Policies and Activities*, 2nd ed. (Baltimore: Johns Hopkins University Press, 1986), 8.
83. This library contained the collection of the Irish chemist Richard Kirwan (1733–1812), which was part of the cargo captured by the Salem privateer *Pilgrim* in the Irish Sea in 1791.
84. Mildred Berman, "Salem's Stellar Scientist: Nathaniel Bowditch—An Appreciation," *Sextant* 7 (1996): 12.
85. Log 935, ship *Tartar*, PLPEM.

86. Vol. B., minutes/records 1824–52, East India Marine Society Records, MH 88. Bowditch served as Society president from 1820 to 1823. He was also a member of the Salem Marine Society. Bowditch excelled in other ventures outside of the scientific community. He was the first insurance actuary in the United States, acting as president of the Essex Fire and Marine Insurance Company, and then became a money manager for wealthy individuals who made their fortunes at sea. Indicative of Salem's changing mercantile climate, Bowditch redirected their wealth from maritime investment to manufacturing investment, creating the mills that built up Lowell, Massachusetts. For an in-depth look at this portion of Bowditch's career, see Tamara Plakins Thornton, *Nathaniel Bowditch and the Power of Numbers* (Chapel Hill: University of North Carolina Press, 2016).
87. Nathaniel Ingersoll Bowditch, "Memoir of Nathaniel Bowditch," in *Mécanique Celeste by the Marquis De La Place*, trans. and with commentary by Nathaniel Bowditch (Boston: Little, Brown, 1839), 4:72.
88. "Art. VI.—The Salem East India Marine Society," *Merchants' Magazine and Commercial Review* 9 (September 1843): 268.
89. Thomas Jefferson and James Madison, letters to the East India Marine Society, box 3, folder 11, East India Marine Society Records, MH 88. Both letters were written at Monticello. Madison also believed that the Society was constructed in such a manner that "will so readily extend itself to the acquisition from countries visited by the Salem Mariners of such new articles belonging to the vegetable and animal domain."
90. Published in the *Portsmouth Journal of Literature and Politics,* April 17, 1824, which notes: "SALEM—The following richly measured tribute of praise to the *first town* in Massachusetts, we copy with pleasure from the *United States* (Philad.) *Gazette.*"
91. Dupree, *Science in the Federal Government*, 39.
92. Ibid.
93. Nathaniel Philbrick, *Sea of Glory: America's Voyage of Discovery, the U.S. Exploring Expedition, 1838–1842* (New York: Viking Penguin, 2003), 18, 20.
94. "Exploring Voyages," reprinted in the *Charleston Courier*, May 9, 1829.
95. Philbrick, *Sea of Glory*, 20.
96. Ibid., 55, 30. Philbrick notes that Reynolds's writings advocating Symmes's theory and an expedition to the Antarctic and the South Pacific appear to have influenced Edgar Allan Poe's *The Narrative of Arthur Gordon Pym of Nantucket* (1838), and his 1839 account "Mocha Dick: Or the White Whale of the Pacific" was part of the inspiration for Herman Melville's *Moby-Dick* (1851).
97. Dupree, *Science in the Federal Government*, 56.
98. Jeremiah N. Reynolds, *Voyage of the United States Frigate Potomac: Under the Command of Commodore John Downes, During the Circumnavigation of the Globe, in the Years 1831, 1832, 1833, and 1834; Including a Particular Account of the Engagement at Quallah-Battoo, on the Coast of Sumatra; with All the Official Documents Relating to the Same* (New York: Harper, 1835), 215. Some scholars characterize this volume as jingoistic.
99. Dupree, *Science in the Federal Government*, 56–57.
100. "Expedition to the Pacific Ocean," *Salem Gazette*, December 2, 1834.
101. Dupree, *Science in the Federal Government*, 64–65.
102. East India Marine Society, "Memorial of the East India Marine Society of Salem, Mass.; Praying That an Expedition be Fitted Out by the Government to Make a Voyage of Discovery and Survey to the South Seas," congressional documents, 2.272, 23rd Congress, 2nd sess. House documents, 75 (Washington, DC: Gales and Seaton, 1834).
103. Vol. B., minutes/records 1824–52, East India Marine Society Records, MH 88. The committee's report was read and approved on January 4, 1837.
104. Charles Wilkes, *Narrative of the United States Exploring Expedition during the years 1838, 1839, 1840, 1841, 1842* (Philadelphia, 1845), 1:xxx.

105. Ernest Stanley Dodge, "The Contributions to Exploration of the Salem East India Marine Society," *American Neptune* 25, no. 3 (1965): 187. Vanderford died during the voyage on March 23, 1842, and Wilkes wrote a tribute to him in his *Narrative*.
106. "The Salem East India Marine Society," *Salem Gazette,* November 9, 1841. The Society was still considered a resource for scientific investigation during the next two decades. In 1847, Alexander Dallas Bache (1806–67), head of the U.S. Coast Survey from 1843 to 1867, visited the museum and donated a set of his charts. He was preparing for a survey of Salem Harbor and the surrounding vicinity and was given "from time to time . . . free excess [*sic*] to the Museum, Library, etc. for the purpose of examining the Journals and other parts of the Museum" upon his request (vol. B., minutes/records 1824–52, East India Marine Society Records, MH 88).
107. William Blake, "William Blake's Annotations to the Works of Sir Joshua Reynolds, 1798," quoted by Lenore Metrick-Chen, *Collecting Objects/Excluding People: Chinese Subjects and American Visual Culture, 1830–1900* (Ithaca: State University of New York Press, 2012), 225; *Salem Register*, November 12, 1804.
108. The Boston Marine Society did form a small collection in the 1830s, ultimately transferred to the Boston Society of Natural History in 1864 and then to the Peabody Museum at Harvard in 1869. See Malloy, *Souvenirs of the Fur Trade*, 124–25.
109. List of subscribers agreeing to formation of organization, East India Marine Society Records, MH 88. Articles 5 and 6 were truncated and renumbered as 12 and 13 for the 1800 printing of the Society's bylaws, and "articles of curiosity" was added to 13 (East India Marine Society, *Bye-Laws and Regulations of the Salem East-India Marine Society, Massachusetts*, 12).
110. East India Marine Society, *The East-India Marine Society of Salem*, 4.
111. Francis Bacon, *Gesta Grayorum*, 1594, quoted in Impey and MacGregor, *The Origins of Museums*, 1.
112. Bentley, *The Diary of William Bentley*, 2:382.
113. *Salem Register*, November 11, 1805.
114. Malloy, *Souvenirs of the Fur Trade*, xi–xii.
115. Labrets fascinated westerners, and objects illustrating their use were desired for display to people back home. The Society owned three labrets in addition to the mask, donated by member Israel Williams in 1803. On the mask and Daniel Cross, see Grimes et al., *Uncommon Legacies*, 150; Karen Kramer, "Intersections: Native American Art in a New Light," *American Indian Art Magazine* 32 (Autumn 2007): 77, 164; and Malloy, *Souvenirs of the Fur Trade*, 73. William Sturgis, one of the ship's owners, borrowed this mask from the museum for a lecture he gave in Boston in 1848, thus demonstrating the Society's willingness to loan objects from the collection. See Mary Malloy, "Author Exposed! Young Sailor Is Revealed as 'Anonymous' Keeper of Excellent Voyage Narrative," *Historic Nantucket* 55, no. 1 (2006). www.nha.org.
116. The Haida mask was recorded as "once used by a distinguished Chieftainess of the Indians at Nootka Sound—said to represent exactly the manner in which she painted her face," but contrary to the description in the museum catalogue, it was a carefully crafted souvenir that appealed to western tastes.
117. Malloy, *Souvenirs of the Fur Trade*, 5.
118. Caroline Howard King, *When I Lived in Salem, 1822–1866* (Brattleboro, VT: Stephen Daye Press, 1937), 29–30.
119. Dane Morrison, *True Yankees: The South Seas and the Discovery of American Identity* (Baltimore: Johns Hopkins University Press, 2014), xx.
120. "East India Marine Society," *Political Repository*, January 20, 1801.
121. *Monthly Magazine, or, British Register*, March 1, 1802, 195.
122. "Boston: Saturday Evening, January 8, 1803," *Boston Weekly Magazine,* January 8, 1803, 47.

123. "To the East India Marine Society," *Salem Gazette*, November 5, 1805.
124. Ibid.
125. Ibid.
126. Bentley, *The Diary of William Bentley*, 3:412–13; vol. A., minutes/records 1799–1824, bills and receipts, box 9, folder 2, East India Marine Society Records, MH 88. The concert cost almost $200 to organize. For a dollar, attendees listened to symphonic and vocal works performed by one of the "best performers from Boston": Catherine (Hiller) Graupner (died 1821), one of the leading Boston soloists of her day and the wife of J. C. Gottlieb Graupner (1767–1836), leader of the Boston Philharmonic Society (1809–24) and a founder of the Handel and Haydn Society. See Christine Ammer, *Unsung: A History of Women in American Music* (Milwaukee: Hal Leonard Corporation, 2001), 15; and David Nicholls, *The Cambridge History of American Music* (Cambridge: Cambridge University Press, 1998), 188. The concert included a Franz Joseph Haydn (1732–1809) symphony; the overture to the romantic opera *Lodoïska* by French violinist and composer Rodolphe Kreutzer (1766–1831); and Thomas Augustine Arne's (1710–78) "The Soldier Tired," an aria from the 1762 opera *Artaxerxes* and a popular selection for performers in the nineteenth century ("The Charity Concert," *Essex Register*, February 1, 1809). It is likely that the Graupners arranged the concert once the East India Marine Society hired them, as most of the works performed by Catherine Graupner were on the playbill of other concerts in Salem and Boston around the turn of the century. See Richard Crawford, *America's Musical Life: A History* (New York: Norton, 2001), 89–90; and Oscar George Theodore Sonneck, *Early Concert-Life in America* (Leipzig: Breitkopf and Härtel, 1907), 306.
127. Whitehill, *The East India Marine Society and the Peabody Museum of Salem*, 26.
128. National Parks Service, *The Salem Project*, 134. Due to the Non-Intercourse Act of 1809, the East India Marine Society's annual meetings of 1809, 1810 and 1811 proceeded without parades before dinner, and during the War of 1812 both were omitted. When the war ended in 1815, anniversary festivities were revived for a four-year period before ceasing to be a regular part of the annual meetings (Whitehill, *The East India Marine Society and the Peabody Museum of Salem*, 26).
129. An excerpt from the *New-York Journal of Commerce* that ran in the *Salem Gazette,* May 21, 1833.
130. National Parks Service, *The Salem Project*, 134.
131. Vol. N, guest book, August 25, 1846–October 25, 1849, East India Marine Society Records, MH 88. See Alan Wallach, "William Wilson Corcoran's Failed National Gallery," in *Exhibiting Contradiction: Essays on the Art Museum in the United States* (Amherst: University of Massachusetts Press, 1998), 22–37.
132. Paul Di Maggio, "Cultural Entrepreneurship in Nineteenth Century Boston: The Creation of an Organized Base for the High Culture in America," in *Media, Culture and Society: A Critical Reader*, ed. Richard Collins, James Curran, Nicholas Garnham, Paddy Scannell, Philip Schlesinger, and Colin Sparks (London: Sage, 1986), 194–211; Allan Wallach, *Exhibiting Contradiction*, 22.
133. "Salem East India Marine Society," *North American Review* 6 (1818): 283–85.
134. Vol. G, guest book, July 2, 1827–March 20, 1829; vol. H, guest book, April 10, 1829–September 20, 1832, East India Marine Society Records, MH 88.
135. Naval Lyceum, *Constitution and By-Laws of the United States Naval Lyceum, Established at the Navy-Yard, New-York* (Brooklyn: Spooner, 1838), 1. See Steven Lubar, "The United States Naval Lyceum, 1833–1889," http://bldg92.org; and William P. Leeman, *Long Road to Annapolis: The Founding of the Naval Academy and the Emerging American Republic* (Chapel Hill: University of North Carolina Press, 2010), 130–34. After it disbanded in 1892, the lyceum's collections were incorporated into the U.S. Naval Academy Museum in Annapolis, Maryland.

136. "16. 'The United States Naval Lyceum,'" *American Journal of Science and Arts* 27, no. 2 (1835): 390–93.
137. "Art. VI.—The Salem East India Marine Society," 268. Freeman Hunt, the founder and editor of this noted nineteenth-century publication, visited the museum two years later in October 1845.
138. Published in "East India Museum," *Salem Gazette,* August 3, 1841.
139. The *Gazette* also pointed out the breadth of the collection, stating that "[t]he captains have procured whatever struck them as new in design or use, whether a razor, a porter's pad or palanquin; and there is many an article of this kind in the Salem collection which has cost but a few cents, and is worth in its present use as many dollars" (*Salem Gazette,* September 12, 1828).
140. George Peabody, *Address at the Opening of the Eastern Rail Road Between Boston and Salem, August 27, 1838* (Salem, MA: Choate, 1888), 13–14.
141. Sally Gregory Kohlstedt, "Curiosities and Cabinets: Natural History Museums and Education on the Antebellum Campus," *Isis* 79, no. 3 (1988): 405, 407.
142. "The Peabody Academy of Science, at Salem, Mass.," *Scientific and Literary Gossip,* March 15, 1883, 37; Peabody Academy of Science scrapbook 3, 1882–84, Peabody Essex Museum General Archive, Phillips Library.
143. In addition, a few Society members served as curators at the Essex Institute in the 1860s. Richard Saltonstall Rogers (1790–1873) and John Bertram were curators of fruits and vegetables at the institute prior to the establishment of the Peabody Academy of Science.
144. Charles W. Upham, "A Circular Letter Issued Pursuant to the Vote of a Convention Held at Topsfield, Dec. 30, 1829, for Establishing a County Lyceum," *Essex Institute Historical Collections* 18 (December 1881): 301.
145. Alfred F. Rosa, *Salem, Transcendentalism, and Hawthorne* (Rutherford, NJ: Fairleigh Dickinson University Press, 1980), 43.
146. "Lyceum Mania in Salem," reprinted in the *Boston Weekly Museum,* October 11, 1851, 141.
147. *Salem Gazette,* December 15, 1865.

Chapter Two: "May resources from the ambition of its members continue to accomplish its design"

1. Dane Morrison, *True Yankees: The South Seas and the Discovery of American Identity* (Baltimore: Johns Hopkins University Press, 2014), xix; Daniel Finamore, "Displaying the Sea and Defining America," *Journal of Maritime Research* 4, no. 1 (2002): 40–41.
2. Obituary of Benjamin Carpenter, *Boston Patriot,* September 26, 1823.
3. John Frayler, "Retired on the Fourth of July," *Pickled Fish and Salt Provisions: Historical Musings from Salem Maritime NHS* 4, no. 6 (2003): 4–7. On Stephen White, see Robert Booth, *Death of an Empire: The Rise and Murderous Fall of Salem, America's Richest City* (New York: St. Martin's Press, 2011).
4. *Salem Register,* March 17, 1864, quoted in George Granville Putnam, *Salem Vessels and Their Voyages: A History of the Pepper Trade with the Island of Sumatra* (Salem, MA: Essex Institute, 1922), 1:30–31.
5. Putnam, *Salem Vessels and Their Voyages,* 1:21.
6. The National Parks Service used the model of the *Friendship* when building a full-scale replica of the original vessel in 1996–98. It is now docked at the Salem Maritime National Historic Site. As no plans of the original exist, the model was the most accurate depiction of this Salem East India trading vessel.
7. In the museum's 1831 printed catalogue, this model is referred to as the *Grand Turk,* the first Salem ship to sail to China. The model was altered between 1821 and 1831 and

was later returned to its original form. Walter Whitehill notes that, at the Society's November 1, 1848, meeting, members "disclaimed any knowledge of 'why this alteration should have taken place,' and voted 'That the Ship bear its original and proper name the Friendship'" (Walter Muir Whitehill, *The East India Marine Society and the Peabody Museum of Salem: A Sesquicentennial History* [Salem, MA: Peabody Museum, 1949], 141–42, n. 17).

8. Caroline Howard King, *When I Lived in Salem, 1822–1866* (Brattleboro, VT: Stephen Daye Press, 1937), 29.
9. Daniel Vickers, with Vince Walsh, *Young Men and the Sea: Yankee Seafarers in the Age of Sail* (New Haven, CT: Yale University Press, 2005), 105.
10. Nathaniel Hawthorne, *The Scarlet Letter: A Romance* (1850), quoted in Vickers, *Young Men and the Sea*, 176.
11. For a complete list of East India Marine Society members and the offices they held, see Whitehill, *The East India Marine Society and the Peabody Museum of Salem*, appendix A and B.
12. *Boston Patriot*, September 26, 1823.
13. See Blaine Edele, "The Allen Family," unpublished paper (1978), 39, Allen Family Papers, MSS 1, Phillips Library, Peabody Essex Museum, Salem, MA (hereafter PLPEM). Edele notes, "Social class endogomy [*sic*] characterized their choice of spouses, as is especially prevalent in upper-class families."
14. Typescript of a memorandum for George Nichols, March 9, 1795, Peirce-Nichols Family papers, MSS 468, PLPEM. Other advice was directed toward physical expectations at sea.
15. Joseph Gilbert Waters, letter to William Dean Waters, November 14, 1819, box 9, folder 8, Waters Family Papers, MH 12, PLPEM.
16. Log 912, ship *Union*, PLPEM.
17. Log 935, ship *Tartar*, PLPEM.
18. George Cleveland's diary, DIA 44, PLPEM. Cleveland states that the recollections in this journal were intended for "my children (if they should have the curiosity to read it)." Cleveland served as East India Marine Society president from 1827 to 1830.
19. Susan Bean, *Yankee India: American Commercial and Cultural Encounters with India in the Age of Sail, 1784–1860* (Salem, MA: Peabody Essex Museum and Mapin Publishing Company, 2001), 43.
20. Entry, November 28, 1817, log 935, ship *Tartar*.
21. Richard Price Northey, "Memoirs of a Yankee Shipmaster," *Essex Institute Historical Collections* 76, no. 3 (1940): 247.
22. Finamore, "Displaying the Sea and Defining America," 42.
23. Ernest Stanley Dodge, "The Contributions to Exploration of the Salem East India Marine Society," *American Neptune* 25, no. 3 (1965): 177.
24. Whitehill, *The East India Marine Society and the Peabody Museum of Salem*, 8–9. This was the forerunner of the coast and geodetic survey (started in 1816). The lack of federally supported scientific organizations in the early republic stemmed from the country's former monarchical ties, which influenced even the staunchest supporters of science, such as Thomas Jefferson, as well as a governmental focus on internal public works projects. Most scientific endeavors, therefore, remained in the hands of individual states. See A. Hunter Dupree, *Science in the Federal Government: A History of Policies and Activities*, 2nd ed. (Baltimore: Johns Hopkins University Press, 1986), 22, 4.
25. Dodge, "The Contributions to Exploration of the Salem East India Marine Society," 177–78.
26. East India Marine Society, *Bye-Laws and Regulations of the Salem East-India Marine Society* (Salem, MA: Pool and Palfray, 1808), 12.
27. Ibid., 3.

28. East India Marine Society, *By-Laws and Regulations of the Salem East-India Marine Society* (Salem, MA: Cushing, 1800), 7–8.
29. *Boston Intelligencer and Evening Gazette*, November 14, 1818 (citing the *Essex Register*).
30. Lloyd A. Brown, *The Story of Maps* (Boston: Little, Brown, 1949), 12.
31. On DesBarres, see G. N. D Evans, *Uncommon Obdurate: The Several Public Careers of J. F. W. DesBarres* (Boston: Peabody Museum and University of Toronto Press, 1969).
32. "History of Essex County Institutions," undated [circa 1842], box 8, folder 1, letters received 1844–46, Henry Wheatland Papers, MSS 464, PLPEM.
33. Vol. A., minutes/records 1799–1824, East India Marine Society Records, MH 88, PLPEM.
34. Ibid. John Churchman's (1753–1805) *The Magnetic Atlas, or Variation Charts of the Whole Terraqueous Globe*, compiled starting in the late eighteenth century, was used to determine magnetic deviation from the reading of a marine compass at sea. The *Independent Chronicle* of January 7, 1802, noted, "The enlightened East-India Marine Society of Salem . . . have taken on their own account, such a number of copies, as to demonstrate their determination to give that support to the improvement which it may be known to deserve."
35. East India Marine Society, *Bye-Laws and Regulations of the Salem East-India Marine Society*, 12.
36. Vol. A., minutes/records, 1799–1824, East India Marine Society Records, MH 88, PLPEM.
37. Transcribed in Dodge, "The Contributions to Exploration of the Salem East India Marine Society," 179.
38. East India Marine Society, *Bye-Laws and Regulations of the Salem East-India Marine Society*, 8–10. No other marine society had such a position.
39. Bowditch worked on six of the twelve volumes created during the East India Marine Society's existence.
40. Inside the journal, Haswell inscribed the words "To the Honorable Salem East India Society, by their Obd[t] Serv[t] William Haswell" in a cartouche on a plan he made of the harbor on the southwest side of Guam.
41. Log 1626, brig *Herald*, PLPEM.
42. Dodge, "The Contributions to Exploration of the Salem East India Marine Society," 180.
43. Log 1628, ship *Cordelia*, PLPEM.
44. Dodge, "The Contributions to Exploration of the Salem East India Marine Society," 178. It was common practice for American and English captains to contact publishers when they found errors in printed sailing directions or send an account of new discoveries to local papers.
45. Dirk Jan Struik, *Yankee Science in the Making* (Boston: Little, Brown, 1948), 109. Forbes was a member of the Boston Marine Society and corresponded with the East India Marine Society on several occasions, even borrowing one of their journals in 1853.
46. Vol. A., minutes/records, 1799–1824, East India Marine Society Records, MH 88.
47. Nathaniel Bowditch, *The New American Practical Navigator*, 1st ed. (Newburyport, MA: Blunt, 1802).
48. *Salem Register*, November 12, 1804.
49. In 1813, the Society determined that Captain Samuel Lambert's charts of Massachusetts Bay, the Nantucket Shoals, and Georges Bank were "the most correct of any within their knowledge." Lambert (1768–1832), a Society member, was also a teacher of navigation and wrote books on the subject, such as *Information Useful for Navigators* (1820). See scrapbooks, box 28(OS), vol. E, East India Marine Society Records, MH 88.

50. "Directions for filling out blank journals for the use of the Society," box 3, folder 20, East India Marine Society Records, MH 88.
51. East India Marine Society, *The East-India Marine Society of Salem* (Salem, MA: Palfray, Ives, Foote, and Brown, 1831), 173.
52. "Directions for filling out blank journals for the use of the Society," box 3, folder 20, East India Marine Society Records, MH 88.
53. *Boston Patriot*, September 26, 1823.
54. Rolfe Ricker, "My Journey. No. 5," *Juvenile Reformer, and Sabbath School Instructor,* September 2, 1835, 57.

Chapter Three: "Gathered, with cost and pains, from every clime"

1. East India Marine Society, *The East-India Marine Society of Salem* (Salem, MA: Palfray, 1821), 4.
2. Ibid. Forty-five percent of East India Marine Society members did not donate a single object to the collection. When including those who gave only one object, this figure rises to more than 50 percent of the membership. The number of objects given by single members ranged from 1 to 137. Some who contributed to the collecting goals of the institution gave objects before they became members (George Schwartz, "'Collecting and Arranging . . . A History of The Globe': A Reconsideration of the Salem East India Marine Society and Antebellum American Museology," Ph.D. diss., Boston University, 2015, 561).
3. East India Marine Society, *The East-India Marine Society of Salem*, 4.
4. Ernest Stanley Dodge, "Early American Contacts in Polynesia and Fiji," *Proceedings of the American Philosophical Society,* April 15, 1963, 102. Fiji is technically in Micronesia but has strong cultural ties with Polynesia.
5. Norman E. Muller, "The Peabody Museum of Salem's Oceanic Collection: An Historical Study," MA thesis, New York University, 1967, 11, N735, M85, Phillips Library, Peabody Essex Museum, Salem, MA (hereafter PLPEM).
6. Douglas Cole, *Captured Heritage: The Scramble for Northwest Coast Artifacts*, 2nd ed. (Vancouver: University of British Columbia Press, 2011), 1.
7. Ibid.
8. Ira Jacknis, "Towards an Art History of Northwest Coast First Nations: I. 'Traditional' Period (1770–1870)," *BC Studies* no. 135 (autumn 2002): 47.
9. East India Marine Society, *The East-India Marine Society of Salem* (Salem, MA: Palfray, Ives, Foote, and Brown, 1831), 178.
10. John R. Jewitt, *A Narrative of the Adventures and Sufferings of John R. Jewitt, Only Survivor of the Crew of the Ship Boston, During a Captivity of Nearly Three Years Among the Savages of Nootka Sound* (Middleton, CT: Beth Richards, 1815), 15.
11. Mary Malloy, *Souvenirs of the Fur Trade: Northwest Coast Indian Art and Artifacts Collected by American Mariners, 1788–1844* (Cambridge, MA: Harvard University, Peabody Museum of Archaeology and Ethnology, 2000), 64, 66.
12. In 1820, Kamehameha II purchased *Cleopatra's Barge*, the first American oceangoing luxury yacht (originally built for the eccentric Salemite George Crowninshield, Jr., at a cost of $100,000), for more than a million pounds of sandalwood. See Paul Forsythe Johnston, *Shipwrecked in Paradise: Cleopatra's Barge in Hawai'i* (College Station: Texas A&M University Press, 2015).
13. Vol. A., minutes/records, 1799–1824, East India Marine Society Records, MH 88, PLPEM. Jeffrie's letter is transcribed in Ernest Stanley Dodge, "An Early Letter to the Salem East India Marine Society," *Essex Institute Historical Collection* 77 (1941): 254–66.

14. William Endicott, *Wrecked Among Cannibals in the Fijis: A Narrative of Shipwreck & Adventure in the South Seas, with Notes by Lawrence Waters Jenkins* (Salem, MA: Marine Research Society, 1923), 26.
15. Ibid.
16. Another object, however, paints Fijians in a different light. A model of a *bure kalou*, or spirit house, donated by Society member Joseph Winn, Jr., (1761–1880) in 1835 denotes an act of kindness recounted by Endicott in his narrative. Endicott noted in his account that the king allowed the shipwrecked crew of the *Glide* to live in a similar temple (ibid., 40–41).
17. Log 32, ship *Concord,* PLPEM.
18. Log 111, ship *Indus,* PLPEM. This passage, dated April 2, 1816, supports speculation that the *Indus*'s crew was creating fake whale's teeth for trade, which was a common practice by the early nineteenth century ("Tabua or Sperm Whale Tooth Neck Ornament from Fiji," https://collection.maas.museum).
19. The Society owned a pair donated by member Nathaniel Page (1782–1823) in 1817.
20. East India Marine Society, *The East-India Marine Society of Salem*, 56. See Daniel Finamore, "'Curiously Carved': Early Collections of Susan's Teeth, 1830–1921," *American Neptune* 60 (2000): 369–80.
21. Rhys Richards, "United States Trade with China, 1784–1814," *American Neptune*, 54, special supplement (1994): 4.
22. Ibid.
23. Immanuel C. Y. Hsu, *The Rise of Modern China* (Oxford: Oxford University Press, 1983), 252–53.
24. The painting of a ship on the exterior and interior of the bowl is taken from William Hutchinson's *Treatise on Practical Seamanship* (1777) and is not of the *Grand Turk*. The same source was used for six other bowls. See William Sargent, *Treasures of Chinese Export Ceramics* (Salem, MA: Peabody Essex Museum), 414. The Society listed the tureens as swans in their catalogue.
25. Robert G. Lee, *Orientals: Asian Americans in Popular Culture* (Philadelphia: Temple University Press, 1999), 28.
26. Dean Lahikainen, *Samuel McIntire: Carving an American Style* (Salem, MA: Peabody Essex Museum, 2007), 83–85.
27. Scrapbooks, vol. E, East India Marine Society Records, MH 88.
28. William Bentley also donated two other examples: one of a monk, originally given to him by Benjamin Hodges; one of a Sufi mendicant (*The Diary of William Bentley, D.D.*, vol. 1, *1784–1792* [Salem, MA: Essex Institute, 1905], 75).
29. Walter Muir Whitehill, "Remarks on the Canton Trade and the Manner of Transacting Business: From a Manuscript of 1809 in the Peabody Museum of Salem," *Essex Institute Historical Collections*, 73, no. 4 (1937): 309.
30. Peabody Museum of Salem, *Michele Felice Cornè, 1752–1845: Versatile Neapolitan Painter of Salem, Boston, and Newport* (Salem, MA: Peabody Museum of Salem, 1972), 79; Carl Crossman, *The Decorative Arts of the China Trade: Paintings, Furnishings, and Exotic Curiosities* (Woodbridge, UK: Antique Collector's Club, 1991), 424, fig. 8.
31. George Cleveland, diary, DIA 44, PLPEM.
32. Susan Bean, *Yankee India: American Commercial and Cultural Encounters with India in the Age of Sail, 1784–1860* (Salem, MA: Peabody Essex Museum and Mapin Publishing Company, 2001), 35.
33. Ibid., 16.
34. Ibid., 17–18, 124.
35. George Cleveland, diary, DIA 44.
36. Ibid. Cleveland wrote that his knowledge of piece goods was particularly useful "in the selection of our cargo, & produced much surprise in the dealers there, as they had been

in the habit of selling cargoes to men who knew nothing of these articles, from their previous modes of life;—it was a trade, they had not learned."

37. Bean, *Yankee India*, 39.
38. Ibid., 16.
39. Ibid., 74.
40. Ibid., 72. Bean states that the shawl was likely Kashmir, often mistaken by Americans for camel's hair.
41. Ibid., 274, n. 30. Washington's likeness was incorporated into Liverpoolware for American merchants and sailors and copied by Chinese export artists.
42. Typescript of Ichabod Nichols, letter to John R. Dalling, September 27, 1805, Peirce-Nichols Family of Salem, Massachusetts, Papers, MSS 468, box 1, folder 1, letters from Ichabod Nichols, 1777–1838, PLPEM.
43. Bean, *Yankee India*, 79.
44. One of these figures was a copy of the Greco-Roman Hellenistic statue *Boy with Thorn,* rendered by an Indian sculptor (see figure 3, no. 6).
45. Bean, *Yankee India*, 185.
46. Ibid., 185, 188. Artisans in Krishnanagar, West Bengal, about fifty miles upriver from Calcutta, crafted both sets of figures from sun-dried clay. They were painted with earth pigments in a tamarind-glue binder, finished with fiber hair, and finally dressed in cloth garments (185).
47. Ibid., 185; Sria Chatterjee, "People of Clay: Portrait Objects in the Peabody Essex Museum," *Museum History Journal* 6, no. 2 (2013): 203–21.
48. Bean, *Yankee India*, 216. Bean notes that these statues were probably made by the most renowned Krishnanagar unfired clay sculptor at the time, Sri Ram Pal. Mitter gave his likeness to his Boston-based client John Parker in 1840, accompanied by a handwritten card: "I remain, Dear Sir, Your very faithful Servant—Raj Kissen Mitter." Eight years later, Dutt presented his portrait figure to T. A. Neal, who was in the India trade with his father, David Neal. The Neals and the Dutts fostered a friendship that spanned several generations (216–17). Both Parker and Neal donated these figures to the Society.
49. 日米交流のあけぼの：黒船きたる / *Worlds Revealed: The Dawn of Japanese and American Exchange*, catalogue of an exhibition at the Edo-Tokyo Museum and the Peabody Essex Museum (Tokyo: Edo-Tokyo Museum, 1999), 60.
50. Nicole Coolidge Rousmaniere, "The Accessioning of Japanese Art in Early Nineteenth-Century America: Ukiyo-e Prints in the Peabody Essex Museum, Salem," *Apollo* 145, no. 421 (1997): 23.
51. Ibid.
52. William Cleveland, diary entry, July 18, 1800, in *A Diary of William Cleveland, Captain's Clerk on Board the "Massachusetts,"* ed. Madoka Kanai (Quezon: University of the Philippines, Institute of Asian Studies, 1965), 18.
53. Ibid.
54. Ibid.
55. Norman R. Bennett and George E. Brooks, Jr., eds., *New England Merchants in Africa: A History Through Documents, 1802 to 1865* (Boston: Boston University Press, 1965), xxiv.
56. John R. Grimes, *The Tribal Style: Selections from the African Collection at the Peabody Museum of Salem* (Salem, MA: Peabody Museum, 1984), 5.
57. Young Waters wrote in his diary on August 11, 1825: "in the evening I visited the museum and saw 16 wax figures among whome [*sic*] was Gen. Washington Gen. Lafayette Gen. Jackson" (Richard Palmer Waters diary, DIA 229, PLPEM).
58. Bennett and Brooks, *New England Merchants in Africa*, xxxii.
59. Grimes, *The Tribal Style*, 7.
60. Mary Lou Curran and John R. Grimes, "Salem and Native America: Toward a Dialogical Perspective," in *Uncommon Legacies: Native American Art from the Peabody*

Essex Museum, ed. John R. Grimes, Christian Feest, and Mary Lou Curran (New York: American Federation of Arts and University of Washington Press, 2002), 58.

61. Evidence for Salem's direct involvement in obtaining African slaves is limited. The art historian Susan Stedman notes, "A slaver is described by Felt in *The Annals of Salem* in 1785, and the diaries and notes of a Dr. Bentley document the activities of eight Salem shipmasters engaged in slave trade during the last fifteen years of that century" ("The Peabody Museum of Salem," *African Arts* 10, no. 1 [1976]: 43, 45–46).
62. East India Marine Society, *The East-India Marine Society of Salem*, 178.
63. More than fifty ceramic pottery vessels were donated to the East India Marine Society.
64. East India Marine Society, *The East-India Marine Society of Salem*, 146.
65. Log 1628, brig *Herald*, PLPEM. The museum's connection to Peru expanded when Manuel Lorenzo Vidaurre (1773–1841), a Peruvian lawyer and politician who advocated for independence, visited in July 1828.
66. Gilbert Farquahar Mathison, *Narrative of a Visit to Brazil, Chile, Peru, and the Sandwich Islands, During the Years 1821 and 1822* (London: Knight, 1825), 269.
67. Karen Kramer Russell characterizes this collection as one that "correlates to larger national movements of museology and, at times, federal policy" ("Over 200 Years of Native American Art and Culture at the Peabody Essex Museum, Salem, Massachusetts," *Tulsa Law Review* 45, no. 33 [2010]: 33).
68. Malloy, *Souvenirs of the Fur Trade*, 128.
69. Christian F. Feest, "Collectors, Collections, and Collectibles: Early Native American Collections in Europe and North America," in *Uncommon Legacies*, 40. Clark's collection grew over the years, due in part to his position as superintendent of Indian affairs in St. Louis from 1821 until his death in 1838. He visited the East India Marine Society Museum toward the end of his life, on June 12, 1837.
70. Catlin toured East India Marine Hall a few months after Clark did (on September 25) during a lecture tour in the northeast that included the Salem Lyceum.
71. Emerson W. Baker II, "Salem as Frontier Outpost," in *Salem: Place, Myth, and Memory*, ed. Dane Morrison and Nancy Lusignan Schultz (Boston: Northeastern University Press, 2004), 36.
72. Anna Boswell, "Re-enactment and the Museum Case: Reading the Oceanic and Native American Displays in the Peabody Essex Museum," *Journal of New Zealand Literature* no. 27 (2009): 54–55.
73. Grimes et al., *Uncommon Legacies*, 88. Corné's allegory was based on the plate *View of the Indians of Terra del Fuego* from George William Anderson's 1784 volume on Cook's voyages of exploration. He added headdresses to the figures, a reflection of the common misperception that all native North Americans wore them.
74. Curran and Grimes, "Salem and Native America," 57. The objects produced for Anglo-Americans, according to Grimes and Curran, were "based on earlier forms and motifs" and "suggest cultural conservatism rather than a lack of Euroamerican contact" (ibid.).
75. Lewis Cass, letter to John C. Calhoun, November 18, 1819, in *American Voyageur: The Journal of David Bates Douglass,* ed. Sydney W. Jackman and John F. Freeman (Marquette: Northern Michigan University Press, 1969), 114–16.
76. Ibid., xiii–xiv.
77. Ibid., 79–80.
78. Elias Boudinot, *An Address to the Whites, Delivered in the First Presbyterian Church, on the 26 of May, 1826* (Philadelphia: Geddes, 1826), 7–10; southeastern Native American documents, University of Georgia Library, http://metis.galib.uga.edu.
79. Russell, "Over 200 Years of Native American Art and Culture at the Peabody Essex Museum," 36–37.
80. Vol. H, guestbook, April 10, 1829–September 20, 1832, East India Marine Society Records, MH 88. Boudinot came to the museum on March 24, 1832.

81. William B. Dinsmoor, "Early American Studies of Mediterranean Archaeology," *Proceedings of the American Philosophical Society,* July 14, 1943, 99. In 1810, the Salem brig *Telemachus* became the first American ship to reach Constantinople.
82. See Joyce Haynes, "America's Earliest Egyptian Collection at the Peabody Essex Museum, Salem," *KMT* 11, no. 2 (2000): 30–41.
83. Correspondence regarding donations of objects, 1799–1838, box 3, folder 1, East India Marine Society Records, MH 88. Tanner, like John Fitzpatrick Jeffrie, apologized for having "nothing of greater consideration to offer . . . your Museum at Salem, for the success of which I have the pleasure of expressing my best wishes & believe me my dear sirs."
84. See Teresa Lynn Barnett, "The Nineteenth-Century Relic: A Pre-History of the Historical Artifact," Ph.D. diss., University of California, Los Angeles, 2008, v–vi.
85. "Curiosity," *Gloucester Telegraph*, October 23, 1830. The tassel was donated by Andrew Wallis of Beverly, Massachusetts, in 1845, and the chain links were presented by Samuel Pearce of Gloucester, Massachusetts, in 1830.
86. A Mr. Muller from Westphalia, Germany, traveling in the United States gave the rosary bead to Derby, and "assured him that he [had] obtained it in Italy and that it was executed as early as the fourteenth century" (East India Marine Society, *The East-India Marine Society of Salem*, 76).
87. Frits Scholten, *Small Wonders: Late-Gothic Boxwood Micro-Carvings from the Low Countries* (Amsterdam: Rijksmuseum, 2016), 612.
88. A visitor recounted asking custodian and Society member Thomas Saul, "'Of whom is that portrait, may I ask.' Going to the nearest sand box and relieving himself of a surplus of tobacco saliva, and then carefully shifting the quid to another corner of his mouth he replied. 'That's Cap'n Eilus Hawsket Derby, one of Salum's most famous murchants.' 'Indeed,' I said. 'I thought at first that it was Ralph Waldo Emerson, it certainly bears a striking resemblance to Mr. Emerson.' 'Yum, it does, it does'" (unidentified article in a scrapbook, PLPEM).
89. On July 31, 1825, Peabody wrote in his journal, "[W]e walked from the Cathedral to the Palace which is in the environs of the town situated in a wood. Here also was an Exhibition, which consisted of pictures of Dutch modern artists and all for sale. Many of them were superior paintings" (George Peabody Papers, subseries C, writings, box 14, folder 1, Joseph Peabody Family Papers, MH 178, PLPEM). This painting depicts Abel after the mortal wound inflicted by his brother Cain, a visual encapsulation of the fall from paradise. It can be read today as an allusion to Salem's diminishing maritime trade and the Society's eventual demise after the Civil War.
90. Bentley supplied Fisher with William Woolett's (1735–85) 1760 engraving of Lorrain's work "from which he has executed this work," and Bentley "urged that it might be displayed in the Athenaeum or E. India Museum" (Bentley, *The Diary of William Bentley, D.D.*, vol. 4, *1811–1819* [Salem, MA: Essex Institute, 1914], 129). Benjamin Merrill donated the painting in 1813.
91. In 1855, two more ship portraits were donated by Nathaniel Brown, who became a member in 1866: one of the ship *Sooloo* (1848) by Domenico Gavarrone (1821–74) of Leghorn, Italy; the other of the Salem ship *Sally* (1802), attributed to Cornè.
92. Michael Kaplan, "America Guided by Wisdom: A Neoclassical Allegory of American Exceptionalism," *New Jacksonian Blog*, December 5, 2010, http://newjacksonianblog.blogspot.com.
93. The later bust was likely a cast of John B. Binon's (flourished 1818–20) bust of Adams commissioned by the Massachusetts state legislature for Faneuil Hall. A manuscript addition to the Society's printed 1821 catalogue notes that it is "modeled by Benor." The current whereabouts of this bust, and almost all those owned by the Society, are unknown.

94. Based on late nineteenth-century sketches of East India Marine Hall (see figure 6), the cast bust of Apollo was likely created after period examples that were based on the Apollo Belvedere. The one of Diana is probably after the statue of Diana by the Greek sculptor Leochares (d. 328 BCE), currently in the Louvre.
95. There was a William Osborn who had been a member of the Society since 1824, but it is unclear if he donated the cast. Because the cast was removed from East India Marine Hall in 1876 and loaned to the Essex Institute (and later the Normal School, today Salem State University), its current whereabouts are unknown, and its importance to the museum during this time has been forgotten.
96. Francis Haskell and Nicholas Penny, *Taste and the Antique: The Lure of Classical Sculpture, 1500–1900* (New Haven, CT: Yale University Press, 1998), 243.
97. Martha B. Amory, *The Domestic and Artistic Life of John Singleton Copley, R.A.* (Boston: Houghton Mifflin, 1882), 53. The letter is dated June 9, 1775.
98. On the Athenaeum's collection, see Hina Hirayama, *"With Éclat": The Boston Athenaeum and the Origin of the Museum of Fine Arts, Boston* (Boston: Boston Athenaeum, 2013). Also see Allan Wallach, *Exhibiting Contradiction: Essays on the Art Museum in the United States* (Amherst: University of Massachusetts Press, 1998), 38–58.
99. Stephen Mrozowski, L. Shaw, M. Holland, and J. Zisk, *Salem, Massachusetts: An Archaeological Survey of the City* (Salem, MA: Prepared for the City of Salem, 1988), 62.
100. Amy Friedlander, *Salem Maritime National Historic Site: Historical Research, 1626–1990* (East Orange, NJ: Cultural Resource Group, Louis Berger and Associates, 1991), 25, 28.
101. Ibid., 34.
102. Schwartz, "Collecting and Arranging," 306.
103. Whitehill, *The East India Marine Society and the Peabody Museum of Salem*, 49–50. Prince worked at the Boston Customs House in 1839 when Nathaniel Hawthorne was employed there, and he visited the museum with his family in October of that year. The figure was possibly acquired by Abraham T. Russell (1806–75), the captain of the New Bedford whaling barque *Bartholomew Gosnold* in the 1840s.
104. Only two other figures of Kūkaʻilimoku survive, both from the same temple. One is in the collection of the Bishop Museum in Honolulu, and the other is in the British Museum. The Peabody Essex Museum's figure is considered to be one of the most important objects in its collection.
105. Malloy, *Souvenirs of the Fur Trade*, 28–29. Cushing came to the Columbia River in 1844 on a family-owned vessel, the *Chenamus*.
106. Interpretation by Dan Finamore, cited in Grimes et al., *Uncommon Legacies*, 156.
107. C. F. W., "CHINA: No. I.," *Gentleman's Magazine* 4, no. 2 (1839): 119.
108. John Haddad, "The Romantic Collector in China: Nathan Dunn's Ten Thousand Chinese Things," *Journal of American Culture* 21, no. 1 (1998): 10–11.
109. Ronald J. Zboray and Mary Saracino Zboray, "Between 'Crockery-Dom' and Barnum: Boston's Chinese Museum, 1845–47," *American Quarterly* 56, no. 2 (2004): 273.
110. Supplement, 1837–55, box 24, folder 8, East India Marine Society Records, MH 88.
111. Lee, *Orientals*, 28.
112. Bettina A. Norton, "This Bridge of the Yankees: Engineers and Indians at the Niagara Frontier," in *Prints and Printmakers of New York State, 1825–1940*, ed. David Tatham (Syracuse, NY: Syracuse University Press, 1986), 133–44. Norton notes that Maungwudaus claimed to cross the bridge when it opened, as there was a small Anishinaabe settlement nearby. He and ten others traveled to Europe in 1844 and were painted by George Catlin for his Indian Gallery (ibid.). Maungwudaus gave a few objects to the Society in 1850 and was likely travelling with Barnum in 1851 when he donated this print.

113. Vol. C., minutes/records, 1853–96, East India Marine Society Records, MH 88. The original sculpture was modeled in Rome in 1860.
114. Ibid.
115. "Valuable Donation," *Salem Observer*, August 13, 1863, reprinted from the *Salem Register.*
116. Daniel Vickers, with Vince Walsh, *Young Men and the Sea: Yankee Seafarers in the Age of Sail* (New Haven, CT: Yale University Press, 2005), 250.

Chapter Four: Exhibition and Display

1. Vol. A., minutes/records, 1799–1824, East India Marine Society Records, MH 88, Phillips Library, Peabody Essex Museum, Salem, MA (hereafter PLPEM). On July 1, 1801, the standing committee and Jonathan Mason were tasked "to compleat a catalog of donations for the cabinets of curiosities."
2. Ibid.
3. Ibid.
4. *Mercantile Advertiser*, January 15, 1802.
5. Vol. A., minutes/records, 1799–1824, East India Marine Society Records, MH 88. This building was constructed by Colonel Benjamin Pickman for the Salem Bank but instead was used by the Salem Marine Insurance Company once completed.
6. William Bentley, *The Diary of William Bentley, D.D.*, vol. 3, *1803–1810* (Salem, MA: Essex Institute, 1911), 93. The image of the "launching of the Essex" on one chimney refers to "4 prints representing the different situations of the Essex from the commencement of a gale to her safe arrival at Bombay," donated by Samuel Gardner Derby in 1803. The British ship *Essex* was dismasted in a storm in 1782 and towed into Bombay Harbor and refitted. The prints by Francis Jukes (1747–1812), after Thomas Luny (1759–1837), were published in 1785.
7. Vol. A., minutes/records, 1799–1824, East India Marine Society Records, MH 88. The Society voted "that the request of Mr. Abbott cannot be complied with consistently with the nature of our institution, and that the President and committee answer his letter through Mr. John Derby to that effect."
8. Bills and receipts, box 9, folder 1, East India Marine Society Records, MH 88.
9. Vol. A., minutes/records, 1799–1824, East India Marine Society Records, MH 88.
10. After 1803, exact years for donations became approximations, with the periods 1804–6, 1810–12, and 1820–21 used instead of annual listings. By 1818, gifts were entered by either the donor or member who received an object, as the handwriting for each entry changes.
11. Walter Muir Whitehill, *The East India Marine Society and the Peabody Museum of Salem: A Sesquicentennial History* (Salem, MA: Peabody Museum, 1949), 36.
12. William Richard Cutter, *Encyclopedia of Massachusetts, Biographical—Genealogical* (New York: American Historical Society, 1916), 12:452; Katherine Wolff, *The Culture Club: The Curious History of the Boston Athenaeum* (Amherst: University of Massachusetts Press, 2009), 173, n. 48.
13. Dorinda Outram, "New Spaces in Natural History," in *Cultures of Natural History*, ed. N. Jardine, J. A. Secord and E. C. Spary (Cambridge: Cambridge University Press, 1996), 250.
14. Carl Linnaeus was deified in his time; he was often compared to Solomon, Socrates, Galileo, and Newton. In actuality, he was more like Nathaniel Bowditch: a classifier who created a system approachable to laypeople rather than theoreticians. See Lisbet Koerner, "Carl Linnaeus in His Time and Place," in Jardine et al., *Cultures of Natural History*, 145, 151. She sees Linnaeus as "a typical Enlightenment improver." Ibid., 151.

15. Christopher Looby, "The Constitution of Nature: Taxonomy as Politics in Jefferson, Peale, and Bartram," *Early American Literature* 22 (1987): 258–59.
16. Ibid., 267.
17. Charles Willson Peale, *Discourse Introductory to a Course of Lectures on the Science of Nature* (Philadelphia, 1800), 39.
18. An artificial classification system is easily applied to any group of specimens or objects in comparison to a natural classification system that uses biological resemblance based on scientific discovery (Stephen G. Saupe, "Phenetic Classification Systems," http://employees.csbsju.edu/). Linnaeus's system, developed for classifying plants, was artificial and easy to use. Both artificial and natural classification systems were pre-Darwinian.
19. East India Marine Society, *The East-India Marine Society of Salem* (Salem, MA: Palfray, 1821), 81.
20. Ernest Stanley Dodge and Charles H. P. Copeland, *Handbook to the Collections of the Peabody Museum of Salem* (Salem, MA: Peabody Museum, 1949), 45.
21. Sir Charles Lyell, *A Second Visit to the United States of North America* (London: Murray, 1849), 1:122–23.
22. East India Marine Society, *The East-India Marine Society of Salem*, 12.
23. The Society's funds at this point were $8,829.16, equivalent to the purchasing power of $181,719.79 today (http://futureboy.homeip.net). Apart from $191.01 in cash, the rest was invested in shares of bank stock in the Merchant, Beverly, and Salem banks; the Union and Salem Marine insurance companies; and U.S. stocks.
24. East India Marine Society, *The East-India Marine Society of Salem*, 4.
25. Report delivered by Nathaniel Bowditch, July 5, 1820, vol. F, East India Marine Society Records, MH 88.
26. East India Marine Society, *The East-India Marine Society of Salem*, 100. Bass believed "it was not possible to make the preceding catalogue so complete as could have been wished" as the "time allowed for the preparation of this Catalogue, (consisting of such a large number and great variety of articles) did not permit a more thorough investigation." He also noted this as "the excuse for any defect or inaccuracy in the work" (ibid.).
27. According to Teresa Lynn Barnett, an object labeled in this way serves as "the ledger of its own history by having its date of provenance or information about the historically significant event with which it was associated painted or scrawled directly across its surface" ("The Nineteenth-Century Relic: A Pre-History of the Historical Artifact," Ph.D. diss., University of California, Los Angeles, 2008, 35).
28. Vol. A., minutes/records, 1799–1824, East India Marine Society Records, MH 88.
29. In regard to exchanges, a practice that continued among American museums until the second half of the twentieth century, the Society noted that any objects donated "by persons who are not members" could not be removed "without the written assent of such persons." Today, most museums would not require a donor's consent for deaccessioning an object unless it was clearly stipulated in the original deed of gift.
30. Vol. A., minutes/records, 1799–1824, East India Marine Society Records, MH 88.
31. Unfortunately, no records of this corporation exist to construct a more in-depth sketch.
32. Stephen Wheatland, "Appendix H: The Salem East India Marine Society: A Report of Its Funds and How They Were Acquired," in Whitehall, *The East India Marine Society and the Peabody Museum of Salem*, 191–92. Wheatland notes that the Society envisioned "the sale of 150 shares at $100.00 each would allow sufficient money for the construction of a building, and that the rental of the ground floor . . . would allow payment of 5% on the investment." This plan did not work out as constituted, "for

when the building was sold in 1867 to the Trustees for the George Peabody Fund, there were 250 shares outstanding, the Society owning 121 of them" (ibid., 191).

33. Philip Chadwick Foster Smith, *East India Marine Hall, 1824–1974* (Salem, MA: Peabody Museum of Salem, 1974), 24.
34. Christopher P. Monkhouse, "Thomas Waldron Sumner: A Biographical Sketch of the Architect of East India Marine Hall," in ibid., 4.
35. "The Independent Congregational Church," *Salem Observer,* December 4, 1824. Another nineteenth-century architect of note who visited the museum was Frederick Law Olmsted (1822–1903), the father of American landscape architecture. He toured the museum with his brother, J. H. Olmstead of Yale College, in May 1845 (vol. M, guest book, September 21, 1843–August 25, 1846, East India Marine Society Records, MH 88).
36. "East India Marine Society," *Essex Register*, October 17, 1825.
37. A portrait of President John Quincy Adams by Charles Osgood was donated in 1834 by Charles A. Andrews (see figure 6, no. 9). The Hudson River School painter Asher B. Durand visited the museum on June 5, 1835, with his patron, Lumen Reed (1784–1836), and Reed's son-in-law, Theodore Allen (1800–50). Reed commissioned Durand to paint portraits of the first seven U.S. presidents in 1835, and he was in the Boston area working on his portrait of John Quincy Adams at this time. It is likely he came to Salem specifically to view the Society's portrait of Adams.
38. "East India Marine Society," *Essex Register*, October 17, 1825. This was not Adams's first visit to the museum, as William Bentley "went with him to the Museum & Athenaeum" in 1818 when Adams was secretary of state (Bentley, *The Diary of William Bentley, D.D.*, vol. 4, *1811–1819* [Salem, MA: Essex Institute, 1914], 548). Adams returned to Salem in 1827 and "visited the Athenaeum, the Essex Historical Society & chamber, and the Marine Society's Hall," and commented in his diary on "the curiosities of which there have been few additions, since I was present at the opening of it two years ago" (John Quincy Adams, diary 37, November 11, 1825–June 24, 1828, in *John Quincy Adams Diary: An Electronic Archive*, http://www.masshist.org).
39. Whitehill, *The East India Marine Society and the Peabody Museum of Salem*, 26–28.
40. "East India Marine Society," *Essex Register*, October 17, 1825.
41. John Remond's invoice lists fourteen musicians, one turtle, etc., at $546.13 (box 1, folder 4, Remond Family Papers, MSS 271, PLPEM).
42. *Salem Observer*, October 19, 1825. Forty-four years later, Remond recalled, "When the East India Marine Hall was dedicated Mr. Adams dined there & I purchased one of the largest fish I could find." One of the attendees came up to Remond after the dinner and said, "[F]riend Remond I don't know of any thing you could have served up more appropriate then that mammoth Codfish—for Mr. Adams is a great defender of our fisheries, & he considered the fisheries the nursery of sailors to be transplanted to our Naval ships" (John Remond, letter to Mrs. Silsbee, March 2, 1869, box 1, folder 2, Redmond Family Papers, MSS 271).
43. Reprinted in the *Essex Register*, October 27, 1825.
44. "East India Marine Society," *Essex Register*, October 17, 1825. The toasts were later published in Lawrence Waters Jenkins and Walter Muir Whitehill. *The Restoration of East India Marine Hall* (Salem, MA: Peabody Museum of Salem, 1944), 8–11.
45. The *Essex Register* reported that "President Adams gracefully proposed: 'The Cape of Storms. To the Navigators and Merchants of Salem, may it prove the Cape of Good Hope.' After fifteen more toasts—Mr. Justice Story of the Supreme Court and Mayor Quincy of Boston having given two each—the President of the United States, having a long journey to Washington ahead of him, retired from the hall, and the company settled down to drink another twenty-five" ("East India Marine Society," *Essex Register*, October 17, 1825).

46. Ibid.
47. "East-India Marine Society," *Salem Observer*, October 15, 1825.
48. *Richmond Enquirer*, October 21, 1825.
49. Scrapbooks, vol. E, East India Marine Society Records, MH 88.
50. Vol. A., minutes/records, 1799–1824, East India Marine Society Records, MH 88.
51. Correspondence, 1807–83, box 3, folder 4, East India Marine Society Records, MH 88. Bass claimed he was not present at the vote requiring approval for exchanging specimens. In May 1825, during a meeting of the committee of observation, the Society did offer a vote of thanks to him "for his devotion to the interest of the Society while their superintendent." After leaving, Bass maintained some association with the Society, writing a letter to his successor, Malthus Ward, in 1829 concerning the exchange of shells.
52. LeAnna Biles Schooler, "Malthus Ward (1794–1863)," in *New Georgia Encyclopedia*, http://www.georgiaencyclopedia.org.
53. Malthus A. Ward, *An Address Pronounced Before the Massachusetts Horticultural Society, in Commemoration of its Third Annual Festival, September 21, 1831* (Boston: Buckingham, 1831), 6–7, 18–19, 26.
54. In 1824, William Luscomb donated a copy of Ennio Quinine Visconti, *Description des antiques du musée royal* (Paris: Herissant le Doug, 1820); and *Notice des tableaux exposés dans la galerie du musée royal* (Paris: Ballaro, 1823). These volumes, both about the Louvre's collections, were likely consulted when cataloging the Society's small collection of antiquities and western art.
55. Caroline Howard King, *When I Lived in Salem, 1822–1866* (Brattleboro, VT: Stephen Daye Press, 1937), 33.
56. "East-India Marine Society," *Salem Observer*, October 15, 1825.
57. This was reprinted as "East-India Marine Hall, Salem," *Salem Gazette,* March 30, 1830, and in *Sailor's Magazine, & Naval Journal,* December 1, 1830, 108–9. The visitor's comments revealed a common bias: "The curiosities are chiefly imported from the East-Indies, and display many of the wonders of these regions of idolatry."
58. This value decreased to $6,000 in 1845 and to $5,000 in 1863; by 1865 the Society voted to cease insuring the collection once the policy expired (vol. B., minutes/records, 1824–52, and vol. C., minutes/records, 1853–96, East India Marine Society Records, MH 88).
59. While at the University of Georgia, Ward created a university botanical garden next to his residence. He was dismissed in 1842 when the university fell on hard economic times and then ran a commercial garden in Athens and helped found the Horticultural Society of Georgia and the Pomological Society (Schooler, "Malthus Ward [1794–1863]").
60. A. H. J., "Obituary. Dr. George Osborne, of Peabody," *Boston Medical and Surgical Journal,* December 28, 1882, 624. Beyond medicine, Osborne had a political career, stepping in to fill a vacant seat in the Massachusetts state senate and serving as a Democratic candidate for Congress.
61. Vol. B., minutes/records, 1824–52, East India Marine Society Records, MH 88).
62. Ibid. The job of assistant superintendent was probably devised in response to questions regarding admission and acquiring tickets that were brought up at the Society's September 2, 1829, meeting. Members agreed that this assistant was not to be paid "in excess of $100.00."
63. Page is best known for his work and inventions related to electricity, specifically his induction coil and circuit breaker patents and his attempts at electromagnetic locomotion. From 1844 to 1849 he was a professor at Columbian College in Washington, D.C. (today George Washington University), and he worked as an examiner at the U.S. Patent Office from 1840 until his death. A trained ventriloquist, he also wrote a work exposing the fraudulent practices of spiritualists. See "Art. 1—Charles Grafton Page," *American Journal of Science and Art*, 2nd ser., 48, no. 142 (1869): 1–17; and Robert C.

Post, *Physics, Patents, and Politics: Biography of Charles Grafton Page* (New York: Science History Publications, 1976).

64. After the publication of the 1837 *Supplement*, all cataloguing was done internally.
65. Quoted in William P. Upham, *Memoir of Henry Wheatland, M.D.* (Cambridge, MA: Wilson and Son University Press, 1895), 12.
66. Ibid., 14. In addition to his connection to these organizations, Wheatland was a member, fellow, and auditor of the American Association for the Advancement of Science; an original trustee and vice-president of the Peabody Museum of Archaeology and Ethnology at Harvard; and an elected member of numerous other local and national societies.
67. Vol. B., minutes/records, 1824–52, East India Marine Society Records, MH 88.
68. Low's donation letter from Canton, addressed to Society president Nathaniel Leveret Rogers (January 6, 1838), states he sent "a Mandarin's dress and appendages complete" via the ship *Asia*, under the aegis of Captain Cale of New York (correspondence regarding donations of objects, box 3, folder 1, East India Marine Society Records, MH 88).
69. Vol. B., minutes/records, 1824–52, East India Marine Society Records, MH 88.
70. Ibid.
71. Eliza Leslie ("Miss Leslie"), "Pencillings of Boston," in *The Gift: A Christmas and New Year's Present* (Philadelphia: Carey and Hart, 1844), 213; Whitehall, *The East India Marine Society and the Peabody Museum of Salem*, 47. Wheatland's installation did not change much, due in part to a drastic decline in donations after 1837.
72. Unidentified newspaper clipping titled "A Day in Old Salem, By a Wayfarer," circa 1878, Peabody Academy of Science, scrapbook 1, 1875–79, PLPEM.
73. Obituary in the *Visitor*, September 3, 1890. Hammond continued in his role as custodian for the Peabody Academy of Science when it formed in 1867.
74. Unidentified newspaper clipping titled "A Day in Old Salem, By a Wayfarer," circa 1878, Peabody Academy of Science, scrapbook 1, 1875–79, PLPEM.
75. Ibid. The custodian also gives the visitor a lengthy and in-depth interpretation of the carved Heaven and Hell rosary bead: "Among the curiosities (not Oriental) . . . which seems to excite more wonder than any other . . . Not usually enjoying showmen's explanations, I should have declined the offer, had not a friend previously charged me to be sure not to lose the ancient mariner's explanation." The visitor's reference to his friend's mention of the rosary bead attests to the object's public notoriety.
76. Thirteen of the approximately 6,400 objects collected by the Society in the antebellum period were what are considered today to be traditional maritime objects.
77. The first donation (Society catalogue number 533) was made by the Boston instrument maker William Williams (1748?–1792) in 1768 for Malachai Allen, who gave it to the museum. The second, number 4978, was made by J. Hutchins, St. Catherine's, London.
78. Captain Henry Jackson donated the mechanical log watch (Society catalogue number 425) in 1803. The life preserver (catalogue number 3876) was donated by Captain Jonathan Neal. Carpenter's machine (catalogue number 2700) was given in 1824 by an unknown donor. In addition to Derby's model (catalogue number 425), he donated one of a European dredge (catalogue number 451).
79. The Magellanic Premium has been awarded only thirty-three times since it was established in 1786.
80. Bainbridge likely visited the museum at this time, and he came back in July 1831 with his daughter. According to the *Boston Daily Globe*, Bainbridge was "fresh from the capture of the *Java*, again by the *Constitution*" ("Model of 'Old Ironsides,'" *Boston Daily Globe*, October 20, 1897), 12.
81. John Robinson, *The Marine Room of the Peabody Museum of Salem* (Salem, MA: Peabody Museum of Salem, 1921), 61.

82. "Model of 'Old Ironsides'," *Boston Daily Globe*, October 20, 1897, 12.
83. Letters received, 1844–46, box 1, folder 7, Henry Wheatland Papers, MSS 464, PLPEM.
84. Letters received, 1847–48, box 1, folder 8, Henry Wheatland Papers, MSS 464, PLPEM.
85. Writing from the Britannic Gardens on August 17, 1846, Gray asked Wheatland to show "the world-famous East India Museum" to his friends Mr. Brownne of the New York Lyceum of Natural History and Mr. Holton (ibid.).
86. This penguin is one of the few extant natural history specimens collected by the Society. John Robinson notes that when the Peabody Academy of Science was formed, "[p] ractically all of the zoological collections of any value came from the Essex institute for those of the East India Marine Society had been so long neglected that they were moth-eaten, or dried up if in spirit,—rum was the preservative mostly used." Others were discarded in the 1940s based on their poor condition. See John Robinson, "Peabody Museum: Random Reminiscences," Peabody Museum of Salem Institutional Archives, PLPEM. One wonders what John J. Audubon (1785–1851) thought of this odd-looking bird when he visited the museum in June 1844.
87. Augustus A. Gould, M.D., "ART. XVIII—Results of an Examination of the Shells of Massachusetts, and their Geographical Distribution (Read February 3, 1841.)," *Boston Journal of Natural History* 3, no. 4 (1841): 483.
88. Lyell, *A Second Visit to the United States of North America*, 122. He also took pleasure in observing that "shells of the neighbouring coast had not been neglected, for people are often as ignorant of the natural history of the region they inhabit, especially of the lakes, rivers, and the sea."
89. Letters received, 1844–46, box 1, folder 8, Henry Wheatland Papers, MSS 464.
90. Wheatland's extant and voluminous correspondence from this period supports Endicott's claims. Very few letters relate to his position as superintendent or the collection of material for donation to the Society. Rather, they focus on his work with the Essex County Natural History Society and the acquisition of specimens for that institution through similar networks of scientists and mariners abroad (Henry Wheatland Papers, MSS 464).
91. Donation lists, 1820–62, box 3, folder 10, East India Marine Society Records, MH 88.
92. Phippen worked in the counting room of Fiske Allen after leaving school and afterward as a bookkeeper and cashier at the Salem Bank until his death. He was a floriculture specialist ("The Late Geo. D. Phippen, Memorial Adopted by the Essex Institute of Salem," *Salem News*, January 8, 1896).
93. Francis Putnam, letter to Henry Wheatland, January 27, 1841, box 1, folder 4, Henry Wheatland Papers, MSS 464.
94. Thomas Saul went to Fiji in 1809 on the ship *Active* with Society members William Putnam Richardson and Benjamin Vanderford. He was master of several ships in the East Indies trade, such as the brig *Java* circa 1822. After retiring from the sea, he spent the last thirty years of his life as a toll gatherer on the Salem turnpike and a constable at the courthouse.
95. Unidentified article in a scrapbook in the PLPEM.
96. King, *When I Lived in Salem*, 29. Martha Nichols, a granddaughter of Society member George Nichols, recalls that she and her sister were "in mortal terror of the janitor, Captain Saul, who glided silently about, every now and then saying to us in a sepulchral tone, 'Don't make so much noise, little girls,' when we had not dared to speak above a whisper." Martha Nichols, "With the Children," in *A Salem Shipmaster and Merchant: The Autobiography of George Nichols*, ed. Martha Nichols (Boston: Four Seas Company, 1921), 29, 112.
97. Vol. C., minutes/records, 1853–96, East India Marine Society Records, MH 88.

98. Donation lists, 1820–62, box 3, folder 10, East India Marine Society Records, MH 88.
99. "Museum of the East India Marine Society, Salem, Mass.," *Sailors' Magazine & Seamen's Friend*, December 1, 1866, 111–12. In the February 1, 1867, edition, a correction was printed for Thomas Saul, who was referred to as "Paul" in the prior issue.

Chapter Five: Visitor Experiences

1. Vols. G–Q, East India Marine Society Records, MH 88, Phillips Library, Peabody Essex Museum, Salem, MA (hereafter PLPEM). No earlier guestbooks exist. For an in-depth list of visitors, see George Schwartz, "'Collecting and Arranging . . . A History of The Globe': A Reconsideration of the Salem East India Marine Society and Antebellum American Museology," Ph.D. diss., Boston University, 2015, app. E.
2. In the following decades, the number of signatures declined annually. This was because the Society began closing its doors during the winter months in response to its dwindling finances. In addition, in the 1840s, attendants instructed Salem residents not to sign the guestbooks. If locals did accidentally write in the book, their names were crossed out and the words "your names are not wanted" written beside them.
3. Other visiting politicians of note were Massachusetts senator and antislavery advocate Charles Sumner (1811–74), who came to Salem in the summers of 1827 and 1849, and Henry Clay (1777–1852), who was speaker of the U.S. House of Representatives when he visited in November 1818.
4. Samuel Longfellow, "Memoir," in *Lectures, Essays, and Sermons,* by Samuel Johnson (Boston: Houghton Mifflin, 1883), 2. Longfellow wonders if Johnson drew inspiration from "that group of painted figures, presenting the various castes and trades of India" for his *Oriental Religions and Their Relation to Universal Religion* (1872).
5. Frazee wrote "Sculptor" next to his name when he visited in November 1833. Tiffany came to the museum in July 1829, two years after founding Tiffany & Company.
6. Jane Franklin Collection, Scott Polar Research Institute, University of Cambridge, GB015, MS 248/160, BJ journal, July–August 1846 [visit to United States], 1 vol. Lady Franklin sponsored several voyages to discover the whereabouts of her husband's expedition.
7. Caroline Howard King, *When I Lived in Salem, 1822–1866* (Brattleboro, VT: Stephen Daye Press, 1937), 31–35. Salem was predominantly a federalist town in the early days of the new republic. William Bentley and the Crowninshield family were among the few local staunch Republicans. The *Salem Gazette* supported federalist viewpoints, while the *Salem Register* sided with Republican policies. See Joseph B. Felt, *Annals of Salem*, 2nd ed. (Salem, MA: Ives, 1849), 2:18–22.
8. Caroline Howard King, *When I Lived in Salem, 1822–1866*, 34–35.
9. "Petty Malignity," *Alexandria Gazette*, September 10, 1834; Lunar, "East India Marine Society," *Salem Gazette*, September 9, 1834.
10. Vol. B., minutes/records, 1824–52, East India Marine Society Records, MH 88.
11. A spat between Bentley and Nathaniel Bowditch over the removal of pro-Republican toasts from the Society's 1802 dinner led to a new article in the bylaws: "Politics shall not on any occasion be introduced into the Society" (East India Marine Society, *Bye-Laws and Regulations of the Salem East-India Marine Society,* [Salem, MA: Pool and Palfray, 1808], 15). Unlike the town and the country at large, the Society agreed to keep politics away from their hall, a decision cemented in an 1810 toast: "Party Spirit—it has no place within these walls. May it be forever banished from our Shores, & the public homage be paid alone to the wise of the virtuous" (toasts, 1808–15, East India Marine Society Records, MH 88).
12. Walter Muir Whitehill, *The East India Marine Society and the Peabody Museum of Salem: A Sesquicentennial History* (Salem, MA: Peabody Museum, 1949), 137, n. 8.

Whitehill noted, "The culprits were not identified until 1937 when the memoirs of Caroline Howard King were posthumously published," but a reference in the *Boston Daily Globe* (December 15, 1899), 4, counters this claim. In an article about the Society's centennial, the *Globe* states, "The old story of the cutting out of the register of the name of Andrew Jackson was recounted, and [the former mayor] Mr. Rantoul declared that the work was not done by an autograph fiend or by any of Pres. Jackson's enemies, but by two schoolgirls."

13. The museum was visited by other abolitionists, such as Sarah M. Grimké (1792–1873) and her sister Angelina Emily Grimké (1805–79), both living in Charleston, South Carolina, when they came in June 1837 (vol. J, guestbook, October 7, 1834–August 26, 1837, East India Marine Society Records, MH 88).
14. Whitehill characterizes Royall's account of the museum as "sober" but does not provide any explanation for his opinion (*The East India Marine Society and the Peabody Museum of Salem*, 44).
15. Anne Newport Royall, *Sketches of History, Life, and Manners, in the United States. By a Traveller* (New Haven, CT, 1826), 360–63.
16. Ibid. Royall notes that the museum held 2,269 objects, the exact number noted in this publication. Most newspaper and visitor accounts of the museum during this period likely extracted material from the catalogue to use in their narratives.
17. Ibid.
18. Ibid., 362.
19. Dorothy J. Rumenik, "Caroline Howard Gilman (1794–1888)," in *Writers of the American Renaissance: An A-to-Z Guide*, ed. Denise D. Knight (Westport, CT: Greenwood, 2003), 142–45.
20. Caroline Gilman, *The Poetry of Travelling in the United States* (New York: Colman, 1832), 181.
21. Ibid., 181–82. In contrast to most of the visitors to the museum, Gilman was drawn to the entomology collection, noting, "It may be that the smallness of the number attracted my admiration, but I have rarely seen a collection so brilliant. . . . Were it not for the savage spears that impaled them, these insects would have seemed ready to fly." She also visited the museum on August 15, 1836, as her name appears in the museum's guestbook.
22. Latin verse cited in Whitehill, *The East India Marine Society and the Peabody Museum of Salem*, 140–41, n. 13. Translation by Daniel Tober, Columbia University, October 28, 2014.
23. "The Salem Museum," *Essex Register*, October 9, 1826. This article also ran in the *Salem Gazette* of October 3, 1826, the *Massachusetts Journal* of the same month, and other publications mentioning the East India Marine Society Museum, such as Theodore Dwight and Henry Dilworth Gilpin, *The Northern Traveller, and Northern Tour: With the Routes to the Springs, Niagara, and Quebec, and the Coal Mines of Pennsylvania; Also, the Tour of New-England: Embellished with Thirty-two Copperplate Engravings* (New York: Harper, 1830), 364–65.
24. Captain Basil Hall, *Travels in North America, in the Years 1827 and 1828* (Edinburgh: Cadell, 1830), 2:144.
25. Harriet Martineau, *Society in America*, 2nd ed. (London: Saunders and Otley, 1837), 2:260–63. Martineau noted that Salem merchants "are hoping to appropriate a large share of the whale fishery," a reflection of the port's short-lived whaling ventures in the 1830s.
26. Ibid., 263.
27. Ibid.
28. Ibid, 263–4. These figures were donated by George W. Abbott in 1827. Three decades later, Martineau memorialized that "the celebrated Salem Museum carries one back

to old times . . . and it used to be the aspiration of every master of a ship to become a member. . . . That feat is now so common that some other qualification is probably added by this time" (Harriet Martineau, "Representative Men. Merchants," *Once a Week,* August 17, 1861, 203–9).

29. James Boardman, *America, and the Americans, by a Citizen of the World* (London: Longman, Rees, Orme, Brown, Green, and Longman, 1833), 72, 192–96. Boardman noted that Scudder's Museum contained an "interesting display of the wonders of nature." Of Peale's Museum, he wrote that it was "particularly rich in Indian costumes and implements; contains many fine specimens in the department of natural history [and] a great variety of portraits of celebrated characters, painted by the ingenious individual who founded the Museum."
30. Ibid., 297–98.
31. Ibid., 298.
32. Ibid., 299.
33. Ibid. Boardman provided the reader with a synopsis of the letter, donated by businessman Augustine Heard (1785–1868) in 1827. According to Boardman, Byron asked his friend to "recommend an advocate to him, to defend a paltry suit brought against him by a tailor, who, as he says, in allusion to extravagant charges, 'has cut his coat according to his cloth, as his brethren do in every country.'" In the postscript, "the noble writer adds, that he expects some packages to arrive soon; and begs that all may be properly specified at the custom-house, for he will not allow any smuggling" (ibid.).
34. Ibid., 299–300.
35. James Silk Buckingham, *The Eastern and Western States of America* (London, 1842), 1:539.
36. Ibid., 1:275.
37. Ibid., 1:271–73. Buckingham's name first appears in the Society's guestbooks on October 17, 1838, alongside those of Elizabeth and Leicester Buckingham.
38. Ibid., 1:270.
39. Ibid., 1:271–75.
40. A few months earlier, on July 29, Samuel Cunard (1787–1865), his son William, Charles Clarke of Halifax, and Captain Henry Woodruff visited the museum. The group had just arrived in Boston on the maiden voyage of the *Britannia*, the first ocean liner of the Cunard Steamship Company.
41. "Parisian Literary News," *American*, September 30, 1882, 397.
42. Adolphe Fourier de Bacourt, *Souvenirs of a Diplomat: Private Letters from America During the Administrations of Presidents Van Buren, Harrison, and Tyler, Translated from the French* (New York: Holt, 1885), 133.
43. In 1852, Kossuth became only the second foreigner to address a joint meeting of the U.S. Congress.
44. "The Magyar in Lynn, Salem, and Danvers," *Salem Register*, May 10, 1852. Pulszky gave a lecture in 1852 titled "On the Progress and Decay of Art and on the Arrangement of a National Museum."
45. Francis Pulszky and Theresa Pulszky, *White, Red, Black: Sketches of American Society in the United States* (New York: Redfield, 1853), 2:189–90. In this book the Pulszkys also discuss their visit to the Patent Office Museum in Washington, D.C.
46. In 1836, Joseph Smith (1805–44) and other members of the Mormon church came to Salem because they had received a tip about a house full of gold in the city. While no reminiscences of their time at the museum have come to light, and no riches materialized, their names do appear in the guestbook. See Alexander L. Baugh, "A Historical Note on Joseph Smith's 1836 Visit to the East India Marine Society Museum in Salem, Massachusetts," *Mormon Historical Studies*, 11, no. 1 (2010): 143–150. They were the first of many Mormon church officials who came to the museum, culminating with

Brigham Young (1801–77) in August 1866. Mordecai Manuel Noah (1785–1851), a Sephardic Jewish playwright, political figure, and proto-Zionist living in New York City, came to Salem with his family in 1832. At about the same time, Andrew Reed and James Matheson of the Congregational Union of England and Wales visited the museum during their travels through the United States to visit churches. Along with a brief description of the Society and the origins of the museum, the pair wrote that it was "the lion of this place" (Andrew Reed and James Matheson, *A Narrative of the Visit to the American Churches by the Deputation from the Congregational Union of England and Wales,* 2nd ed. (London: Jackson and Walford, 1836), 1:323–24.

47. Rolfe Ricker, "My Journey. No. 5," *Juvenile Reformer, and Sabbath School Instructor,* September 2, 1835, 57.
48. Ibid. Similarly, J. Lewis Shack, in a letter to G. G. Newhall in 1850, referred to the museum as one of the "many links in the golden chain of our common Christianity which is erelong to unite the nations of the earth in one great and glorious Brotherhood" (papers relating to objects, 1841–83, East India Marine Society Records, MH88).
49. Eleanor Broadhead, "A Brief History of the Negro in Salem," unpublished paper prepared for the Committee on Racial Understanding for the Confrontation on Racism, April 11–12, 1969, 1, PLPEM.
50. Rebecca R. Noel, "Salem as Nation's Schoolhouse," in *Salem: Place, Myth, and Memory,* ed. Dane Morrison and Nancy Lusignan Schultz (Boston: Northeastern University Press, 2004), 144–45.
51. Arthur O. White, "Salem's Antebellum Black Community: Seedbed of the School Integration Movement," *Essex Institute Historical Collections* 108, no. 2 (1972): 109.
52. George Schwartz, "'The Chief Spirit . . . Our Venerable Fellow Citizen': The Life of John Remond in Antebellum Salem, Massachusetts," in *The Dublin Seminar for New England Folklife Annual Proceedings,* ed. Peter Benes (Boston: Boston University, 2012), 127–28.
53. The letter was written to the abolitionist Reverend Samuel Eli Cornish (1795–1858), a co-editor of *Freedom's Journal.* It was reprinted in the *Salem Observer,* November 17, 1827, which stated "In a late number of Freedom's Journal, we found the following notice of this town, which was probably written by one of the Editors, who visited us a few weeks ago."
54. "Letter No. XV," *Freedom's Journal,* November 9, 1827, 139. In it Russwarm wrote, "Salem is the residence of our friend R. [Remond] who by uniform propriety of conduct, and an undeviating attention to business has gained the respect of all classes of the citizens." He also noted that Remond was too sick to accompany the men around town.
55. Ibid. Cornish and Russwarm were certainly not the first African Americans to visit the museum. Prince Saunders (1775–1839), a teacher, diplomat, and advisor to Emperor Henri Christophe of Haiti, came in 1818 while he was in Salem encouraging free blacks to immigrate to Haiti. William Bentley noted in his diary on this date, "Mr. P. Saunders who was with me last Evening, breakfasted & dined with me this day. I went with him to G. C[rowninshield]'s barge & to the Museum" (*The Diary of William Bentley, D.D.*, vol. 4, *1811–1819* [Salem, MA: Essex Institute, 1914], 516–17). Bernard Soulié, a wealthy merchant and banker from a prominent free family of color in New Orleans, came to the museum in August 1866 (vol. P, guestbook, August 4, 1856–September 14, 1866, East India Marine Society Records, MH 88).
56. Vol. B., minutes/records, 1824–52, East India Marine Society Records, MH 88. Only resolutions related to amending the Society's bylaws required the vote of all living members.
57. Vol. C., minutes/records, 1853–96, East India Marine Society Records, MH 88.
58. "For the Register," *Salem Register,* July 22, 1850.

59. Ibid.
60. Vol. O, guestbook, August 26, 1849–August 1, 1856, and vol. P, guestbook, August 4, 1856–September 14, 1866, East India Marine Society Records, MH 88. Wadia had been in the United Kingdom, studying for his civil service exams at the University of London in 1856–60, before traveling to the United States, where he spent time in New York and Boston before returning to Bombay in early 1862 (Jenny Rose, personal communication, October 1, 2018).
61. *Essex Register*, November 9, 1807.
62. Ephraim Emmerton, letter to Dr. George Choate, G. G. Newhall, James King, J. T. Allen, and Nathan Fry, May 31, 1849, box 1, folder 4, Emmerton Family Papers, MSS 24, PLPEM.
63. Edward Sandford Martin, *The Life of Joseph Hodges Choate as Gathered Chiefly from His Letters* (New York: Scribner's, 1920), 1:43–44. James Buffington Briggs shared the quotation when he donated a set of figures from India to the Society in 1823.
64. King, *When I Lived in Salem*, 29–30.
65. Ibid., 29. King would later meet the real-life descendent of one of these figures, Rustomjee Hirjeebhoy Wadia: "Among the strange foreign visitors of those days, we were somewhat startled one evening by a friend's bringing a real live Parsee, with a tall calico headdress, to take tea with us. It was rather a revelation to me that a fire worshipper could take tea like ordinary mortals. But he was a harmless lion, and roared very gently, and drank his tea and ate his bread and butter quite like other folks and told us many interesting thing about his life in Bombay. I remember we all spoke very distinctly, as if we were talking to a child, and that he answered us in a very low cultivated refined voice, using much better English than we did" (37; identification courtesy of Jenny Rose, personal communication, October 1, 2018).
66. Ibid.
67. Martha Nichols, "Chapter VII. With the Children," in *A Salem Shipmaster and Merchant: The Autobiography of George Nichols*, ed. Martha Nichols (Boston: Four Seas Company, 1921), 111–12.
68. E. H. F., "For the Observer. A Visit to Salem," *Salem Observer*, August 4, 1860.
69. Ibid.
70. George L. Chaney, "The Brahmo Somaj," *Old and New* 5, no. 6 (1872): 679. Chaney's story focuses on Rammohun Roy (1772–1833), the Bengalese reformer known as the father of modern India, and Chunder Sen (1838–84), who attempted to incorporate Christianity into Hindu teaching.
71. Jee Yoon Lee, "'The Rude Contact of Some Actual Circumstance': Hawthorne and Salem's East India Marine Museum," *English Literary History* 73, no. 4 (2006): 950.
72. Charles E. Goodspeed, *Nathaniel Hawthorne and the Museum of the Salem East India Marine Society, or The Gathering of a Virtuoso's Collection* (Salem, MA: Peabody Museum of Salem, 1946). Hawthorne scholars have largely ignored or dismissed this story as one of his lesser works, and few individuals have connected it to the museum. The antiquarian book dealer Charles Elliot Goodspeed (1867–1950) noted that the origins of "A Virtuoso's Collection" date to 1828, when Hawthorne retreated from Salem society for seven years after the underwhelming reception to his first published work, *Fanshawe* (6).
73. In 1832, Hawthorne visited the museum, probably for the first time, even though his late father had been a member and he knew the former superintendent, Malthus A. Ward, from his days at Bowdoin College. He was accompanied by Samuel Dinsmore, Jr. (1799–1869), clerk of the New Hampshire state senate and later governor of the state, and by future president of the United States Franklin Pierce (1804–69), a close friend from Hawthorne's college days. At the time of their visit, the museum was in its most prosperous phase, even though Salem's mercantile trade was declining. Still, ten years would go by before "A Virtuoso's Collection" was published.

74. Nathaniel Hawthorne, *A Virtuoso's Collection, and Other Tales* (Boston: Osgood, 1877), 8–9.
75. Goodspeed, *Nathaniel Hawthorne and the Museum of the Salem East India Marine Society*, 13.
76. Hawthorne, *A Virtuoso's Collection*, 37.
77. Ibid., 18.
78. Ibid., 38, 42.
79. Alfred F. Rosa, *Salem, Transcendentalism, and Hawthorne* (Rutherford, NJ: Fairleigh Dickinson University Press, 1980), 44.
80. Ibid., 84.
81. Bradford Torrey and Francis Henry Allen, eds. *The Journal of Henry D. Thoreau* (New York: Courier Dover, 1962), 2:178. Several Society members purchased the first bay lynx for the collection in 1821, and Ebenezer Aborn, Francis Spinny, and David A. Swasy of Lynnfield, Massachusetts, donated the other in 1832.
82. Ibid.; Henry David Thoreau, *The Writings of Henry David Thoreau,* vol. 11, *July 2, 1858–February 28, 1859,* ed. Bradford Torrey (Boston: Houghton Mifflin, 1906), 170. Pickering Dodge donated the sword in 1826, Benjamin Carpenter and Benjamin Blanchard gave the mortar and pestle in 1802, and the Honorable Nathan Reed presented the stone knife blade circa 1804–6.
83. Publishers also visited the museum, including Charles Scribner (1821–71), who came in July 1841.
84. Hannah Flagg Gould, "The Greek Antique," *Godey's Lady's Book,* January 1, 1847, 28. The majority of this article recounts the story of the Greek boy, "which is gathered from among the long-buried Telies of an early period in the Christian era." Gould concluded her piece by commenting, "[I]t is not strange that one of them should have ultimately found its way to our western world, and planted itself down in the City of the Witches" (85).
85. Ibid., 28.
86. Eliza Leslie, "Pencillings of Boston," in *The Gift: A Christmas and New Year's Present* (Philadelphia: Carey and Hart, 1844), 213.
87. Ibid., 213–14.
88. Ibid., 215–16.
89. Ibid., 216.
90. Ibid., 214.
91. Paula Bradstreet Richter, "Lucy Cleveland, Folk Artist," *Magazine Antiques* 158 (August 2000): 206–7. Richter notes that *The Sick Chamber* was Cleveland's most complex ensemble, probably based on life experience and a lithograph of George Washington on his deathbed. She may have also worked from an English engraving titled *The Sick Chamber*, after the French painter Jean-Baptiste Greuze (1725–1805), which was sold at auction in Salem on September 9, 1831, by T. Deland and Company.
92. Leslie, "Pencillings of Boston," 214–15. E. H. F. mentioned this object in his/her account as "the sick woman in bed" (E. H. F., "For the Observer. A Visit to Salem," *Salem Observer*, August 4, 1860).
93. Leslie, "Pencillings of Boston," 215.
94. Ibid., 216.
95. Ibid. Outside observers and visitors never seemed to grasp the concept of an American museum that did not charge an entrance fee. An article that ran in the *Boston Galaxy,* April 11, 1828, warned those coming to the museum to "take a caution. It is not opened for profit, and what you give at the door is a gratuity to the keeper. I was unreasonable enough to require change for a cool ten, and nine dollars were disgorged reluctantly." The next day, the *Salem Observer* corrected the *Galaxy*'s "statement respecting admission money received at the door" as "utterly false. We do not believe that a cent has

ever been received for admission." During the Society's November 7, 1838, meeting, President Richard Saltonstall Rogers reported that a visitor "offered to the asst. Superintendant [*sic*] a gold coin as a fee for admission," and while being told it was "contrary to the rules of the Society," the coin was still left in East India Marine Hall. Rogers passed a resolution that "the same being repugnant to the feeling of the society that the gold coin be deposited in the museum until called for by the person to whom it belongs," and hoped it would not happen again (vol. B., minutes/records, 1824–52, East India Marine Society Records).

96. Day Kellogg Lee, *Merrimack: Or, Life at the Loom* (New York: Redfield, 1854), 196. Lee, inspired by the soapstone maitreya Buddha donated by William Ward in 1800, returned to it later in the book when another character, "the proud Sheriff," is likened to "the alabaster image in Salem Museum, with its bald, flattened head, and its great shiny lump of a face" (252). Lee was born in Sempronius, New York, and was a Universalist pastor in many towns, including Salem, when he likely visited the museum. He was also a frequent writer for Universalist newspapers and other periodicals. *Merrimack* was part of a series of books under the general title *Tales of Labor,* comprising four volumes ("The Rev. Day K. Lee, D.D.," *New York Tribune,* June 4, 1869, 5).
97. School groups often visited the museum, as noted in contemporary newspapers and recorded in the visitor guestbooks. The *Salem Gazette,* September 2, 1834, reported a visit from a "bevy of fair young ladies, between forty and fifty in number, all in their gala dresses, . . . the pupils of a flourishing Female Academy in Andover, under the care of Mr. Samuel Lamson." The *Salem Register,* July 12, 1847, described a visit of the Chelsea Congregational sabbath school to Salem, whose members "marched to the East India Marine Hall, where a half hour was spent in examining the fine collection of curiosities there." In addition, the Harvard Street Baptist School of Boston visited in 1844 according to a short article in the *Daily Atlas,* August 5, 1844.
98. Henry Gally Knight, *Lottie Wilde's Picnic by Grandmother Hope. Founded on Facts* (New York: Crowell, 1867), 136.
99. Ibid., 165–66, 171.
100. Ibid., 169–70.
101. Ibid., 173–74.
102. E. D. Eliot, "The Lost Deed: A Legend of Old Salem," *Graham's Magazine* 40, no. 1 (1852): 20–21.
103. Ibid., 21.
104. "Art. I.—Salem Witchcraft; with an Account of Salem Village, and a History of Opinions on Witchcraft and Kindred Subjects," *Edinburgh Review* 128, no. 261 (1868): 3. The focus of this article is a review of Charles W. Upham's *Salem Witchcraft: With an Account of Salem Village, and a History of Opinions on Witchcraft and Kindred Subjects* (1867).
105. Ibid., 2.
106. From an excerpt entitled "Salem" that ran in the *Salem Gazette,* May 21, 1833.

Conclusion: "That thus their exploits, on the ocean wave, from age to age might still be handed down"

1. Nathaniel Hawthorne, *The Scarlet Letter, A Romance* (1850), accessed from University of Virginia's Electronic Archive of Early American Fiction, 4–5. John Frayler, a historian for the Salem Maritime National Historic Site, believes, "One of the stereotyped hapless recipients of Hawthorne's stinging imagery" in the "Introduction" to *The Scarlet Letter,* "though not identified by name," was William Story. See John Frayler, "Retired on the Fourth of July," *Pickled Fish and Salt Provisions* 4, no. 6 (2003): 2.
2. Octavius Brooks Frothingham, *Recollections and Impressions, 1822–1890* (New York: Putnam, 1891), 41–42.

3. A. Friedlander, *Salem Maritime National Historic Site: Historical Research, 1626–1990* (East Orange, NJ: Berger, 1991), 25.
4. Box 1, folder 4, Henry Wheatland Papers, 1629–1903, MSS 464, Phillips Library, Peabody Essex Museum, Salem, MA (hereafter PLPEM).
5. Vol. B., minutes/records, 1824–52, East India Marine Society Records, MH 88, PLPEM.
6. Stephen Wheatland, "The Salem East India Marine Society: A Report of Its Funds and How They Were Acquired," in *The East India Marine Society and the Peabody Museum of Salem: A Sesquicentennial History,* by Walter Muir Whitehill (Salem, MA: Peabody Museum, 1949), 191.
7. Vol. B., minutes/records, 1824–52, East India Marine Society Records, MH 88.
8. In 1809, William Ives (1756–1814) became the first member to be expelled from the Society for failure to pay dues.
9. Whitehill, *The East India Marine Society and the Peabody Museum of Salem*, 33. Nathaniel Silsbee, the last founding member, died in July 1850.
10. Vol. B., minutes/records, 1824–52, East India Marine Society Records, MH 88.
11. The next attempt at a festive dinner came in 1869, for the occasion of the seventieth anniversary of the Society. Although the dinner was almost unanimously approved, a committee later found it would be too expensive, and the vote of approval was removed at a special meeting on October 1 (vol. C., minutes/records, 1853–96, East India Marine Society Records, MH 88).
12. "The Salem East India Marine Society," *Salem Gazette,* November 9, 1841.
13. Ibid. Nathaniel Silsbee was the only original member who was still alive to attend the meeting.
14. *Celebration of the Introduction of the Water of Cochituate Lake into the City of Boston. October 25, 1848* (Boston, 1848), 14.
15. Vol. B., minutes/records, 1824–52, East India Marine Society Records, MH 88.
16. "Celebrations of the 4th," *Salem Observer*, July 5, 1851.
17. Vol. C., minutes/records, 1853–96, East India Marine Society Records, MH 88.
18. "East India Museum," *Salem Register*, May 7, 1855.
19. Wheatland, "The Salem East India Marine Society," 193.
20. Vol. C., minutes/records 1853–96, East India Marine Society Records, MH 88.
21. The full version of the legislative committee's report appears at the end of the records/minutes (1853–96) along with the original letter request. The attendance figures given in this report are inflated.
22. On May 3, 1848, the East India Marine Society passed a vote of thanks to Maury for his "splendid Chart of the North Atlantic Ocean from New York to the Equator . . . [which] was presented by the National Observatory to this Society." Eight years later, in late December 1856, Maury, working for the National Observatory in Washington, D.C., visited the Society's museum. According to the *Salem Register*, he "expressed a very high appreciation of its value," and the newspaper noted that Maury had "years ago, made use of the extensive collection of journals and log-books belonging to the Society, and has been indebted to many Salem shipmasters for assistance in conducting his important studies" (December 22, 1856).
23. Vol. C., minutes/records, 1853–96, East India Marine Society Records, MH 88.
24. Letter from Maury to the East India Marine Society, May 27, 1859, in ibid.
25. Salem Marine Society Collection, letter book, 1771–1872.
26. Vol. C., minutes/records, 1853–96, East India Marine Society Records, MH 88.
27. Ibid. The picture was found in the drawer of a table that came from the Essex Institute in April 1907. It was likely removed from East India Marine Hall in 1867 and deposited there.
28. The Salem Marine Society, which owned a smaller portrait of Maury donated by Ripley Ropes, similarly displayed its dissatisfaction with him. Maury was expelled from

their society on May 30, 1861, as "a Traitor to his Country." His portrait was hung "head down" and facing the wall, where it remains today (minutes for the monthly meeting, May 30, 1861, at Essex House, Salem Marine Society Collection, record book, 1860–87).

29. Donation lists, 1820–62, box 3, folder 10, East India Marine Society Records, MH 88.
30. Ibid. The Essex Institute was located in Plummer Hall from 1857 until 1992, when it merged with the Peabody Museum of Salem. The Salem Athenaeum owned Plummer Hall but eventually sold it to the Essex Institute in 1905.
31. Wheatland, "The Salem East India Marine Society," 194.
32. Ibid.
33. Robinson did not become a member until 1869, two years after the Society sold East India Marine Hall. Honorary membership was first discussed in 1824. Honorary members were allowed all the rights of regular members, apart from voting and receiving charity. Robinson served in many capacities at the Peabody Academy of Science and the Peabody Museum of Salem, wrote and lectured on horticulture and botany, and was a numaticist. See Whitehill, *The East India Marine Society and the Peabody Museum of Salem*, 83–94, 102–9, 113–14; *The Opening of John Robinson Hall in the Peabody Museum of Salem, Massachusetts* (Topsfield, MA: Peabody Museum of Salem, 1930); and Albert P. Morse, "John Robinson, Botanist, of Salem, Massachusetts," *Rhodora* 31, no. 372 (December 1929): 245–54.
34. Portions of the report presented at the November 29, 1865, meeting were published in the *Salem Register* on December 4. All parts of this report were accepted, except for the sale of the collections, which was postponed. In 1802, the Society forbade publication of internal affairs "without the express consent of the President and being duly signed by him" (vol. A., minutes/records, 1799–1824, East India Marine Society, MH 88).
35. "The Salem East India Marine Museum," *Salem Register*, November 30, 1865.
36. Whitehill, *The East India Marine Society and the Peabody Museum of Salem*, 53. The *New-Orleans Times* incorrectly noted on May 17, 1866, that "[t]he East Indian Marine Hall, at Salem, Mass., has been destroyed by fire."
37. His childhood town of South Danvers was renamed Peabody in his honor after his death. See Franklin Parker, "The Legacy of George Peabody: Special Bicentenary Issue," *Peabody Journal of Education* 70, no. 1 (1994).
38. Wheatland, "The Salem East India Marine Society," 194–95, 202.
39. "Agreement with the East India Marine Society," *First Annual Report of the Trustees of the Peabody Academy of Science* (January 1869): 8–9.
40. *Cape Ann Light and Gloucester Telegraph*, May 18, 1867.
41. Putnam was serving as superintendent of the Essex Institute at the time.
42. The relationship between academic scientists and natural history museums soon began to decline. See Steve Conn, *Museums and American Intellectual Life, 1876–1926* (Chicago: University of Chicago Press, 1998), 32–74.
43. Lawrence Waters Jenkins and Walter Muir Whitehill, *The Restoration of East India Marine Hall* (Salem, MA: Peabody Museum of Salem, 1944). On this period of the museum's history, see Whitehill, *The East India Marine Society and the Peabody Museum of Salem*, 54–82.
44. Eleanor Putnam, *Old Salem* (Boston: Houghton Mifflin, 1886), 8.
45. Jenkins and Whitehill, *The Restoration of East India Marine Hall*, 12.
46. "Historical Specimens," in *First Annual Report of the Trustees of the Peabody Academy of Science* (January 1869): 49.
47. Alice M. Guernsey, "Sights in Salem," *Household* (October 1871), Peabody Academy of Science, scrapbook 1, 1875–79, PLPEM.
48. Ibid. The museum is also referred to as the East India Marine Society Museum in a short article titled "The East India Marine Society," *Cape Ann Advertiser*, June 19, 1874.

49. Brown was a Salem Marine Society member and served as master from 1870–79. According to his obituary in the *Salem Register*, he commanded the ships *Rome* and *White Swallow*, finishing his career on the *Shirley* in 1863. He was an alderman from 1866 to 1868, Salem mayor from 1870 to 1871, and city treasurer in 1879.
50. Vol. C., minutes/records, 1853–96, East India Marine Society Records, MH 88. Brown was part of the dissenting opinion on the committee formed to look into this matter.
51. Ibid.
52. Wheatland, in fact, had planted the seeds for this change in 1867. Although his tenure as superintendent was strained at times, he "expressed a desire to secure the portraits of . . . those persons who have been intimately connected with the East India Marine Society, as a fitting accompaniment to our hall" (Additions to the Museum," in *First Annual Report of the Trustees of the Peabody Academy of Science* [January 1869]: 48–49).
53. See L. O. Howard, "Edward Sylvester Morse, 1838–1925: A Biographical Sketch," *National Academy of Sciences Biographical Memoirs* 17 (1935): 4–28; and Dorothy Godfrey Wayman, *Edward Sylvester Morse: A Biography* (Cambridge, MA: Harvard University Press, 1942).
54. Director's report, Peabody Academy of Science, 1880, box 1A, folder 7, Peabody Essex Museum General Archives, PLPEM.
55. Maritime Art and History Department files, Peabody Essex Museum. These were dated "East India Marine Hall, December 1, 1884."
56. Vol. C., minutes/records, 1853–96, East India Marine Society Records, MH 88.
57. Peabody Academy of Science curator James Henry Emerton (1847–1931) created these drawings. Emerton was known for his natural history illustrations and his books on arachnids, and he had previously worked at the Boston Society of Natural History and the Essex Institute. In addition to Wheatland, George D. Phippen and other individuals provided oral accounts to aid Emerton. In 1890, Peabody Academy of Science assistant and librarian Arthur Robinson Stone—John Robinson's cousin—produced another set of drawings with an overhead schematic of the hall and a key identifying more objects on display. This aided in the creation of figures 3 to 6.
58. John Robinson, "East India Marine Society. Sketch of the Scientific History of the East India Marine Society, Suggested by an Examination of Old Manuscript Records and Documents Belonging to the Society," *Salem Gazette*, January 30, 1885, Peabody Academy of Science, scrapbook 3, 1882–90, Peabody Essex Museum General Archive, PLPEM.
59. Peabody Academy of Science, scrapbook 3, 1882–90.
60. "Fresh Life in Old Salem," *Evening Transcript*, July 2, 1887, in ibid. The article also notes, with a touch of Boston bias, "It is furthermore understood that the town is pervaded by an air of grass-grown gentility and antique aristocracy, and it is believed that the wharves are dropping to pieces and curtained with sea-weeds fatter than those of fabled Lethe."
61. These travelogues were reprinted and published as a two-volume set by George Edward Wright of the *Times*.
62. "A Visit to the States. Part LIII. The North Shore of Massachusetts," *Times of London*, January 12, 1888, 8.
63. Dan Finamore, personal communication, October 25, 2013. While no one knows when the attic was first used to store collections, Thomas Saul signed his name on one of the crossbeams in 1842 and started a tradition still in place. The historical graffiti in East India Marine Hall's attic includes the names of museum staff and others who worked on installations in the gallery.
64. Whitehill, *The East India Marine Society and the Peabody Museum of Salem*, 104–5. From director's reports, it appears that the president of the board of trustees, George Augustus Peabody, suggested a new gallery for the maritime collections in the early

1890s but that John Robinson spearheaded the effort (Edward Sylvester Morse, "Director's Report 1893," draft, Peabody Essex Museum General Archives, PLPEM).

65. See John Robinson, *The Marine Room of the Peabody Museum of Salem* (Salem, MA: Peabody Museum of Salem, 1921).
66. John Robinson, "Marine Room Opening," typescript, circa 1905, Peabody Essex Museum General Archives, PLPEM. Robinson recalled, "The ship masters of the East India Marine Society" showed great interest in the Marine Room, and "several of them have made valuable contributions to the collections" (John Robinson, "Report on the Marine Room for 1905," typescript, Peabody Essex Museum General Archives, PLPEM).
67. Wheatland, "The Salem East India Marine Society," 195.
68. Ibid., 195–96.
69. Ibid., 196.
70. East India Marine Society, *History of the Salem East India Marine Society* (Salem, MA: Newcomb and Gauss, 1916), 4.
71. Katharine Holland Brown, "Brewster Blood," in *Scribner's Magazine* 57, no. 1 (1915): 77
72. Four years later, the novel was turned into a silent film with the same title. Directed by George Medford (1877–1961) and distributed by Paramount Pictures (then on Long Island, New York), the film stared Leatrice Joy (1895–1985) as Princess Taou Yuen. Many scenes were filmed in Salem, including some that were set on dilapidated Derby Wharf. The *Charles W. Morgan*, the only extant nineteenth-century wooden whale ship, was incorporated into the production and made to look like a square-rigged East India trading ship. See John Frayler, "Java Head is Missing," *Pickled Fish and Salted Provisions* 8, no. 1 (2006): 3–7.
73. Ibid. Fuller (1804–86) made this model of the U.S.S. *Ohio* during a voyage in 1849–50 and donated it to the East India Marine Society in 1850.
74. Agnes Edwards Rothery, *The Romantic Shore* (Salem, MA: Salem Press, 1915), 32–46.
75. Ralph D. Paine, "Old Salem Ships and Sailors," *Outing Magazine* 51, no. 4 (1908): 389.
76. Donna Cassidy, *Marsden Hartley: Race, Region, and Nation* (Lebanon, NH: University Press of New England, 2005), 156–57.
77. The art historian Donna Cassidy believes that Hartley's *Birds of the Bagaduce*, painted in 1939, was one of these works (ibid.).
78. John P. O'Neill, ed., *Barnett Newman: Selected Writings and Interviews* (Berkeley: University of California Press, 1992), 58–59.
79. Ibid. Newman and Adolph Gottlieb had been close friends since 1922, after meeting at the Art Students League, and they shared an interest Native American art (ibid., 58). The Chilkat blanket was donated by Robert Bennett Forbes in 1832 and is the earliest known example of its kind.
80. Jenkins and Whitehill, *The Restoration of East India Marine Hall*, 15. Augustus Peabody Loring, Jr. (1885–1951), a descendant of Joseph Peabody and president of the museum's trustees in June 1942, led the charge to restore the hall to reflect its original design.
81. Robert Maynard Hutchins, "The Value of the Museum," *Science*, new ser., 98, no. 2546 (1943): 332.
82. "PEM Launches Contemporary Art Initiative," September 27, 2010, http://www.pem.org. *FreePort* was developed by the PEM's first curator of contemporary art, Trevor Smith.
83. "FreePort [No. 001]: Charles Sandison," http://pem.org.
84. "FreePort [No. 003]: Susan Philipsz," http://pem.org.
85. Other contemporary artists working with PEM curators have also recognized the roots of the museum. Kent Monkman (born 1965), a Canadian artist of Cree descent who makes films, installations, performances, and paintings that "invite interpretation as satirical reimaginings of North American art history," noted, "Everything in the

collection came off of these ships, . . . the people, the goods, all of it. And I like the symbolism of the sea, the mystery of what is on the other side of the ocean" (Elizabeth Pochoda and Eleanor H. Gustafson, "Talking Past and Present at the Peabody Essex Museum," *Magazine Antiques* [January 2014], http://www.themagazineantiques.com).

86. Organized by academy trustee General Francis H. Appleton (a grandson of Society member Nathaniel Appleton [1778–1818]), this event was also viewed as a fundraiser for constructing a new museum gallery, Weld Hall (named after Charles Goddard Weld), which opened in 1906.
87. "Museum Centennial," *Boston Daily Advertiser*, December 16, 1899, 8.
88. "$10,000 Gift For East India Marine Society," *Salem News*, December 16, 1899, Peabody Academy of Science, scrapbook 4, 1890–1903, Peabody Essex Museum General Archives, PLPEM.

INDEX

Page numbers in italics denote figures.